"SHARP, TIMELY, CANDID AND ARTICULATE."*

Sisters from all walks of life—celebrities along with homemakers and secretaries, married and unmarried, old and young—have contributed their most closely guarded secrets and experiences to this ground-breaking study.

SISTERS is meticulously researched, beautifully written, and profoundly felt. It is *about* sisters, but it encompasses any life that is shared with another.

"Insight into sisterhood itself . . . Also an attractive portrait of the submissive and will-ful, tender and callous, loving and hating, perceptive and self-centered, intelligent and exciting women of America today."
—*Los Angeles Times Book Review**

SISTERS

LOVE AND RIVALRY
INSIDE THE FAMILY
AND BEYOND

ELIZABETH FISHEL

BANTAM BOOKS
NEW YORK · TORONTO · LONDON

TO MY PARENTS, EDITH AND JAMES,
AND MY SISTER, ANNE FISHEL

*This low-priced Bantam Book
has been completely reset in a type face
designed for easy reading, and was printed
from new plates. It contains the complete
text of the original hard-cover edition.*
NOT ONE WORD HAS BEEN OMITTED.

RL 8, IL 8+

SISTERS
*A Bantam Book | published by arrangement with
William Morrow & Company*

PRINTING HISTORY
Morrow edition published April 1979
3 printings through April 1979
Literary Guild edition April 1979
Macmillan Book Club edition July 1979
Serialized in LOS ANGELES HERALD EXAMINER *April 1979*
Bantam edition | February 1980

The lines from "Older Sister" by Carly Simon © 1974 C'Est Music. Used
by permission. All rights reserved.
The lines from "You've Got Me Flying," words: Holly Near; music: Jeff
Langley, © 1975 by Hereford Music. Used by permission. All rights re-
served.
The lines from "For Claudia, Against Narrowness" from *Loveroot* by
Erica Jong. Copyright © 1968, 1969, 1973, 1974, 1975 by Erica Mann Jong.
Reprinted by permission of Holt, Rinehart & Winston, Inc., publishers.
The lines from "Transcendental Etude" and from "Sibling Mysteries"
from *The Dream of a Common Language, Poems 1974–1977* by Adrienne
Rich, are reprinted with the permission of W. W. Norton & Company, Inc.
Copyright © 1978 by W. W. Norton & Company, Inc.
The lines from the poems by Ntozake Shange originally appeared in
*For Colored Girls Who Have Considered Suicide When the Rainbow Is
Enuf.* Shameless Hussy Press, San Lorenzo, California, 1976.
Some portions of Chapter 1 ("Person-to-Person: My Sister and I")
originally appeared in slightly different form in *Ms Magazine*, January
1979.

ISBN 0–553–13467–1

Published simultaneously in the United States and Canada

PRINTED IN THE UNITED STATES OF AMERICA

ACKNOWLEDGMENTS

FIRST, I WOULD TO THANK THE MANY WOMEN WHO SHARED their life-stories and their sisters' stories—both those whose names you will recognize and those who remain anonymous. I would also like to thank all the women who answered my Questionnaire in such depth and detail. Without their honesty, concern and thoughtfulness about sisters and sisterhood, this book would never have been possible.

My thanks to Mike McGrady, who first encouraged me to write about my sister for *Newsday* almost ten years ago—and has encouraged me in countless ways ever since. And thanks to Pat Berens, Phillipa Brophy and Sterling Lord, who believed in this project from the first, and throughout its progress were helpful, interested and enthusiastic. And special thanks to my editor, James Landis, whose thoughtful questions and incisive comments helped shape this book at every stage, and whose interest and support made the task of writing it immeasurably easier.

Many people gave important advice, generous suggestions and encouragement while I researched and formulated this book. I want especially to thank Nancy Chodorow, Joanne Edgar, George Goethals, the late Margaret Mead, B. K. Moran, Tillie Olsen, Gregg Thomson and Gloria Steinem. Special thanks as well to Sheila Ballantyne and Philip Spielman, who helped me define my intent and ideas at various points along the way. I also want to thank those people who read drafts of chapters and whose careful comments, questions and criticisms helped me clarify and improve the manuscript: Sheila Ballantyne, Merry Blodgett, Ann-Marie Hogan, Susan Manuel, Leah Potts, Dusky Rhodes and Hy Spotnitz. And special thanks to Franny Taliaferro, who made many lucid and valuable comments on my work-in-progress, as she has for so many years.

Judy Baugh and Meg Holmberg did the extensive job of

transcribing the tapes of interviews with admirable patience and accuracy. Meg Holmberg's unflappable and thorough assistance in preparing the footnotes and bibliography aided the progress of the book as well. My thanks to both of them.

Finally, I want to thank my family for their love and support throughout this project. My parents, Edith and James Fishel, whose encouragement for my writing began long, long before this book and continued to sustain me throughout. My husband, Robert Houghteling, who was not only my first, most painstaking and supportive reader, but also made my life infinitely happier while I was writing. And my sister, Anne Fishel, who was, of course the first inspiration for the book and a constant inspiration throughout. Out of our conversations, our reading and our shared observations about ourselves and other sisters, the idea for this book was born, and Annie's suggestions, insights and ideas influenced its progress from beginning to end. The finished book only begins to express my boundless appreciation and love.

CONTENTS

INTRODUCTION

WHEN THE PHONE RANG TO TELL ME MY SISTER WAS BORN I was sitting on the pot, overalls crumpled at my feet, a five-year-old with a fat, overindulged and overprotected face. Our tiny New York City apartment was not exactly the Garden of Eden, but in my early bloom of tyranny, I felt it was all mine, bristling with the dense underbrush of my worldly possessions, a child-size rocking chair, dollhouse and at least five apple-cheeked Ginny dolls, monogrammed silver spoons, embroidered Parisian dresses, fingerpaints and every Dr. Seuss extant. The snake in the grass, if there was one, was a plastic dentist set bought to coax me to the dentist without tears.

Into this airtight world, Anne was carried, and for the first months of her life before we moved to more expansive quarters, she was set in a bassinet in the windowless, airless dining room. I made her a necklace out of many-colored buttons, which she was never allowed to handle because "She might swallow it" (the double-edged threat and promise of Mother's words were menacing and spellbinding). But I was allowed to shake the necklace over her bassinet, and I did for hours on end, steadily, stealthily gazing at this tiny being, this giant who had once invaded the privacy of my garden and saved me from it. I stared at her for hours, her clenched and unclenched fists, her perfect periwinkle nails, her face, smooth as an eggshell in repose, twisted as a rag in tears, and all the while, I tried to decipher the mystery that my life had inalterably and forever changed.

Once I asked a five-year-old girl, the youngest I talked to for this book, how things were different after her sister's recent birth. Her eyes widened to full moons and clouded with private visions. Usually talkative and inquisitive, all she could say was "Very different." She said it with the self-possession of someone who knows a great deal more than she's telling.

I understood her silence, her reserve. For I, too, at five, had no words for my sister's birth. But even without words, I knew it to be the single sharpest joy and trauma since my own.

What I did not know then was that lying in the cradle was my dearest friend and bitterest rival, my mirror and opposite, my confidante and betrayer, my student and teacher, my reference point and counterpoint, my support and dependent, my daughter and mother, my subordinate, my superior and, scariest still, my equal.

She could as likely have been a brother, a Thomas (for the name was all picked out, ready to weave into the family mythology), and I suspect the Thomas who was never born would have altered my vision, too. But Thomas would never have been flesh of my own flesh, never shared the guts of common experience, the dreams, the fears, the mannerisms, the quirks of fate, the primitive bond of blood. What Annie and I were to grow into giving each other was the intimate, exhilarating and spooky knowledge of someone who was utterly like and utterly unlike the other. Our relationship was simple as breath, complex as circulation. She was only the first person I could tell the truth to.

How does a girl's life change when a sister is born and how is a woman's life ever after altered by having sisters? Those were the questions that began this book.

One afternoon, I asked the questions of a group of women friends, of various ages and stages, with one bond in common: all of them had sisters. Ostensibly we were to try out a questionnaire I was formulating, but we were also to formalize what we do anyway when we get together: gossip about our families. And by gossip, I mean simply make sense and symbol of our lives. It was to be a quilting bee of our identities.

Each friend, as it happened, was hovering delicately, nervously on the cusp of a life-crisis. Each was about to choose which of two roads to follow into the fabled yellow woods. For Rachel, the choice was having a child, for Margaret, staying with a flagging marriage, for Lisa, graduate school in political science, and for Julie, running a business that was presently running her.

As they unraveled their family secrets, the interstices with parents and sisters, patterns began to emerge, idiosyncratic as the crazy quilt, common as the Star of Bethlehem. Rachel, on the ambivalent brink of pregnancy, reviewed her own family constellation: an authoritarian father, a capitulating mother, a brother, three years older, whose "bad case of stubbornness turned out to be psychosis," and a sister, four years younger, whose birth Rachel remembered, even now at thirty-three, with keen distaste. "My baby sister got my room, and I was moved to a room down a long hall that was at least three blocks long. My mother was always fussing with the baby, and I felt displaced and cut off from her." As the two sisters grew up, Rachel recalled guiltily, "My sister put enormous energy into being the 'good sister.' But I was constantly irritated with her and spent a lot of my childhood in a bad mood. I think I had a lot of jealousy of my mother, which I couldn't express, so I took it out on a littler version of my mother—my sister." After that revelation, the next was no surprise: "It's very difficult to think about having kids who would have brothers and sisters."

Margaret traced a sister's dream to the complex of motives for marrying the man she was now brooding about leaving. "He and I went to England to visit my sister and her husband. While we were there, she dreamed that I died and left my closets a mess, and she and my mother were so happy, because they could finally clean up after me." The dream epitomized her own blackest fears of family intrusiveness: into her closets (which she kept messy on purpose to keep the family out), worse, into her thoughts and spirit. What she needed, she had to conclude, was a comrade and confidante outside the family, someone to entrust with her literal and figurative closets. She married the man she was willing to make her executor, but over the years, the dream of a protector was fraying around the edges.

For Lisa and Julie, the pieces of sibling patchwork fit piecemeal with the uncertainty of their careers. Lisa's deliberation about graduate school had been unhinged the month before by a panic-chilled call from her mother: "Your sister has disappeared." There was not a word, not a trace left behind in her sister's apartment in a working-class ghetto, where she lived in line with her stern Marxist beliefs. There were just rumblings of rumor that she knew too much, that certain people were after her, that she'd gone underground, a left-wing refugee.

Lisa's swarm of memories (the hot arguments about Lenin and Mao, her sister's affairs with ex-cons and junkies, her "hypochondriacal" illnesses) mingled wearily with dreams of mutilation (her sister walking with her head cut off, saying, "I can manage," the two undressing and her sister with no feet). Lisa ricocheted between guilt and embarrassed relief, self-searching and painful feelings of responsibility for her parents. As for her own future as a political scientist—the quandary had become stagnation.

Finally, Julie, the overburdened businesswoman and oldest girl in an Irish working-class family of two brothers and two sisters, saw the closest synapse between her sibling position and her professional malaise. "I think I felt that my parents had had a baby because I wanted a sister," she wrote on her questionnaire, "so she was 'mine' in some sense. I don't think I ever really felt like a child after she was born, and I was put in the role of 'second mother,' not only to her, but to the whole family." Playing "second mother" to her sister made that a tempestuous relationship, still stormy with outbursts, though both sisters had long since left the nest. So playing "little mother" in her business—both with her partner and her employees—was a role she was suited for just as doggedly as she resisted it.

Four women thinking about four sisters, by chance filling out questionnaires, patching together their memories, secrets, dreams. Four women at the crossroads, and for each, her route was unextricably crossed with her sister's, their scripts connected, their lives inalterably shaped by each other's. For each of my friends, the presence of a sister, and whether she was younger or older, ambivalently loved or ambivalently feared, ally or enemy, success or disappointment was a tangible integer in the tallying of her own life's choices. Her sister's presence marked her as ineffably as her mother's red hair and perfect pitch, her father's temper and her grandfather's fortune in shirts.

What surprised me when I left my impromptu circle of friends and questionnaires and went to consult the libraries was that none of these instincts about sisters was in any complex or systematic way studied, analyzed or corroborated by mainstream psychological literature. Freud, Deutsch, Adler, Horney, Jung: an occasional reference to sibling rivalry, but usually in a neurotic patient and, if then, likely to be male. More recently, Erikson, Eric Berne, Robert White: an intermittent reference to sibling patterns along the life-cycle, but no real framework or overview in which to place my friends' and their sisters' life-stories.

There was, admittedly, a profusion of data on birth order, much of it contradictory, correlating one's ordinal position in the family with everything from success in college and bliss in marriage to extrasensory perception and expressed interest in becoming a college professor. And twins had been obsessively researched, an anomaly for psychologists like black holes for scientists. I also found a promising volume called *The Sibling* by Brian Sutton-Smith and B. G. Rosenberg, which turned out to be a dense maze of technical data on sibling relationships in childhood and adolescence. The authors unabashedly referred to their subjects as F1FF (the oldest of three girls), FMF3 (the youngest girl with an older brother and an older sister), etc. But for the four thoughtful and complicated women in my living room, that was hardly a fitting conceptual scheme.

Even in the personal and passionate recent outpouring of feminist literature, where I expected a resource when all else failed, I was disappointed. There were certainly reams on political "sisterhood," and in the past year or two, almost a subculture of studies on mothers and daughters. But any mention of blood sisters was at best fragmentary and incidental.

Why so glaringly little on this relationship that, next to a girl's relationship with her parents, is the most primary of any? Why, in short, no *Sisters Karamazov?* First and most obviously, until the recent renewal of feminist consciousness, women just didn't matter too much—either as research subjects or as researchers. (Healthy, active women, that is. "Hysterical" women have always had a macabre grip on the male medical imagination.) Second, and particularly from the perspective of academic methodology, studies of siblings are notoriously difficult to control. The number and range of variables can be as mercurial as an adolescent's moods: How many were there in a family and, of these, how many sisters and how many brothers? Were all the children wanted and how many miscarriages occurred between births? Any multiple births or step-siblings? What about the differences between families of all sisters and those with sisters and brothers?

Finally (and most elusive to pin down), I think there is something disconcerting and oddly threatening where the balance of power is as undefined and fraught with ambivalence as between siblings. In a girl's relationship with her parents, the perimeters of power are clearly drawn. But in relationships with siblings, the sharing of power is often in constant flux: at times, a relationship of equals; at times, any one or the other may take control. If these early scripts stay unresolved, any research by a sibling of siblings retains the stigma of self-justification (even the academics Sutton-Smith and Rosenberg are human enough to dedicate The Sibling to "our older siblings who will undoubtedly regard this as just another form of harassment").

Not until I turned to literature did I find stories and themes that reinforced my own thinking about sisters and began giving shape to this book. Where academics floundered because the subject was too unwieldy or too tenuous to reduce to theory and generalization, novelists pierced to the heart of the matter by breathing life into the specific, the unique and the extraordinary—and inadvertently finding the universal. Many of the topics this book will consider have analogues in stories, novels and plays, from the rivalry of Rachel and Sarah and of Cinderella and her stepsisters to the unassailable friendship of Ursula and Gudrun in Women in Love, or the eager solidarity of the March sisters in Little Women; from the polarities of youth in "Snow-White and Rose-Red" to the sympathies of old age in Jessamyn West's memoir of her sister's death in The Woman Said Yes. Still, there were holes, gaps, subjects skimmed or overlooked.

Gradually it dawned on me, in a sort of subterranean way, like realizing the man you are going to marry is the one you have been loving for years. The book I was looking for I was going to have to write myself. I had the outline, the metaphor: my own experience as a sister of a sister was the seed; the psychological literature, the roots and the trunks, was the centuries of novels, stories and plays. But the final flowering was to be my own: an exploration of sisters from youth to age, from rivalry to solidarity, from family to family, and a search for the connections between sisters within the family and without, between blood sisters and the feminist ideal of sisterhood.

I wanted a complex and varied cross-section of sisters and began with long, thorough and emotionally charged personal interviews. For every family of sisters described here, I met and talked with many others: in all about fifty sisters from thirty families. I also took a classified ad in *Ms.* and placed a notice in the newsletter of the national organization of Mothers of Twins Clubs, asking for women to fill out a questionnaire on sisters, to broaden my scope and hear from people I couldn't meet in person.

The Questionnaire was detailed, probing and intense (see Appendix). Several women wrote apologetically that it was too painful to fill out. Yet I received more than one hundred and fifty voluminous, passionate, completed Questionnaires, and the large response testified to the depth and breadth of feeling women had about their sisters, which many admitted had long gone unexamined and unexplained.

Thinking about how different this book would be had my sister written it or had we written it together was, in a curious way, the starting point of the Questionnaire. Annie's vantage point, her birth position, her emotional, intellectual and sexual history, her sense of humor, of propriety and of the outrageous would have taken the broad outlines of our story and shaped it into another portrait entirely, with different shading and coloration, points of emphasis, starkness and subtlety, seriousness, silliness and wit. Knowing she would read my version kept me honest and prematurely chastened.

A conversation with Kate Millett's sister Mallory (five years younger than Kate as Annie is five years younger than I), haunted my thoughts on the subject. Some years ago, Kate Millett made a film, *Three Lives,* and one of the lives portrayed was Mallory's. I saw it in a women's film festival when it came out, and found it boldly dramatic and, I thought, deeply revealing. But Mallory, who is an actress, a Bohemian and an outspoken and independent spirit in her own right, told me, "I don't feel that the film was me. It's as if you took a photo of me, cut it into pieces and put it together again as a picture of Kate." That image became a kind of totem, a warning against looking into the lives of others and seeing only one's own face reflected, over and over.

By using the Questionnaires, I wanted to allow the differ-

xviii   SISTERS

ences, the varieties of point of view to emerge and to watch
the mosaic of family life change according to which sister
was pasting in the pieces. Since often several sisters in one
family answered the Questionnaire, it provided a sounding
board in the midst of a set of sisters, a means for sisters to
talk to each other indirectly and, occasionally, at bewildered
cross-purposes. I had no initial stake in whose side was the
"right" one or the "true" story (I knew from experience that
within the same family, each has a different set of parents, a
different childhood, a different vision and future). But, like a
friend, my sympathies could be drawn from one side to the
other, depending on the pull and persuasion of the story.
Mainly, I wanted to track down as many different sides of the
story as possible, a kind of *Rashomon* of sisters and sisterhood.

The one hundred and fifty respondents turned out to be a
diverse group, including:

* Number of families: Thirteen family sets, including
thirty-five women, and one hundred and fifteen unrelated
women from different families.

* Family composition: About half of the respondents had
brothers, about half came from all-girl families.

* Birth position: About one-third of the respondents were
oldest children, one-third, middle, and one-third, youngest.

* Background: Of the *Ms.* respondents, about two-thirds
came from middle-class or professional families, about one-
third from working-class families; of the Mothers of Twins
Clubs respondents, about two-thirds came from working-class
families and about one-third from middle-class.

* Occupation: Among others, student and professor,
housewife and mother, truckdriver and psychologist, actress
and computer programmer.

The average age of the respondents was thirty-two (though,
overall, their ages ranged from eighteen to eighty-two).
The sample, therefore, emphasized the woman who had
emerged from her family of birth and was involved in the
process of establishing an independent identity, vocation,
style of life and, in many cases, a family of her own. This
seemed a crucial juncture to examine, since it is a time when
sibling relationships (as well as parent-child) are often dramatically shifting gears. (And though the Questionnaires
highlight this development transition, the interviews for the
rest of the book follow women through the full range of the
lifecycle.)

The chief difference in the two sample groups—*Ms.* readers and Mothers of Twins Club members—was their consciousness about feminism and the Women's Movement. It was this crucial difference in attitude which led me to choose these two disparate groups. Most of the *Ms.* readers considered themselves feminists and were open to exploring how feminism influenced their relationships with their sisters; most Mothers of Twins Club members did not define themselves as feminists and did not seek out the same connections. But as it turned out, the spectrum of emotions described—the close, the distant and the ambivalent relationships—was quite similar in both groups, regardless of the women's attitudes about feminism. Awareness of the politics of sisterhood in no way meant that a woman's personal experience of being and having a sister was uniformly or arbitrarily positive. And many of the women who had no strong ideological feelings about sisterhood still often realized how powerful their relationships with their sisters were or could be.

My final criterion for choosing a subject to interview was my own responsiveness to her story and my instinct for whether it was representative enough to provide the breadth of commonality or eccentric enough to provide the depth and quirkiness of truth. I wanted enough shadings of experience for readers to find at least some images of themselves and some of their own families.

One imbalance, inadvertent at first: My interviews favored all-girl families, rather than mixed-sex families. I did interview a number of brothers about sisters and vice versa, but primarily, I focused on all-sister families in order to study the sister bond isolated and at its most intense. Also I found that particularly strong and creative female personalities often emerged from these families, a phenomenon corroborated by Margaret Hennig and Anne Jardim's study, *The Managerial Woman.* Of the twenty-five women they studied (chosen from among the top hundred businesswomen in the country), *all of them* were the eldest of families of all girls.

Why include well-known women in the same? My hunch was that their more publicly known stories and talents would epitomize the delicate balance of competition and camaraderie among all sisters. I wanted to gauge the influence of family, and particularly, of the sister bond on the intellectual and creative flowering of some of the leading women in this country in the arts, politics and education. But since our conversations centered around sisters, not arts, politics or education, I was able to glimpse a more intimate and perhaps more vulnerable side of these women. For many of them had meticulously etched a public persona, but it was tricky to wear it talking about a sister who knew her when.

I also wanted to draw on these women's professional expertise to conjecture theoretically about sisters and sisterhood: Carly Simon, for instance, had written a song about sisters (and she sang professionally with her sister Lucy before she made it on her own); Margaret Mead had studied the theme in other cultures; Gloria Steinem had given speeches and founded a magazine about sisterhood; Flo Kennedy had litigated and campaigned ardently for the rights of her black sisters; and Kate Millett had made the film *Three Lives* about her sister Mallory.

I was sounding out the resonances that having sisters made on these celebrated women's personal and public lives. I was also, of course, listening for the resonance that rang the other way. What was it like, under the skin, for instance, to be the fifty-three-year-old older sister married and raising six children in the suburbs, when your younger sister was an internationally known figurehead of the Women's Movement, barnstorming against many of your most precious values? What about being the fey and slightly visionary younger sister ("I can read a whole book about astronomy," she told me, "and afterwards remember three rainbows colliding"), with an older sister an anthropologist who systematized other cultures with the precision of a seismograph? Or a middle sister with a sweet style and a mellow voice, when your younger sister, whose voice and style are no more mellow and sweet, rockets to the top of the pop charts by the force of circumstance and charisma?

Less schooled in (and less foxy about) answering questions, the lesser-known sisters were often a richer resource than their more public siblings. They had more time and energy for an interview, drank tea or beer with me in their homes, rather than scheduling me into an appointment in their offices. And their censors were not as vigilant. So my conversations with Susanne Steinem Patch, Elizabeth Mead Steig and Lucy Simon Levine were among the most enjoyable and valuable of any for the book.

What about the sisters I approached for interviews who said no? There were plenty of them, and their reasons were a Rorschach of the complexity and density of the subject. A modestly well-known folksinger, for example, makes no secret, chatting during performances, of her rivalry with her infinitely better-known sister. But when I asked to talk with her, she didn't want to expose the silver dagger between them for publication. "It will take me at least five years before I even figure out what I think about my sister," she demurred.

A photographer who freely takes pictures of her two younger sisters in a bleak and unflattering spectrum of moods was at first eager to talk with me, then got psychogenically cold feet and changed her mind. "Words are so much more dangerous than pictures," she protested. "Right now I feel my sisters are an enormous drag, and talking about them would depress me for weeks."

And this, from a world-famous chef, worded as artfully as she bakes a pie crust:

> I adore [my sister], but we are five years apart, she being the younger. We never really knew each other until we were both grown, so she had little influence on me—but perhaps I did on her because I was older. We've lived apart almost all our adult lives, love seeing each other when we do, which is rarely more than a day or two or a week or so at a time. Thus I don't think I would be of much use to you.

Too painful, too private, too fraught with ambivalence, too hot to handle—the reasons people said no became signposts for me, clues to what to dig for, what was denied and feared. I realized that sisters' influence on each other was often elusive to pin down and varied in intensity and involvement from family to family (from what family therapist Salvador Minuchin calls the "disengaged" family to the "enmeshed" one). Sibling influence was also often most interesting where it was least recognized or defined. And predictably, one sister's motive for silence could easily be another's reason to speak.

The passionate response to my request for respondents to the Questionnaire testified more than anything to the power of feeling that many women have about their sisters. Painful, private, fraught with ambivalence, yes, but the women who wrote to me, I had to conclude as their emotions sizzled on the page, relished thinking about their sisters: some to discharge anger, some to unmask and disempower jealousy, and some simply to brag about love. But most answered me for the most obvious reason of all: No one had formally asked them before about a relationship they knew in their hearts to be crucial.

Through reading, interviews, questionnaires and endless hours of brooding about sisters, I began to formulate the contours of this book and define its objectives. I wanted to begin with the relationship I knew best and one which began my search: my relationship with my sister, Annie. I wanted to look at our influence on each other at each stage of our journeys, the sharing and diverging of interests and identities at each juncture growing up, the widening and closing of the five-year age difference between us. I also wanted to puzzle out the mysterious process by which we negotiated from fierce rivals to dearest friends.

Then I wanted to examine the web of ways that sisters in every family influence and shape each other at each stage of development, each "passage" (to borrow Gail Sheehy's phrase) along the life-cycle: from the hammering-out of identities growing up through the choices and decisions of adulthood. Within the spectrum of the life-cycle, I wanted to describe the constant changes and fluctuations, ambivalences and resolutions, competition and camaraderie between sisters over time, for as psychologist Robert White explains, "The influence of any given sibling, taken over time, may consist of a complex pattern of benefits and harms."[1]

Then drawing specifically on the Questionnaire material, I wanted to focus on the dynamics of the family crucible. I wanted to look at sisters' places in the family constellation and study the messages of birth order. I also wanted to probe the complex issue of influence both inside the family crucible and beyond: parents' and brothers' influence on sisters' relationships, and sisters' direct and indirect influence on each other.

Using models from stories and fairy tales, I also wanted to present three distinct patterns of sister relationships, exploring when and how they begin, change or haunt sisters till old age. Using *Little Women*, I wanted to describe the creation and function of roles in the large family of sisters. Using "Cinderella," I wanted to trace the roots of sibling rivalry and the intricate *pas de deux* (*trois* or *quatre*) by which rivals may become friends. And using "Snow-White and Rose-Red," I wanted to look at patterns of opposition and polarities, whether harmonious or discordant.

Then I wanted to examine two crucial areas of sisters'

influence on each other, beginning as early as the nursery and continuing often till the grave: sexuality and art. I was especially curious about the process by which sisters become models for each other, both in their sexual and creative development, offering and receiving a lifetime's worth of messages and mores, alternately serving as complements or counterparts to each other's explorations. This section would close with portraits of sisters in old age, sisters who had weathered the closeness and distance, the rivalry and polarity, the sexual and creative influence of the years—and emerged as most loyal friends. And knowing that any of these issues alone could fill a book, I decided to bring them to life throughout by story, portrait and example.

Finally, I wanted to tread the emotional terrain outside the family and explore how having a sister affects a woman's attitude toward other women and her capacity for closeness and friendship with women. I wanted to speculate on the connections between sisters within the family and without, between blood sisters and sisters in the Women's Movement, between the subtleties and varieties of actual sister relationships and the political ideal that "Sisterhood is powerful."

This is a book that's grounded in the conversations that go on between sisters, which I have listened to for hours from my own precarious perch as go-between. At times I have listened, as a parent might, for the similarities and differences between sisters, for the clues to the mysteries of growing up, the first spreading of wings. Other times, I have listened as a friend might, for the roots of pain and jealousy and the comfort of friendship; and still others, I have kept a distance, a detached observer looking for patterns, the common thread.

I have heard two sisters in a row insist they are absolutely honest with each other, then spend hours telling me secrets, grudges they have never shared with each other. I have heard sisters who swear they are never jealous or angry at each other remember, in detail, dreams of each other's mutilation and death. But I have also heard sisters who candidly admitted the ambivalences of dreams but also knew unambivalently that a sister's friendship was an irreplaceable gift (and many who preferred their sisters' company to anyone else's on earth).

The content, the words of our conversations have not usually surprised me. What surprised me was that within a family, the voices of sisters as they're talking are virtually always the same. The same inflections, nuances, cadences. Now what that means, that two or four or seven sisters talk with the same voice, I did not at first understand. But after hearing the voices repeat themselves enough, I knew that no matter how much the words diverged, the voices spoke the common, irrefutable and inextricable connection of family.

1

PERSON-TO-PERSON: MY SISTER AND I

I know when I was nine, feelings between my sister and me changed. I became her most loyal admirer, and she became my staunchest supporter. Still, most relationships that have had to weather nine years of intense rivalry and resentment, a few years of idolatry and eight years of separation would have dissolved long ago. How did our relationship survive these odds?

—ANNE FISHEL

I HAVE BEEN TOLD BY FRIENDS WHO HAPPEN TO OVERHEAR my side of the weekly phone conversations between my sister and me that ours is a private language, barely discernible even to those who know me best, a thick brew of intensity and high hilarity, baby talk and worldly counsel, sophisticated allusions, salty Yiddish and a patois of strange inflections and phraseology almost primitive in its litany. The ritual of these calls is smoothly formalized so that the content can be free-form, unpredictable, as certain flowers are meticulously planted and cultivated so that their wild beauty can bloom, a surprise no matter how planned for. The calls come late at night, in the seductive zone when the rates drop, usually, but not always Thursdays, announced by the promising crackle of the long-distance wire hooking New York to Berkeley, and an operator calling person-to-person for "Elizabeth Rose." That is the code to which I reply, "She's in the shower," another code which signals Annie to hang up and redial directly, thus wrangling a few, extra precious minutes from the tight fist of Mother Bell. These calls go on as long as they must and longer than they should. They are subsidized by a too-generous father who must realize at the same primitive level where Annie and I make the calls that they are crucial family lifelines. (The habit of phone codes, at least, we learned from him. When we were younger, and he traveled on business, he would check in to announce his safe arrival in a distant city,

3

by calling person-to-person for "Charlotte or Emily Brontë." So inextricably are the phone wires tied up with our roots and our destinies.)

Ever since I left home, I have come to rely on these phone calls as a talisman at the crossroads, a reminder of the girl I have been to the woman I am becoming. The calls are as reliable as my mother's Hannukah gelt and mushy, old-fashioned valentines, my father's clippings of the obituaries of second-rate novelists whose creative and procreative output is equally prodigious. But while the message of my parents' totems is stability and continuity, the theme of the phone calls with my sister is change. In the ten years since I left home and the phone calls began, we have seen each other through pains and *coups*, fallings in and out of love, early radicalization (hers) and ambivalent defloration (mine), waiting to get into college, chomping at the bit to get out, therapy, women's groups and privacy, *Sturm und Drang* with our parents and the mending of fences between us, her undying series of devotions to astrology, Marxism, clowns, Freud, vegetarianism and the gradual embracing of turkey, and my equally wholehearted and sequential dedication to Dylan, dance, Henry James, Joan Didion, journal writing, free-lancing and junk food. We are each other's reference point at our turning points. And the dance between us is also a delicate balance of influence, between leader and led, teacher and taught, soother and soothed. We alternately give a shoulder and need one.

How this delicate balance emerged from the hair-pulling helter-skelter of childhood is one of the curiosities that began my search.

I have few early memories of my sister, Elizabeth. Photographs reveal a childhood relationship that is warm and loving: the two of us dressed in matching taffeta outfits or naked together in the bathtub, always our arms around each other and wide smiles to the camera. The display of sisterliness recorded in these photos masked the true feelings we had for each other then. For Elizabeth's hand, seemingly benign in its clasp around my waist, was often furtively pinching me just as the picture was being snapped. The hidden sentiment in the photograph was part of a larger emotional pattern of my feeling subordinate to my sister and, consequently, jealous. Months of shining her shoes in return for a small charm, and playing her student by taking a battery of tests that she

*created and administered, left me humiliated, though eager to
please. Daily I asked my parents which of their two daughters
they liked the best, although I was never comforted by their
equivocal responses. I did have two reliable sources of comfort. The first was the delight I experienced when my mother
was angry at my sister but not at me; "You not yelling at me,
Mommy" was my frequent refrain. The second was the
writing of secret stories in which I reduced my sister to a
baby eating bananas and sucking her thumb.*

Every leap and bound of our early years was meticulously
recorded by our mother, who had given up her own work as a
professional photographer to raise us. Mostly the pictures tell
the story of the efforts made by parents and grandparents to
force our common bond. Here we are, age seven and two, in
our matching red-and-white striped bathing suits, clutching
each other on the Long Island sand dunes. Here again, at
eight and three, in the yellow cotton sundresses with the tiny
pink flowers, which I thought were far too babyish for me.
And then at nine and four, in the black velvet party dresses,
which Grandma Mollie had given her two princesses. And
this time I was indignant that Annie's outfits were as sophisticated as mine. (I was already beginning to balk at the link
with her more childish state, knowing it was still my own, yet
chafing to break free of it, to soar into the world of stockings
and heels and Littlest Angel bras. Even today I cringe when
our ages are confused, an atavistic need not yet lost for
acknowledgment of those extra years, that evanescent edge of
maturity.)

During that early period of enforced and ersatz twinship,
the differences in age and temperament were still inalterable.
As the elder, I was prone to capitalize on my power, privilege
and self-proclaimed superior cache of wisdom. The five years
of unlimited parental favor I had accrued before Annie was
born had left me with an inflated view of my powers that I
was not easily going to trade in. (Only years later did I
realize, chastened, that her presence taught me how to share,
how to hammer out a settlement of differences, how, in short,
to enter into the human race.) But then, I shamelessly bossed
her around, made her do favors for me, played teacher and
gave her and her friends batteries of tests. As the baby, she
rarely took the blame, was reserved and secretive, her nose
buried in a fuzzy sweater she sniffed for years to give her

comfort, quietly mobilizing her resources. I myself sucked my thumb until I was fourteen and gingerly took to kissing boys. Ours was a nervous childhood.

There was once a time (I shrink to remember it) when I took my baby sister lovingly in my arms, walked to the open window of our fourteenth-floor apartment and pretended I was going to throw her out of it. When she wailed, I immediately retreated, shamefaced but having tasted omnipotence. The appeal of the fantasy was not so much that I wanted to get rid of her, but rather that I needed her as the means to assert my will. For beneath my show of bravura and the swagger of my inflated powers, I was still just a five-year-old whose actual power was severely (and understandably) circumscribed by the adults who still ran the show: parents, grandparents, teachers, mothers and fathers of friends. Dominating Annie allowed me the transitory illusion of power in an unfree world. (And coincidentally, when Annie reached the same age that I was then, she indulged in some omnipotence fantasies of her own: the secret stories in which she reduced me to a banana-eating, thumb-sucking baby.) Only when we both grew up a little, only when each of us began to find her own resources, the glimmer of her own real strength, was it possible to think about forming a friendship of equals.

When we fought, like couples who've lived together for years, we knew the most tender nerve to strike. But when we decided to cooperate, we became a force to reckon with.

Who could say when our solidarity began? Was it making silly faces in the pantry mirror when we were supposed to be observing our table manners? Was it the trip to Europe when I was fourteen, she was nine, or was it coming home and discovering boys? Was it the weeks she coached me practicing my walk in high heels or when I coached her recitation of "Tarantella" for the school poetry contest? Was it when we discovered the power of a united front against the badgering and caviling of our too-well-intentioned parents? Was it the songs, the rhymes, the private language we made up, the burgeoning knowledge of shared history and shared mythology we could create and re-create, more powerful for us than for any outsiders? Was it corroborating each other's experience of the family and therefore making each other's world more understandable? Was it the year I was sixteen and she eleven, when I became Elizabeth, not Lizzy, and she changed her middle name from Katherine to Cassandra? Did we find ourselves or each other first?

Just as it's impossible to point to the very moment one falls in love, so it was with becoming sisters. An accumulation of shocks of recognition, gradual but irrevocable, until we could not imagine how we had survived before.

It is the June Annie graduates from college, and we are strolling the streets of Cambridge, laughing and absorbed in each other's company, in the muggy early-summer sun, in the charged atmosphere of the rite of passage. Both of us have lived and gone to school here in succession, never overlapping, so it is a kind of metaphor for our common ground, where we have separately sown our seeds—and our wild oats. First it was my terrain, the hole-in-the-wall bookshop, papered with stately portraits of poets whom the crusty old proprietor knew by name, though swore he'd never read a word they wrote, and the cafeteria that was open all night for displaced New Yorkers and that finally went under (because Cambridge, after all, was just not New York), and the odiously hip boutique that hawked blue jeans and tie-dyed shirts and then had the execrable taste to hawk mass-produced memorabilia from the Harvard strike. Then it became Annie's terrain, and the crusty old bookstore proprietor died, and the glossy bookstore around the corner mushroomed, and people who actually wanted to buy books instead of revel in atmosphere started going there instead. And the café and pastry scene exploded like a tasty cream puff, so there was one place to go for the best capuccino and another for the best chocolate-chip cookie and yet a third for the best piece of cheesecake (so good it also tasted like New York). And the odiously hip boutiques began pushing Frye boots and delicate shoes that tied around the ankles, and instead of the blue jeans and tie-dye, clothes that (God forbid) matched.

But for all its self-consciousness and artifice, Cambridge was the place that allowed each of us to come into her own. It was a peculiar form of nurturing, hardly a kind mother, breezy and disinterested in the fall, black and discontent in the winter, and in the spring too sweet, too pretty, so that the expectations raised could never possibly be met. Still, it was the place I had my first lover, my first bank account, my first inkling that writing was more than a private fantasy, could even earn a person a living. (My first writing teacher held up the novel he had published at twenty-three and said, "Anyone in this room could do the same.") It was the place the

Vietnam War came home to me, when I realized the cops could as easily have reduced me to a bloody pulp as the next one (had I been in the wrong building at the wrong time), and thus became my first tentative link between the personal and the political. It was also the place that first introduced me to feminism and to sisterhood.

For Annie, in the next era, a mere five years later (first lover, first radicalization, first consciousness-raising already behind her), it was nevertheless the first place to read Marx and Freud, study and teach women's labor history and think of herself as a scholar, and still in another psychic breath to don a red nose and motley layers of secondhand togs and join a clown troupe in the guise of Pinky. It was also the first place to find a love that lasted and lasted and the first occasion to live on her own, pay the phone bills, serve quiche for company and have a cat. It was also the first opportunity to learn to administer a Rorschach and to work in a hospital with a teen-age mute who, after weeks of silent walks and volleyball games, turned to Annie and said, "That's a nice watch you're wearing," and the first place to consider becoming a therapist.

As we wander the familiar streets, we talk of the common ground traveled together yet five years apart, the separate routes that have from time to time veered in opposite directions, only to converge again farther down the road. We talk of the differences that have been allowed to flourish, only to etch out and underline the similarities, the five years' distance between us that has actually narrowed the gap, so that we lose track of older and younger, exchange ages and places. We consider our roles in the family, once as sharply defined as salt and pepper. Now they have lost their borders, their constraints; there are no polarities, and, scrupulously, no favorites, each allowed her center stage, her retreat.

We walk the common streets, talking about the eras passing and dreaming a little of the future, of what we will become, where we'll live, whether we'll marry and whom, whether our children will walk these same streets. And though I am making this walk sound serious and portentous, that was only later, with the symbolism of hindsight. Had you happened to pass us walking along in the early-summer sun, you would have seen two laughing and chattering young women, engaged in that patois of strange inflections and private phrases, wrapped in each other's company and oblivious to the world.

When I left for college, flashing my *Songs of Innocence and Experience,* my Marimekkos and my suede boots, Annie was still a little girl. When I came home a half-year later, she had miraculously grown up. The little girl had gone to see *The Sound of Music* seven times, sung the theme song from "The Patty Duke Show" all over town and collected Halloween pennies for UNICEF. Her involvement with the opposite sex was limited to a faithful correspondence with a pen pal in India. The grown-up (and she insisted at fourteen on being called a woman) was into astrology and smoked dope, went to political demonstrations, studied feminism and argued about the revolution. She had even given up her Indian pen pal (who by then was proposing marriage) in order to handle the more or less full-time barrage of phone calls from New York City's radical high-school underground.

Despite our closeness during the years before I left the nest, my clearing out was also pivotal. No longer was Annie forced to be the "little sister," either at home or at school. She was now a strong lady in her own right. She strode through the city in her farmer jeans and her hiking boots with a new bounce in her step and loosened her childhood ponytail in masses of head-turning chestnut waves. (By this point, we had also lost whatever slight physical resemblance we had as kids: Annie forever taller and slimmer, I, rounder and more freckled in the face, although we still share certain facial expressions, mannerisms and the habit of saying "Definitely.")

As in many relationships, this period of separation was necessary to reestablish ourselves as equals. For many years, our birth order had hampered us both. I had to be the leader, the counselor, the responsible one. Annie was the follower and the faithful. But when, at the grand and tender age of fourteen, she stood up on her own feet, the power radically shifted and became shared. From then on, I turned to her for advice, ideas and inspiration as often as she turned to me. I may have introduced her to Dylan, Hermann Hesse, Kate Millett. But she introduced me to the Grateful Dead, Chairman Mao and the guerrilla art of plastering "THIS AD EXPLOITS WOMEN" stickers throughout the New York subway system.

The radicalization in manners and mores of her generation, compared with mine, was another great equalizer in our relationship. Though five years younger than my college friends, Annie's friends dressed as we did, listened to the

same music, went to the same demonstrations and more or
less read the same books. Her friends were light-years beyond
my schoolgirl coterie, who, even as seniors at our New York
City girls' school, were virgins in every sexual and political
sense of the word. Already, at fourteen, Annie's friends were
women of the world.

My friends tore their hair and hearts out for Paul McCartney. One of Annie's classmates happened to bump into Paul
McCartney on a New York City street corner and ever so
suavely agreed to join him at the Plaza for tea.

*My world fell apart when Elizabeth left for college. No
breakup of a love affair or falling away of a friendship has
since equaled the sense of loss I felt at age thirteen when my
sister first went away. Abandonment was coupled with the
changing of my family role from younger sister to only child.
This meant that I had to carry the weight of dinner conversations instead of listening attentively on the fringes and had to
defend myself against a two-on-one attack from my parents
instead of acting as a buffer between them and my sister. My
refrains of "You not yelling at me, Mommy" no longer rang
out.*

*I like to look back on my early adolescent years as
extremely rebellious ones, years of trouble and havoc for
everyone involved with me at home and at school. But my
rebellion was not so dramatic. Perhaps if I were still convinced that the revolution was on its way, I would not be so
cynical. Now I look back on the demos I went to, often
knowing there would be violence, the raising my voice to my
parents about politics, the befriending of bus drivers, Cuban
revolutionaries, chestnut vendors, and other street strangers,
and I realize there were personal motivations as well as
political ones.*

*For the first time, I was doing things Elizabeth had never
done and might even have disapproved of. The cultivation of
a somewhat wild, reckless identity was the beginning of my
development as a person distinct from her. Our family,
schooling, clothing had been almost identical, but rebellion
was mine.*

Two front-page clips from our political histories; the year
was 1971. One, Annie's article in her school newspaper,
"Womanna From Heaven," an impassioned first-person account of the Feminist March on Washington for abortion on

demand. Her women's group was with her, and some had already had secret and illegal abortions. Even at sixteen, they knew firsthand why they were demonstrating.

The other, from the *Boston Globe*, about the proud and defiant march of Radcliffe women to protest Harvard's demolition of the women's center. I am one of three students in the photograph, holding a banner that reads "THIS IS FOR THE SISTERS." The other two women are also chanting and raising clenched fists, but I somehow manage to look, well, polite. As the eldest and so-well-reared daughter, I always had trouble raising my voice.

Unlearning to not speak—Marge Piercy's phrase that could have been my own political credo. A tentative beginning in the anti-War movement when, as a high-school student, I stood among the crowd shouting along with Stokely, "Hell, no, we won't go." Then a confused Radcliffe freshman during the strike of '69, agreeing with all the SDS demands, yet psychologically unable to seize a building. And finally, gradually, finding my way into the Women's Movement, experiencing the *Click!* of the personal made political and beginning to write about it. The girl who dreamed only of becoming Louisa May Alcott had finally discovered her sisterhood with Margaret Fuller and Emma Goldman.

For Annie, the learning to speak out came years earlier, I think, her anger closer to the surface, her feistiness less overlaid with social conditioning. My high-school rebellion was mostly a retreat into the fantasy world of "The Universal Soldier" and "What Have They Done to the Rain?" But while I was a brooder, lost in folk visions, Annie at the same age was creating visions of her own. Organizing a sit-in at her proper girls' school to protest uniform regulations, raising money for an experimental school of her own called Fern Hill, mobilizing a women's group and school assemblies on feminism, joining demonstration after demonstration (almost getting clobbered by construction workers during the infamous Wall Street debacle). And throughout it all, endlessly defying or having to defend herself against the united parental front. Che Cassandra, our father called her, a *nom de guerre*.

The accident of birth order was the early imprinting of our political roles. For the five uninterrupted years of parental attention I'd had before Annie was born made me anxious, approval-seeking and rather uneasy about rocking the boat. While Annie had her five years alone under the parental gaze as an adolescent and during a time of political upheaval, so her response was to challenge, argue and make waves. Now our modes have converged, given way to the changes of time, lapping against our attitudes like the sea against rocks. But every so often, the waves will part in such a way that I can see straight to the bottom, the way we once were and will somehow always be.

The night before my sister's graduation, we go to a party together, a huge extravaganza thrown in the courtyard of the futuristic Science Center, complete with a bottomless pit of booze, a continuous tape of disco music and hundreds of about-to-be graduates in stripes and sports coats and shoes that tie around the ankles, hustling and bumping and boogy-ing the night away in ritualized anticipation of entering the real world. In my day, there would have been more beards and blue jeans, more grass than booze and less of a sense of purpose, more anomie about the next step. Had there been a Science Center we would have been allowed to use it only under the sharp eye of a security guard.

Annie is at home here, slips into the crowd in her glitzy red satin pants and black leotard, dancing and laughing and making the rounds of friends. I, meanwhile, float around the periphery, not exactly the wallflower at the orgy, but an observer from a different era of a scene that is not my show.

Once Annie tiptoed in the shadows of my teen-age parties, round-eyed with wonder at the shady underworld of nervous-ly blooming sexuality. Then I was the slightly prim teenager, wishing passionately to be cool, who tried out the steps I had faithfully practiced in front of the bathroom mirror, alter-nately feeling the lure of the party and trying to stifle it. The good girl and the growing girl were caught in their own awkward fandango, and I was teetering under the burden of being the older sister, the first daughter. For along with the ephemeral power and prestige of my role went the burden of a sex education, from which Annie was shielded by the alleged innocence of her youth. By and large, the messages were tacit, not explicit, slipped to me by innuendo or between the punch lines of jokes theoretically *"nicht* for the *Kinder."* "Sex is something you should keep, you shouldn't give it away to just anyone." "Tampax can be dangerous." "If you must use words like penis and vagina, at least lower your voice." Before I left for college, my mother showed me a diaphragm, while strongly cautioning me never to find myself in a situation where I'd have to use one—or at least not until I was safely married. Long before Annie even reached the age of consent, Mom seemed to have lost this zeal to overprotect her honor. Perhaps her attitude shifted with the generations, perhaps it merely mellowed with the years. Still, somehow I feel our parents will forever think of me as a virgin, probably long after I have children of my own. Whereas Annie's sexuality was a little less tended, allowed to blossom more at her own risk.

So tonight it is my turn to dawdle in the shadows and gape, as Annie sashays and spins and saunters among the crowd. I am at the same time watching our differences at a distance and watching through Annie's eyes, immersed in the scene, the way a parent who can hardly carry a tune relishes vicariously a child's operatic solo. And then we are dancing together, and the steady, primitive beat of the disco music drums the differences away, and there is just the tap of our shoes that tie around the ankles and the sway of our stripes and the merging of our mannerisms and our grins.

The ceremonial march to Annie's graduation is heralded by trumpets and led off by the oldest Harvard graduate still extant, a bone-dry and determined hundred-and-three-year-old gentleman, marching a proud straight line, though the lenses of both his glasses are shattered, a dubious symbol of our endurability against odds. Falling in line behind him are the representatives from most of the classes since his, a motley and triumphant parade of successes and ne'er-do-wells, lawyers and ladies' men, leaders and followers, bankers and drinkers and an especially hearty and well-heeled sampling of elder Radcliffe stateswomen, dressed almost like sisters in their tailored summer dresses and matching jackets.

Bringing up the rear of the line, yet of course dominating it, is Annie's class, a proud array of caps and gowns over would-be doctors and stockbrokers and union organizers and teachers of the deaf. And finally, Annie and her friends veer into sight, hair wafting in the breeze beneath their mortarboards. One friend has gotten high for the occasion and is dragging rakishly on a cigarette, thumbing her nose a little at it all, but beneath the poses they are sheepishly proud. I am standing in a thicket of parents, aunts and uncles, shutters snapping, and I, too, am proud, the way a parent would be proud, but there is a different quality to it, another charge to the identification. Like a parent, I can watch the marching parade and see the spectrum of time unfurl, the stages of heartiness and frailness. But unlike the parent who is buffered from the child by the cushioning zone of twenty or thirty years, the distance between my sister and me suddenly seems perilously small. Only five years before, I was marching in the same procession, feeling worldly-wise, and Annie was agape on the sidelines. Now I am more and less worldly, more and less wise.

As I watch her transition, my own five years unfold in front of me, the breakthroughs and setbacks, dilemmas and dawdlings. I wonder if Annie watches me for clues as I puzzle, blunder, navigate the next step, the way I watch our two older cousins, raised almost like sisters to us, for signs and hints as they work, marry, have children, separate, carry on. "Only be afraid of the big things in life," said one of my cousins, in all seriousness, when she was fourteen, I was nine, "like going to the dentist." Later I asked them whether it hurt the first time and how they decided whom to marry and what it felt like to give birth and to raise a son. I planned and measured my script against theirs. Now I wonder if they felt as ambivalently worldly and wise as I do on the sidelines of Annie's passing parade. I wonder whom they watch for clues.

The ceremony passes in a flurry of diplomas and a blaze of heat (even the speaker, indefatigable Barbara Jordan, faints), and I hover between laughter and tears. Evidently, Annie does, too, because by the end of the day she has lost her voice, and the whole family loads her four years of records and books into the car in exhausted silence. Later that night, I cannot help myself, I call her on the phone on the excuse I left something or other I need behind. Person-to-person to Anne Cassandra, and when the scratchy residue of a voice reappearing answers, "She's in the shower," that is all I need to hear.

2

THE FAMILY CONSTELLATION

As I was growing up, I was absolutely certain that I was the favorite. I mean I just considered myself more important [than the other siblings]. I was very conscious of my role in the family. My parents made a great to-do about the fact that I was first. For instance, on Christmas, when we came in to the tree in the morning, I was always the one allowed first in line. I was older and smarter and stronger, and I think my mother also gave me an unusual amount of responsibility, so that I learned to think I could do a lot more things than [my younger siblings] could do. I saw myself as a surrogate mother and loved it.

—LUCILLE FORER, author of
The Birth Order Factor

How did (does) your birth position affect your sense of yourself, asked the Questionnaire, *for instance, your self-image, your relationship with siblings, your relationship with friends, your work?* This chapter will explore the theories and conjecture that surround each of the major birth positions: the myth and mystique of the dominating oldest sister, the compromising middle sister, and the spoiled and babied youngest sister. Then, drawing on material from the Questionnaire and interviews, the chapter will consider how a variety of women respond to the fate and accident of their birth position, whether they follow or resist its inner script—or are confounded by ambivalence about it. For just as astrologists recommend knowledge of the constellations to help us rule the stars rather than be ruled by them, similarly with birth order: What we make of the birth position we are born to is at least as illuminating as what it makes of us.

"The position in the family leaves an indelible stamp upon the style of life,"[1] wrote Alfred Adler, who, early in this century, was the first psychoanalyst to probe in depth siblings' influence on each other, the first to look beyond the tight-knit father-mother-child unit and examine the complex relations between *every* star in what he termed the "family constellation." Student, friend and later rival of Freud, Adler is generally considered the founding father of birth-order research. A self-proclaimed feisty and ambitious "youngest," he emphasized the competitive striving among siblings in the family and was the first to name the terms of birth order and to take seriously the effect of birth position on every nook and cranny of personality development. "The situation is never the same for two children in a family," he pointed out, "and each child will show in his style of life the results of his attempts to adapt himself to his own peculiar circumstances." [2] How each child's adaptation to the circumstances of birth position influences ego development, intelligence, creativity, need for power, sociability and family relationships became the broad outlines of the birth-order picture. Within those outlines, Adler sketched the styles of behavior commonly associated with the various birth positions inside the family constellation.

> Every oldest child has experienced for some time the situation of an only child and has been compelled suddenly to adapt himself to a new situation at the birth of the next oldest. . . . The first-born child is generally given a good deal of attention and spoiling. He has been accustomed to be the center of the family. Too often it is quite suddenly and sharply, without any preparation, that he finds himself ousted from this position. . . . Other children may lose position in the same way; but they will probably not feel it so strongly. . . . Sometimes a child who has lost his power, the small kingdom he ruled, understands better than others the importance of power and authority. . . .

> The second child is in a quite different position. . . . Throughout his childhood he has a pacemaker. There is always a child ahead of him in age and development and he is stimulated to exert himself and catch up. . . . He believes as if he were in a race, as if some one were a step or two in front and he had to hurry to get ahead of him. He is under full steam all the time.

> All other children have followers; all other children can be dethroned; but the youngest can never be dethroned. . . . He is always the baby of the family and probably he is the most pampered. . . . Sometimes a youngest child will not admit to any single ambition, but this is because he wishes to excel in everything, he wishes to be unlimited and unique. [3]

Consider the three Simon sisters, for example—Joanna, Lucy and Carly—three musicians, born three years apart, each with a different history and destiny according to the fate and accident of her birth. The oldest is Joanna Simon, thirty-eight, the opera singer, with frosted blond coif and smoothly, stagily made-up face. She wears blue-and-white gingham-checked slacks in a flowery blue-and-white living room, everything matching, meticulously rehearsed, her aura almost from another era, her parents' era, her interests and mores drilled into her by her upright and erudite father, publisher Richard Simon, of Simon and Schuster. Last of the three to marry (a year before our conversation, after eight years of psychoanalysis), last to break the tie with home and youth, she is still the prima donna, the benevolent despot, dispensing her worldly wit and wisdom, never minding if it falls on deaf ears; the maternal pose is the thing. While she talks, smoothly, stagily as her skin, under her piano hunches a small stuffed rabbit, a child's toy, a wedding present, a symbol of a past dream, a lost promise of eternal splendor that has not entirely panned out.

"I really don't know anything bad about being the oldest. I liked it enormously. It gave me a position of power over my sisters which I enjoyed very much. Because I was the oldest, and my father died when my sisters were fairly young, I had more exposure to him. I knew that he wanted me to grow up to be something special, and he was teaching me. I think I was supposed to teach my sisters.

"I've always felt that since I was the oldest, I was the protector, the one to set the example, and the one who tried to be sure that everybody was all right, that things were under control. I still feel exactly the same way. I feel basically very motherly toward my sisters. That hasn't changed at all. If I thought they were doing something drastically wrong with their lives, making a huge mistake, I would advise them about it."

Calm, controlled, keeping carefully to the surfaces of things, only occasionally peering into the cracks in the veneer, then quickly smoothing the covers again, plumping the pillows of the psyche.

"Since I was the oldest, I thought I should be doing everything first, so when Carly got married, I felt very sorry for myself. And then I figured, everybody has to go at their own pace. And I just got married last year. It took a long time. But I don't regret having waited, and I feel that I was terribly lucky to find the man that I did find. I feel that that was the way it was supposed to be and that's how it happened."

The second is Lucy Simon, thirty-five, the compromiser, the go-between, ingratiating, the caretaker from childhood who followed her tracking and became a nurse, though her heart was never in it:

"Since nursing was something I'd always been interested in as a child, [I thought] maybe I should do it. It really was one of those dumb things. So I am, in fact, a nurse. I didn't spend much time doing it. But that was where my self-image was. It took a lot of years of analysis to realize that it wasn't what I was."

She is the softest, the gentlest of the three, trim and lithe, all light-brown curls and a powdering of freckles, nonchalant chic, carefully unstudied, unhurried. Her world is perhaps the most classic of the three, a nurse married to a doctor, a psychiatrist, with two lovely children, an elegant New York City apartment, a maid, and a skittish poodle named Rosie whom she holds and comforts as she talks, as if she were cuddling protectively the shaggy part of herself.

Once she and Carly were folksingers together, a matched set, the Simon Sisters. Now she's on her own, a pop singer whose career is a ripple, compared with (as it invariably is) the tremendous wave of her younger sister's stardom. And though Lucy Simon is very circumspect, very gracious about the ways her path diverted and diverges from Carly's, her own dreams and ambitions sputter beneath the surface, and when she lets them out, they rip the silky sheen with a vengeance:

"When Carly became successful on her own, there was a kind of distance put between us, because of whatever feeling of guilt that she had made it commercially and Joanna and I hadn't. I think that there goes through so many families—and I don't know if it's ever possible to eliminate it totally—[the feeling] that if one person has something, the other one feels entitled to the same thing. When we were children, it was doled out evenly, and now, as adults, it should stay the same."

Even as an adult, and against her will, the second sister clings to the myth of the equal dole, while the girl within remembers the hurrying to catch up with an older sister and the frantic running from a younger one who was every minute gaining on her.

The third is Carly Simon, thirty-two, youngest of the girls (though brother Peter, twenty-nine, is the family baby and adored pet of his sisters, a photographer and old-time hippie, who, according to Carly, is "completely out of his mind," guileless almost to a fault). Carly Simon is not only overwhelmingly the most successful, but also the loosest, the brashest, the kookiest and, with all the fame and fortune and fears that go with it, the most honest.

"One strength that I seem to have is being in touch with how I feel about things, as complicated as they get, and not trying to avoid unpleasant things that do exist. But one failure that I have is to share these feelings with the people they're about and therefore clear the air. One of Lucy's great qualities is that she's as reassuring as anyone I've ever known. She has the best bedside manner, so consoling and compassionate, a great listener. Joey's also a great listener, but she has to bring things back to herself."

Carly's looks are the most eccentric of the three. Her face appears to be all mouth, wide and toothy and awkward, but sensual. Her body, draped in silk and wool, liquidly unwinding to its full impressive height, is sexy, but oddly hermaphroditic, that hint of Mick Jagger between the lines. She slinks into the black leather couches in her enormous New York apartment (really two apartments, with the walls knocked out between) surrounded by all the symbols of her success (glass and chrome and Oriental rug, fluttery lace tablecloth, jarring modern canvases and everywhere instruments: trombone, marimba, autoharp, guitars). In the midst of all her comfort she still remembers absolutely vividly the pain and delicacy of growing up the third of the sisters.

"[My older sisters] were nice to me, and there were certain of their friends that I emulated more than others. But it was mainly Lucy; she was like the queen. I followed her through all the generations of her poses. Whatever she was trying on, I tried on, too: the cheerleading, the Bohemian and then the guitar playing. I picked up the guitar as a result of her. So that to say we were close is an understatement."

Three sisters, three musicians, three years apart—and what Adler calls "the peculiar circumstances" of their birth begin to tell their story, provide the lines of music on which the melody is played. Later we will look at some of the other forces and circumstances which influence their themes, for birth order, of course, is only part of the story. But since Adler it has teased and attracted a multitude of researchers, so that a kind of pseudo-science of birth order has sprung up, using the same broad outlines and definitions that Adler used. But recently birth-order research has been aided and abetted by the advent of a sophisticated computerized technology (so that in a flash any variable from alcoholism to anxious laughter to compatibility and success in marriage can be correlated with birth position) and by a balmy social climate for identity-seeking and self-scrutiny. It seems no coincidence that birth-order research and astrology are flourishing in the culture at the same time. Like astrology, birth order provides a game and a game-plan to position ourselves in relation to others, a series of clues to guide us through the mysterious process of growth. However, birth order has been studied and explored in an abundance of carefully controlled experiments, and in my opinion the factors governing its influence are significantly more measurable and persuasive than the stars.

A multitude of factors come into play when considering the effects of birth order: shifting parental attitudes from child to child (what birth-order specialist Lucille Forer calls the "psychological aging" as well as the physical aging of parents[4]); power struggling between parents and children as well as among the children themselves within the sibling hierarchy; whether a child is wanted or whether one birth is preceded by a miscarriage or even another sibling's death. One psychoanalyst described a woman patient, an only child, who was haunted by the specter of a sister who had died before she was born. Immediately after the death of her first child, the mother became pregnant to replace the beloved daughter she had lost. And for her whole life, the second daughter was dogged by comparisons to the first—and was always judged inferior. Nor did it help that the first daughter looked just like her mother and that the second was the image of her father. In this woman's case, her apparent birth position masked a complex of extenuating circumstances.

The spacing between children is another factor which influences the effects of birth position and relationships within the sibling hierarchy. Siblings born five or more years apart often share some of the characteristics of only children, for instance, and a middle child may also be the oldest of a second set of siblings. While parents often hope to plan the ideal spacing between children, psychologists disagree about what to consider "ideal." One early study showed that "jealousy occurred most frequently when the age difference between the two children was between 18 and 42 months," and gave the explanation that presumably "before 18 months the child's cognitive development does not permit a true grasp of the situation, whatever discomfort he may feel, whereas after 42 months, his repertory has enlarged to a point where many alternatives are available."[5]

Alfred Adler was typically definitive about what spacing between children he recommended:

> From my experience I should say that the best distance is about three years. At the age of three a child can cooperate if a younger child is born. He is intelligent enough to understand that there can be more than one child in a family. If he is only one-and-a-half or two, we cannot discuss it with him; he cannot understand our arguments. We shall not be able, therefore, to prepare him rightly for the event.[6]

More recently, a psychologist compared the reactions of three children—ages three, two and one—to the birth of another sibling and made these conclusions about the spacing of children in his family:

> Martin at age three was able to organize an integrated and varied system of defense in comparison to the fragile maneuvers of two-year-old Anne, while one-year-old Bernard had only an unorganized and non-specific response as though his development had not yet reached the point where he was able to grasp the nature of the event. . . . The specific ways in which Martin and Anne learned to deal with the dangerous affects and impulses that were stirred by the birth could be the basis for successful handling of future realities.[7]

What spacing makes for most harmonious sibling relationships? Less than one year? between one-and-a-half and three-and-a-half? exactly three years? Dr. Hyman Spotnitz, a New York City psychoanalyst, summed up the controversy this way: "Obstetricians generally agree that for the health of the mother and a child, the ideal space between children is four years. But the psychological argument varies from family to family. One year has an advantage because the older child is not so aware of the new sibling's birth. Also, the older the child, the more resentful she'll be of the new baby and the more she'll feel deprived of maternal affection.

"But still, there are advantages and disadvantages to any number of years between siblings, and it is difficult to generalize. There is no substitute for individual analysis of case histories." What follows, then, is a brief discussion of each of the major birth positions, with evidence for each based on individual cases and interviews. There is rarely seamless consistency in birth-order findings—and the specific seems more illuminating here than the general.[8]

Fascination with the mystique of the firstborn can be traced to a British scientist, Sir Francis Galton, who in 1875 studied eminent English scientists and found a preponderance of firstborn and only sons represented. He credited the noteworthy success of first sons to several influences of their birth position: the especially close relationship between parent and firstborn child, the extra responsibility the first son often bore (and, I would add, the custom of primogeniture, which gave the eldest the family fortune—and the *noblesse oblige* of the family name).

Birth-order theorists are still sampling and speculating about the eminent, and though primogeniture is generally outmoded, the social hierarchy reorganized and sexual identities radically reshuffled since Galton's era, there still seems to show up a preponderance of firstborns in studies of the renowned. A century after Galton, Margaret Hennig and Anne Jardim's recent study of twenty-five of the country's top one hundred businesswomen shows that even in a radically different climate of social and sexual mores, *all the women were firstborn,* either only children or the eldest in an all-girl family of no more than three female siblings. That all the subjects turned out to be firstborn Hennig (in a study prior to *The Managerial Woman*) called "the rather typical finding in all research on professional women," and explained this pattern, citing Douvan and Adelson's extensive studies of adolescents:

> Anecdotal accounts, clinical observations and empirical studies concur: the first child is likely to be the recipient of pressures, hopes and anxieties that later children are more apt to escape. The parents will generally be overattentive and overambitious; excessively eager that the child validate their worth as parents, excessively fearful that the child may depart from some ideal standard, overstern yet overindulgent.[9]

In *The Birth Order Factor,* psychotherapist Lucille Forer qualifies the prevalent correlation between firstborn girls and high-achievement motivation. Firstborns, she concedes,

> are often high achievers, it is true, but not necessarily happier, whether they achieve or not. One research study found that firstborn girls of families of six or more children were outspoken about their adult discomfort, and they were the ones least envied by other children in their families. While being oldest confers many advantages, it does not guarantee better social or emotional adjustment.[10]

"Generally speaking," she adds, "in relation to vocational aptitudes, firstborn children benefit intellectually from their birth position, while laterborns benefit socially."[11]

Dr. Forer, herself the eldest of a family of two girls and two boys, chose a response tyical of many firstborns to the birth of younger siblings: She became a "surrogate mother." How the crisis of the birth of the second child is handled is, naturally, a turning point in the life of the firstborn, an event which reverberates not only on the siblings' relationship, but on personal relationships ever after, with classmates and colleagues, friends and lovers. To become a surrogate mother is a way (not always conscious) for the older child to transform the pain of displacement, the agony of rivalry and the disappointment of no longer being the baby into a psychological advantage. Parents may often foster this surrogate mothering, by various ways and means. When my sister was born, my mother bought me a doll exactly my sister's size and suggested we raise the two of them together. For a while, we bathed, coddled and cooed at our charges together. But though my doll never made a peep, I sensed I had the worst end of the deal. Long before the doll's stuffing gave out, I threw her aside and turned the full force of my bossy, lonely, wanting-to-be-loving five-year-old self upon my little sister.

Adler explains the surrogate-mother phenomenon in a chapter in *Understanding Human Nature* called "Aggressive Character Traits":

> It may happen that an older sister will express her love, treat a younger brother like a mother, yet psychologically, this need not be different from [a case of obvious jealousy]. If an older girl assumes the mother attitude to younger children, then she has regained a position of power where she can act and behave as she will; the trick enables her to create a valuable asset out of a dangerous position.[12]

In Freud's study of "Little Hans," his analysis of a phobia in a five-year-old boy that coincides with the birth of a little sister, he notes in passing a kind of footnote to the surrogate-mother response. First, he describes little Hans's feeling of privation upon the birth of his sister (the temporary loss of his mother's care while she gave birth and the more sustained loss of her undivided attention while she is occupied with the baby). Then, Freud theorizes that Hans "made up for the loss which his sister's arrival had entailed on him by imagining he had children of his own"—first, real summer playmates, later imaginary playmates who became the stuff of his autoerotic fantasies.[13] In Han's case, "imagining he had children of his own" was stressful and troubling. For many firstborns, it is a pleasurable and bearably powerful fantasy. (Here again, I can corroborate from personal experience, remembering how I tried to convince my best friend—within my mother's earshot, no less—that my newborn sister was *my* child. A provocative Freudian drama that luckily never developed to phobic proportions.)

Two of the formidable and formative thinkers of our time, Simone de Beauvoir and Margaret Mead, both firstborns with sisters, point to their surrogate mothering and caretaking of younger sisters as critical events in the birthing and shaping of their intellectual lives. In *Memoirs of a Dutiful Daughter*, Simone de Beauvoir recalls the forging of what was to become a lifelong bond with her two-and-a-half-year younger sister, called Poupette. Not until Simone's sixth birthday did the young Poupette "play a considerable role in my life." Here, de Beauvoir describes the delicate hierarchy between herself and Poupette and shows how her younger sister imbued her with a sense of authority she had not known before:

> I owe a great debt to my sister for helping me to externalize many of my dreams in play: she also helped me to save my daily life from silence, through her I got into the habit of wanting to communicate with people. . . . What I appreciated most in our relationship was that I had a real hold over her. The grown-ups had me at their mercy. If I demanded praise from them, it was still up to them to decide whether to praise me or not. . . . But between my sister and myself things happened naturally. . . . Her tears were real, and if she laughed at one of my jokes, I knew she wasn't trying to humour me. She alone endowed me with authority; adults sometimes gave in to me: she obeyed me. . . .[14]

Besides a clue to her own authority, Poupette endowed Simone with an inkling of her efficiency, her capability, her power as a thinker and a human being:

> Teaching my sister to read, write and count gave me, from the age of six onwards, a sense of pride in my own efficiency. . . . When I started to change ignorance into knowledge, when I started to impress truth upon a virgin mind, I felt I was at last creating something real. I was not just imitating grown-ups: I was on their level. . . . Until then, I had contented myself

with responding dutifully to the care that was lavished upon me: but now, for the first time, I, too, was being of service to someone. I was breaking away from the passivity of childhood and entering the great human circle in which everyone is useful to everyone else. Since I had started working seriously time no longer fled away, but left its mark on me: by sharing my knowledge with another, I was fixing time on another's memory, and so making it doubly secure.[15]

Simone de Beauvoir captures the memory, at age six, of the birth of the artist in her role as older sister.

Then, in her autobiography, *Blackberry Winter*, Margaret Mead describes her birth as an anthropologist within her sibling hierarchy. Mead was the eldest of five children: Richard and Katherine (who died an infant), born two and four years after Margaret, then two and four years later, Elizabeth and Priscilla, who "were treated almost like a second family." After Priscilla's birth, their mother suffered a severe post-partum depression and the ten-year-old Margaret exuberantly joined her grandmother in filling in the mothering gap. Although the chapter "Sisters in Old Age" will discuss Margaret Mead's family constellation in more detail, I include the following as one more piece of evidence of the influence of an eldest sister's surrogate mothering on her intellectual flowering as an adult:

[Elizabeth and Priscilla as babies] were already beginning to show clear contrasts in temperament, which Grandma pointed out as she set me to work taking notes on their behavior—on the first words Priscilla spoke and the way one echoed the other. . . . I learned to make these notes with love, carrying on what Mother had begun. I knew that she had filled thirteen notebooks on me and only four on Richard; now I was taking over for the younger children. In many ways I thought of the babies as my children, whom I could observe and teach and cultivate. I also wanted to give them everything I missed.[16]

Not every firstborn, of course, breaks free of the nursery walls to become a world-famous philosopher or anthropologist. But still the force of being first—both the burden and the pleasure of it—plays upon a woman's development and her relationships with others, whatever her ultimate destiny. Shouldering responsibility and parental expectations, feeling righteous, ambitious and, at times, morally rigid, identifying with her parents and courting parental favor—these are the birthright of the oldest sister. The responses in the Questionnaires range from luxuriating in the birthright, as if it were a perfectly tailored coat of many colors, to floundering under its overwhelming weight—and even being driven berserk by it.

On the one hand is the woman who, at twenty-six, is comfortable with her role as elder of two sisters, even crows about it: "assertive, inquisitive, won't settle for any shit, protective, a social person, outgoing, brassy and bold. I want to be the best and will be!" And at the far end of the life-cycle, an eighty-two-year-old oldest of four sisters, two brothers, born into poverty and an era when caretaking by the olders of the youngers was an irreplaceable thread in the weave of family life. She writes in more measured tones about the deeply etched and deeply felt mark of being firstborn. "I cannot say that my self-esteem comes through my being the firstborn," she demurs, but the words that follow contradict her protest:

> At an early age I felt responsible for the younger children in our family. I believe that my mother's mother helped me to believe in myself. She praised every move I made. I could sew when I was twelve. Good or bad, she always praised my work.

"I am aggressive, loud, and most often capable of all the responsibilities I take on," writes a thirty-five-year-old recent mother. "I need this place as much as my family needs me to be in it." She revels in the snug fit between her psychological needs and the demands of her role; self-satisfaction is written into the subtext of her answers. For another woman, in her early forties, with a younger brother and sister, the fit of the role is also snug—with a dangling thread or two:

> I love being the oldest and think my birth position gives me a particularly strong sense of self. I may or may not be the favorite of my parents, who scrupulously do not play favorites; the important thing is that I *feel* favored. It's interesting that many of my close friends are also First Children.

Later, she adds an apparent contradiction, but does not elaborate on it. "My sister is always being taken care of. I'm always out there succeeding."

Between the lines of many of the proud eldests lies the shadow side of their birthright, the tug between dependence and independence, between mother and father, between parents and the world, that the firstborn tends to internalize more severely than any of her siblings. Dr. Forer's explanation: "The oldest girl tends to identify with her father's values as soon as her brother is born." The little girl turns away from her mother, who in her daughter's eyes has turned away from her by bringing home the baby, the intruder. Instead, the daughter forms an alliance with her father, adopting his values, his drive for success, his worldliness. But inside, the need for mother love has not been altogether quieted. "Often in growing up," remembers an oldest of four, "I was called upon to be the biggest child in emotional support, and I feel I had to grow up too fast because of it."

For another woman, the fit between birth position and her own psychic requirements is similarly awkward and unsatisfying:

> I am the eldest of six children, and I think the responsibility I felt toward my younger brothers and sisters helped mold my image as a person responsible for other people, nurturing them and making things easier for them. Sometimes I feel like I don't get the sort of affectionate care that my brothers and sisters get from me, because I am regarded as the competent one who can take care of herself and everyone else too.

Ambivalence about wearing the mantle of being first surfaces in various psychological guises. A twenty-three-year-old, oldest of a family of six (and the first grandchild to boot), describes herself as "outgoing, bossy, self-righteous *and guilty*." A familiar reaction to the ambivalence of being first, "older-sister guilt" is the label writer Jane Lazarre gives this pattern. Author of *The Mother Knot,* Jane Lazarre is a self-avowed loving but dominating elder of two sisters whose mother died when they were young. Here the push-pull internalized by the eldest surfaces as guilt: She revels in the bossiness, the righteousness, yet feels sheepish about it; she is proud of her surrogate mothering, her crimson cloak of extra authority, yet feels a little ashamed, as if stepping across the line between sibling and mother is too thrilling to be safe, too overwhelming to be handled without punishment. Or as another eldest puts it, "In whatever I do, I feel an extreme sense of responsibility. I can never be tired or rest. As a result, I tend to get myself in situations which stretch me to

the limit. When I'm out there, it's very intense." So another
nagging quality of older-sister guilt, as Lucille Forer appraises it,

> is a lingering concern that [she is] not achieving enough. Emo-
> tional disturbance related to this concern often reveals itself in
> dreams about test situations, even years after a person has com-
> pleted school. Such dreams may have to do with being unpre-
> pared, or facing unexpected questions, or failing to take the
> test.[17]

When not dreaming, but in waking life, the older sister
feels as if she has utterly failed the test, the result is not only
guilt, but soul-shattering, ego-tormenting rage. A twenty-
eight-year-old pours out her unambiguous passions on the
subject with the burning desperation of one who until several
years ago could not even say the word "father" without
crying:

> My parents had a set of expectations ready and waiting for
> me when I was born. I did not meet them. Things were
> okay until I was about eleven years old. At that time, the
> whole relationship went berserk. I couldn't make them
> happy. There was "family therapy" and endless sessions of
> heart-to-heart talks that tortured me. I know, as my mother
> has told me, that "no child was ever more loved," but
> somehow the love went astray as the child grew up. The
> ideas of right and wrong that my parents, especially my
> father, gave me turned into terrible barriers as I got older
> and went in new directions. And my father's dissatisfaction
> with me extends even into the present. I am probably the
> most moral person I know, and yet my father sees me as
> very irresponsible. There is no one I want more to please
> and no one with whom it is more impossible.

Her feelings of being overwhelmed by the demands of her
birth position, of course, reverberated on her relationship
with her sister, an indirect but inescapable limit on the
friendship between them. Here is her younger sister's appraisal of the family's syndrome:

> My sister and my father were feuding so often that it was
> very hard for me to feel comfortable. She and I never had
> problems with each other, but she was too busy trying to
> cope with the situation with my father to worry about me.

And I was too busy trying to understand what was going on between them to try to develop a strong relationship with my sister.

The younger sister mentions how it is difficult to "divorce" her own feelings about her father and her birth position from feelings about her sister's volatile place in the family constellation. Most likely, as long as she and her sister live within the family nexus, they are "wedded" to its requirement and expectations. Only with age, with distance, with therapy, in this case, and the deep-rooted process of change can the real separation begin—and only then the real possibility of a freely chosen bond as sisters.

The middle or in-between sister has traditionally been the trickiest to research, her characteristics most evasive to pin down, because so many variables—psychological and circumstantial—affect her development along the way. She may be the middle of three sisters or somewhere in between a large brood of girls. She may be sandwiched between an older brother and a younger sister or vice versa. If she's in the middle of a large family, the age differences between siblings influence her, too, because she may also be an "oldest" for a second set of children and share the characteristics of a firstborn. Another variable is the shift of parental attitudes and expectations from first- to laterborns: more or less interested or involved, fearful or relaxed, vigorous or laissez-faire. And still another factor is how much time in the limelight the child gets before the attention switches to or is shared by the next in line.

Nevertheless, mythology and conjecture swirl about the middle sister, much of which she internalizes as truth for better or worse. "Second place in a family of three is often considered the most difficult of all birth positions," suggests Lucille Forer. "The second of two children generally is not openly competitive, but the second of three is wedged in a situation which stimulates maximum competitive potential."[18] She cites as evidence of the crunch of growing up between two siblings a survey of three-children families in which children and their teachers picked the middle position as "most vulnerable to maladjustment," although the parents claimed not to favor one child over the other (a monumental "although," I'd add, and virtually impossible to prove). Among nursery-school children from three-child families, secondborn children had the highest ratings on verbal aggression toward peers and on seeking assistance from adults.[19]

The most treacherous slot, past research has found, is the middle position in a family of siblings all the same sex, and in particular, "the parent's favorite child is *least* likely to be a daughter both preceded and followed by a girl."[20] On the positive side, however, the middle sister may be more even-keeled and hang-loose than her more driven older sister, more gregarious and sociable, and a good negotiator, hammering out a middle path, a compromise between extremes. In the large family (of six siblings or more), researchers James Bossard and Eleanor Boll found that being a middle child was a highly valued slot. "One leaves the whole body of material with one impression," they report, "middle place in the birth order is the most coveted position among children in large families"—buffeted against the burdens and responsibilities of the eldest and against the second-class citizenship of the youngest.[21]

Given how the birth-order game is balanced both for and against the middle sister (the cards of parental favor against her, the cards of conviviality and temperament on her side), when she chooses to distinguish herself, she's likely to succeed. Her arena may be personal (she may be the first of the sisters to marry or the first to have a child), professional (special notoriety or excellence in her particular career), or flamboyantly antisocial (the family rebel or outlaw, but executed with panache). Charlotte Brontë, for instance, was nestled in the middle of a family of five, as is feisty and peerless black activist attorney Flo Kennedy. And Joan Baez, Kate Millett and Bonnie Parker (of Bonnie and Clyde fame) are all middle sisters of three.

Kate Millett describes her sister constellation as a "series of gradations," with Kate at age forty-four exactly five years younger than the oldest sister, Sally, and exactly five years older than the youngest, Mallory: "I've always felt that I was the medium between the two. Since my older sister's a lawyer and in politics, and my younger sister is in the theatrical and art world, and I, being sort of in politics and much longer and more retiring an artist—I'm as reasonable as the elder and as sort of detached from the world as the younger."

Like many middle sisters, Kate Millett defines herself as a medium or go-between, splicing together the differences between younger and older sisters, between different generations, different temperaments, different professional and creative milieus, with a toehold in each world—while solidly standing her own turf.

A twenty-five-year-old middle sister of three echoes Millett's positive sentiments with embellishments of her own:

> Being in the middle, I can see both sides, and a way to compromise, in most arguments—that is, I tend to get in the middle of fights that aren't mine. I think that, to some extent, my need for privacy comes from being neither the first nor the last in the house. I don't know if it's due to birth position, but I'm never uncomfortable being one of three, even when I'm with a couple.

For others, the middle slot is not so comfortable a niche, but a rather awkward point between two generations, not wholly belonging to either, yet ambiguously sharing qualities with each. In some families, a large age gap between the middle sister and those flanking her on either side may provoke or reinforce the sense of displacement, as in this portrait of a twenty-five-year-old with sisters thirty-three and fifteen:

> In a way I was both the younger and older child in my family. My older sister had left home before my sister was born. I was an only child for a year, I guess! My position has caused conflicts since I started out feeling inferior and then had the opportunity to learn what it's like to be the older, "superior" one too. But I had so much responsibility for my younger sister after my mother left [when I was fourteen] that it forced me to grow up too fast—I was expected even to give up my dreams for my adulthood in order to provide a solid home for her.

Though an extreme case (a rare fourteen-year-old completely takes over the family mothering), her story throws into high contrast the potentially painful double bind of some middle sisters. Simultaneously "older" and "younger," "superior" and "inferior," she squirms in either role. Forced to assume the mantle of mothering, she still craves mother love herself—and fears, like the firstborn, that having been "forced to grow up too fast," she may never grow up at all.

Whether a middle child feels comfortable or cramped depends on the particulars of her situation. In Margaret Mead's family, as I have described, there were two sets of two children and, between them, a child who died an infant.

Elizabeth was "the next-to-youngest," who now can joke, with an irony perhaps peculiar to the survival instincts of the middle child, that when she dies, she will leave everything to "the next-to-youngest." At seventy, an artist and a retired and gifted teacher of other art teachers, Elizabeth Mead Steig sits one afternoon in her small Boston apartment and muses about her birth position. Her mind drifts a little when the pain of memory threatens to become too acute, and the drifting makes the memory all the more poignant.

"You see, I really don't have the same mother and father that [Margaret] has. She was a first child, a wanted child who was born when my mother was writing her doctor's thesis and writing articles for the encyclopedia and going on with her professional life. And my father was a young and extraordinarily energetic professor at the University of Pennsylvania." These are the parents she heard about, probably had glimpses of, but the parents whom Margaret and her brother, Richard, knew firsthand and unspoiled.

"Richard had tuberculosis of the hip, I think, and he was very delicate, and my father paid an enormous amount of attention to him. And then I came along, and my mother was never ready for— Oh, no, then my sister Katherine was born. I never saw her because she died two years before I was born, but I didn't know it was two years before I was born until a couple of years ago, because I telescope time, and my feeling was that she had died and then they didn't want the next baby because they were so sorry for the last one."

She describes how she listens "in clusters," just as now she remembers "in clusters," because remembering the whole truth is too hard to bear. "After I was born, mother had a postpartum neurosis, and doctors in those days sent you to live in the country. So the first six months of my life, more than six months, there was a nurse looking after me. My grandmother was there and Margaret was there. I don't have any memories of lack of tenderness. But I have memories that sound like doves cooing, She's coming, she's coming. But she didn't come. And finally, at Christmas, they let my mother come home."

Seventy years later, memory merges with mythology, and she still feels the legacy of her birth position, like a sharp sting on the psyche.

Some middle sisters, like this fifty-five-year-old, second of four, reckoning the mark of birth, resist or circumvent its mysterious hold:

I was much aware my older brother was more easygoing than I and that both brothers were brighter than I, and that my sister was cuter than I, therefore all more favored. I don't remember that being second of four had any significance other than that.

Others feverishly rebel to win negative distinction rather than none at all:

My older brother, because he is male, did not get the same restrictions from my parents as I did and was pretty much left alone. [My younger sister] was the family baby and thus avoided a lot of crises that I went through before she did. She was also real good in school, and my parents loved her for it. I, being female, not doing very well in school, and constantly told by my mother that I was worthless, rebelled against my parents. I got in most of the trouble, got caught smoking dope, got caught with birth-control pills, got busted for shoplifting, had long-haired "hippie" boyfriends, stopped wearing a bra, etc. Thus my brother and sister look "good" in comparison.

She concludes with a cool distance that it is hard to believe she feels:

I think middle children rebel frequently to get the attention that they may not get because of their birthplace.

Some middle sisters do not even struggle to keep the cool, analytical distance between birth position and deep-buried need, but give in desperately to the full force of its prerequisites. This thirty-four-year-old woman has a sister, thirty-six, and a brother, eighteen:

Being the middle child was hell. My sister did all the cutesy baby things first. She set up goals my parents wanted me to reach or exceed, and her temperament was supposed to be mine also. I rebelled and struggled for my own identity and developed the most sadistic sense of humor. I laughed my way through life while in great pain. I would joke at my own faults to stop the possibility of someone else doing it. Everything I did was old hat.

Bad enough being second to her path-breaking older sister—worse when her brother was born:

Being male, everything he did was recorded and watched with such joy. Boys are so different, you know. They are brighter, stronger, smarter, cuter, devilish, daring and all these other great things. I imitated them, outdid them and yet they loved me for it. I had to become one of the boys. I felt physically out of touch with my own body until I was nineteen, and only now am beginning to feel really feminine.

Every one of her jobs involved struggling to achieve notice in a "primarily male dominated area," and she adds she hasn't settled this conflict yet—she's a housewife who has just become a truck driver.

The brush and palette of her birth position still color every corner of her identity: sexuality and marriage, work and relationships and, notably and unsurprisingly, her relationship with her sister. "I refused to be a Xerox of my sister and made waves. This unfortunately caused us to feel we have little in common and has created a gap which we are finding hard to close." Her anger at her sister for the audacity (if accident) of being first steams up from underground and creates a "gap" too cavernous, too treacherous to close.

Nor has it been possible for her to build a bridge to her brother, for her bitter history of envying him still obstructs the way:

My brother was the personification of the Holy Grail. He became the end-all and be-all. When he appeared, I disappeared. Up until that time, I was visible as a thorn in my sister's side but now nothing. He could do no wrong, and I hated him for it. As a child, I wished him dead many times. However, I instinctively protected him and cherished him. I think this was to get our parents' love. If I treated him as they did and saw in him all they did, they would love me. My sister was still indifferent to me and had the privilege because of her age of taking care of my brother. I now envied the time and energy spent on him. I don't think I ever envied any one person more than him.

Sisters' relationships with their brothers (and brothers' with each other) could, of course, be the subject of a whole other book. But the presence of a brother or several among sisters so alters the chemistry of the family, the bearings of the family constellation, and relationships between sisters themselves that I want to look briefly at the topic here.

The middle sister quoted above etches a dramatic picture of how the birth of a brother changed the balance of her family. Already overshadowed by an older sister who did everything "first," she felt altogether snuffed out when her brother was born. "When he appeared, I disappeared" is how she puts the crushing blow to her identity. Immediately and seemingly forever after, her brother became the preferred, revered, even "holy" child of the family: the focal point of parental attention and of the rivalry between the two sisters.

Although this woman's reaction is more exaggerated than typical, the pattern of preferential treatment for brothers is nevertheless a common one. Even with the influence of the Women's Movement on sex roles and child rearing, a recent U. S. study done by the Population Reference Bureau showed that a huge majority of parents still prefer boy children over girls. Demographer Nancy Williamson surveyed 1,500 married women and 375 of their husbands. Although many responded that they would like one child of each sex, *twice as many* women preferred boys over girls, and husbands favored boys over girls by as much as *three or four to one*.[22]

My interviews and Questionnaires showed that even in families in which boys were not overtly preferred to girls, the different set of messages and expectations given to the brothers was invariably experienced as preferential by their sisters. A fifty-five-year-old middle sister with two brothers and a sister remembers the differences this way:

> Dad said, "I want my boys to be brilliant and successful and my girls to be beautiful and happy." It was a joke but he meant it, too. We all were pressed to be socially successful with the "right" people, but the boys were also supposed to be captains of industry or senators.

Here is what another, differing set of expectations felt like to a brother, with two sisters and an older brother:

> My brother and I were treated differently from my sisters from the beginning. We had different tasks from them, we were given bigger helpings of food, we were expected to be more capable, stronger, louder, braver, and so on. I was told that my sisters were special, fragile creatures whom I

should appreciate and help. My brother, of course, I knew all about since he was the jerk in the next bed.

For a thirty-five-year-old woman, third in a line of sisters when a brother was born, the acute differences in parental expectations for the sisters and brother have had a lasting and devastating effect. "When Tom was born," she writes, "I was sent off to live with an aunt for a month or so, can you imagine? I was fifteen months old and just did not understand. I am now thirty-five and still do not understand." She continues:

He got MY attention. I hated him actively, all my life. When I wanted to go to medical school, I was told, "We only have enough money for one person to go, and after all, your brother is a boy." Aaaaaghgh! Anyway, I went to nursing school (three years, cheap program), and he went to medical school. Needless to say, he is now, at thirty-four, a well-to-do young cardiologist with a house and a swimming pool and two nice cars, and I struggle for every cent. I still am very jealous of everything he's got, and try to overcome it.

The struggle to "overcome" her jealousy has been a life-long process which she still has not successfully resolved. It has been marked by inner turmoil (at twenty-two, she was hospitalized for a "psychotic break") and continuing doubts and conflicts about her own sexuality (though married, she has had a string of lovers—both male and female). Her brother did not feel comfortable with his sexuality for a long time either. She remembers forcing him to practice French kissing with her—"which he hated"—and "he dated late and was very shy with girls. Was engaged once, broke off, then married after graduation." His marriage was the occasion for a sisterly prank whose symbolism was so obvious that it was certainly not lost on the newlyweds. "I sewed open all the flies on his undershorts and pajama bottoms and packed them for his honeymoon. It was two years or so before he forgave me." All the jealousy and infatuation, the fury and desperation was sewn into those open flies. The gesture shouted without words: Your maleness has tormented me for all these years —now I'll force you to make it show.

Naturally, not every family in which sisters also have brothers becomes as polarized and as fraught with tension as this one. But the presence of both boys and girls in the same family almost invariably raises the question of differing expectations—and how that question is resolved deeply influences the peace or agony of sibling relationships. "It's incredible to me," summed up Gloria Steinem in an interview, "that a boy and a girl can come out of the exact same household with two very different cultures." In some families, the "two different cultures" knock painfully against each other to the discomfort of both sides. Lucille Forer feels that "sisters with brothers seem more influenced toward adoption of opposite-sex characteristics than are brothers with sisters. If brothers have sisters close in age, their own male characteristics may be intensified, while the sisters often adopt male interests and attitudes. This may occur in the girls because male attributes still seem more prestigious in our society."[23]

In many families, the two different cultures are experienced by both sides as eye-opening, valuable and cherished, with alliances formed between brothers and sisters that are as powerful and enduring as those between sisters. Writes one man who had both sisters and brothers:

> From my experience with men who had no sisters or who had very peculiar sisters, I am convinced that little girls need brothers and little boys need sisters. They hold up half the sky, after all.

Then this, from a woman who also has both sisters and brothers, voices a common theme shared by many women from many different places in the family constellation:

> Toward all my brothers and sisters I feel a lot of love and tenderness, but I must admit that with my brothers, there is a certain distance that comes from the sex difference. With my sisters, I share both blood and womanhood. With my brothers, that sense of understanding common experience just isn't there.

The youngest sister is the family baby and, the larger the family, the more likely to be coddled, since older brothers and sisters as well as parents will provide extra strokes. For better or worse, she may remain so way beyond the age of consent—and at an age where her pose is no longer seemly or cute, merely rooted in and reinforced by the habit of years.

The younger sister may be used to special privileges and always getting her own way—or she may be worn down by having to wait her turn at the end of a long line of elders who come first and matter more. "Depending on the family situation," observes Lucille Forer, she "grows up either spoiled, in the sense of always demanding more, or deprived, in that everything [she] gets was used by [her] predecessors."[24] According to Walter Toman, another birth-order theoretician (whose categories in most cases seem too rigid), youngest sister of sisters is "charming, quick, capricious, and yet gullible," and "her family and friends must always be ready for surprises and ready to pay for them if they entail costs."[25]

A quintessential youngest both for charm and skittishness is Bisa Williams. She has an older brother and two older sisters, one of whom is playwright and dynamo Ntozake Shange, author of the recent classic about black sisterhood, *For Colored Girls Who Have Considered Suicide, When the Rainbow Is Enuf*. At twenty-four, Bisa lives in California, busily trying to find herself, a part-time comparative-literature student at UCLA, a part-time film-maker and, in the time that's left, assistant director to the Los Angeles production of *For Colored Girls*. Born Andrea Williams, Bisa was given her African name several years ago by Ntozake (who was born Paulette), and until recently "had a block" on what it meant. Now she'll admit it means "greatly loved." "It sounds funny," she says shyly. "Now whenever people ask, I tell them it's because I'm the youngest in the family." Being the youngest cuts the sting of the boast; it is a rationale she can live with, because she always has—either preening in its glow or teetering under its obligation.

When the four were growing up, the elder ones envied her special privileegs and occasionally teased her to tears because of them. Once they put her on trial in a kangaroo court, which an instinct for self-preservation warned her not to attend. "It didn't hurt my feelings," she insists, "I was just blocking them out." But they brought her the verdict anyway: "Guilty of being a crybaby." The older she gets, the more willing she becomes to stand on her own feet against the encroachments of her older siblings, especially those of her oldest sister, also quintessential in her role as my-will-be-done firstborn.

"In order to make a point Ntozake will encroach it on you all the time, impose it: 'We're gonna be this way, and we're gonna do this now.' Either you do it or you can stand out like a sore thumb 'cause you're not—and more often than not, I'll stand out. She's gotten into the habit of being able to move people around, 'cause she's very convincing. And as a baby, I was pushed around, and everybody said, 'Shut up and do it.' But I don't have to do that anymore. I think that really aggravates her. It aggravates all of them, because sometimes I just turn off all of them."

Despite the defiant surge of her words, she is still hooked into the old patterns, the turn-the-other-cheek defense of the youngest. *I just turn off all of them,* she insists, for in some remote psychic recess, she is still the baby who cannot trust herself to decide to confront her elders—and win. Nor can she trust her vision of the future, for when I ask her about her optimal fantasy for her work and art, she hedges: "My optimal fantasy is to be, let's see, I don't think I have one. Which is part of the problem in the way I was raised. [I was] given every advantage [my parents] could afford and that we could muster. I never ran into any problems with what I was going to be in the world. I was going to be somebody. But I never decided what it was that I wanted to be, because I knew that whatever it will be, I'll be able to do it. Circular logic."

Another youngest, about the same age as Bisa and equally undecided about her future, puts the dilemma this way:

> Being the youngest has tended to make me less motivated in the area of work. I feel I can always "slide by" as I have in the past. With friends, I seem to choose those who are my equals or those I can dominate (positions I didn't hold in my family).

The youngest of three sisters names similar themes, but with an additional charge of bitterness:

> I felt I had to fight with my whole family to keep a sense of myself: they were all older and thought they could boss me around. As youngest, I often became lazy and used my age as a way of getting out of things. My sisters treated my ideas as if they weren't as good as theirs. That has accustomed me to being either passive, expecting help from others, dependent or ready for a fight, which does not really lead to having many friendships.

Another youngest faces and appraises her role as the family baby with relative equanimity, born of hours of scrutiny. "Oh, boy!" she begins, as if taking a psychic breath before taking the plunge:

> I was definitely the baby in the family and a sickly five-year-old to boot. Apparently my sister mothered me a lot. I was given much more freedom than my siblings, and there is slight tension about that. I wasn't pressured to be a responsible citizen—I went to art school. My parents have given me more money and supported me longer than my siblings. I think being the sickly youngest has made me slightly more adventurous, lonelier, more interested in learning and using my brains and with a slight sense of being *both favored and deprived* [italics mine].

Favored and deprived says the youngest, specially singled out, she feels, and yet somehow neglected, too, so that her life becomes a puzzling-out of those poles and her relationships maneuvered gently, gingerly around and between them. And similarly for her sisters, both within and without her family, how often their responses to the niche of their birth echo the ambivalence of the youngest: The oldest sister, who is proudly and flashily succeeding, while inside she still yearns to be taken care of, or the middle sister, who artfully negotiates between extremes, while bitterly resenting the sisters sandwiching her in on either side. These ambivalences, common to every star in the family constellation, play upon each other from star to star and sister to sister in patterns of roles, rivalries and polarities, as later chapters will explore. These are the paradoxes of family life, and their unraveling is part of the mystery of growing up.

3

INSIDE THE FAMILY
CRUCIBLE AND BEYOND

The love between Joyce and me is very strong and
very important to both of us. It has always been a
priority that we maintain that bond throughout all
our other struggles. I could write a book on my sister and how she influenced my life. Let it suffice that
I love her deeply and want to make a life with her.
. . . [We have both dreamt about] the two of us making love and discussed it as a possibility. I guess Joyce
pretty much rules it out of our relationship, but I'm
not too sure how I feel about it. I love having her
meet my women friends and letting them see how incredible she is.

—DELIA, *Twenty-five*

When I meet [my sister's friends] they somehow
don't recognize me standing in her bold shadow. I
feel that women will always like her better than me;
that she is more worthwhile than me and even that
her friends are more worthwhile than my friends.
When we're both around a woman, I expect to be
left out of a lot of what is shared. . . . I have dreamt
of making love with her. It was a sensual and pleasant
dream, but when I woke up and recalled it, I was surprised. . . . I'd like to add that my sister is my best
friend as well as my sister.

—JOYCE, *Twenty-three*

Are you satisfied with the relationship with your sister?
asked the Questionnaire, and this chapter will explore the
enormous range of response, of interpretation, of emphasis
from sister to sister and family to family. As the Questionnaires piled up, the variations in the quality of relationships
emerged in patterns of closeness, distance and ambivalence,
and this chapter will first look at a sampling of these responses. Then we will go on to probe the complex and
interwoven play of influences inside the family crucible and
beyond: the influence of age, the mellowing that often comes
with time, and the fluctuations in the quality of relationships
throughout a lifetime; the influence of parents, their encouragement and pressures; and the influence of sisters on each
other's scripts. Finally, we will listen in on the special, private
language often shared between sisters, the language of words
and deeds, of whispered secrets and common dreams.

Of the patterns of closeness, distance and ambivalence
described by the Questionnaires, the close relationships were
characterized by a spirit of intimacy, openness, loyalty,
friendliness (often described as being each other's "best
friend"), emotional vitality (room to express anger and
jealousy, as well as joy and coziness) and sheer pleasure in
each other's company. This, for example, from a social-work

student who describes her family as a kind of Amazonian "Little Women":

> My sisters and I have a strong sense of how powerful and attractive we are as a group, and when we're together in threes or fours we get high and crazy and brave. People look at us because we look like sisters, because we're all tall and healthy and vibrant and have pride in ourselves and in our family. We're all devoted to our father (to Daddy). We talk about our mother [who died when Laura was five] often and have kept her alive in our lives. My sisters fascinate me, amaze me, impress me, excite me.
> —Laura, twenty-four, third in family of four sisters, one brother

Or these identical twins, who also have two older sisters and are close to them, but exceptionally, almost supernaturally tight with each other in a kind of symbiotic bond, which may be sensed by other sisters, but peculiar in its intensity to twins:

> I love [all my sisters]. I get along with Gwen the best, because even though we are very different, we are as much the same. I love her as a sister, and she is my best friend.
> —Gail, thirty-three

> Emotionally [with my two older sisters] I am close more in a sisterly way. With Gail, my twin, we are akin emotionally and spiritually—we've hunted UFO's together, drunk in bars, shared similar life-styles, and we can sense each other's inner feelings without even communicating sometimes.
> —Gwen, thirty-three

Or this lighthearted, fullhearted exuberance from an artist who finds it hard to be "wacky" with people besides her husband—and sister:

> My sister and I are very close and have been since we entered our early teens. She is my closest female friend, and there isn't anything I would hesitate to tell her. Though we are very different in our outlook on life, we usually can understand where the other is coming from.

Our happiest times are when we're just being silly together. We tend to get a bit crazy, and it usually escalates. Like when we remembered switching food. That was this thing we did when one of us liked something served for dinner and the other didn't. We'd trade with each other and pray my mother wouldn't notice because she was a stickler about cleaning your plate.

—Ellen, twenty-three, elder of two sisters

At the opposite end of the emotional spectrum were the descriptions of distant relationships, equally emotionally charged, but full of bitterness, pain, desperate rivalry, unbridled and often unexpressed anger, invective and awesome disappointment. The first Questionnaire that arrived was the most bitter, the most furious of all of them, as if emotions buried for years had at last been given permission to leap out:

My sister and I do not see each other, are very far apart emotionally, and I will be satisfied to have nothing to do with her, although I will always wish that things could have been different. I have always experienced her as a vicious, terroristic individual. The angriest I've ever been at my sister is when she said that my being sent to a hospital (and my wanting to go to get away from the family) was nobody's fault. I felt that she harassed me into a nervous breakdown and disclaimed responsibility for her actions, so I improvised a weapon from a rotting bannister and leaped for her with it. When my father started yelling, "What the hell are you doing?" I drew back out of fear of him.

—Nora, twenty-eight, younger of two sisters

Or these, from two different middle-aged women, both ambitious, driven and outwardly successful (one a businesswoman, the other a lawyer), but inwardly haunted by seething sister rivalries that the years neither changed nor softened:

[My sister and I] are so utterly different in character, temperament, interests and sociopolitical outlook that we get along only at moments of great trouble. Our life experiences have been so completely opposite: she married one day after high-school graduation and had a sheltered, dependent marital relationship, with two healthy, intelligent sons. I had to work since I was fifteen, married at twenty-one, had a hysterectomy at twenty-two, was forced to adopt children, because I wanted them so desperately. My son is decent and hardworking, but not terribly intelligent; my daughter was found to be brain-damaged, is probably schizophrenic, became epileptic, and, while warm-hearted and bright, will probably never be able to lead a normal life.

—Doris, fifty-six, older of two sisters

(My sister) lives in France, and I have seen her once since I was nineteen: for two hours when I was thirty-four. I told her I was pregnant with my first child, and she said, "Too bad you've had them so late—they'll never be able to be friends with mine." It is a sad thought that she obviously means we shall go to our graves without seeing each other. She knows I had cancer a few years ago, yet even in the face of oncoming death, her neurosis prevents her from seeing me. I once loved her when we were young and would be good to her in her sad loneliness if she would let me. Blood ties are strong, but others can take their place—almost.

—Bertha, fifty-three, youngest of
two sisters, one brother,
who died before her birth

Caught midway between the poles of closeness and distance are the ambivalent relationships, fraught with a mixture of love and hate, bitterness and delight, affection and withdrawal, ease and anxiety, laced with questioning and bafflement at why things between sisters did not go better than they did. A nurse who admitted she "always felt I should have been an only child and wanted badly to be one" concluded pages of arguments with herself this way:

My mixed feelings toward my sister, my irradicable love-hate mix, have been almost the longest-standing puzzle of my life. It's nice to write some of it out. Thanks for the chance to take part.

—Melanie, thirty, older of two sisters

Two of the most poignantly ambivalent responses came from a set of sisters thirty-six and thirty-four. The older is mentally retarded and epileptic and cannot read or write well, so she dictated her answers to her younger sister. First, the younger sister, who is an actress:

Because [my older sister] is retarded and epileptic, we did everything together, except school. Until I went away to college at eighteen, I never slept soundly. I would immediately awaken if she turned over wrong in bed. I hated her for being sick and getting attention, and I hated myself for not being perfect to her. My relationship with Ginna has left me with a feeling I must ease everyone's hurts. Surprisingly enough, Ginna gave me the most precious gift: that awareness, that extra sensitivity that makes me an actress. The trials of living with her very scary seizures made me yearn to have been born in another time and kept me ever-cultivating my vivid imagination.
—Sarah, thirty-four, younger of two sisters

Ginna's dictated answers are brief and cautious. "No comment, too private," read half the responses. (Comments her sister, the amanuensis, in a covering letter: "I was shocked that she was so suspicious. My guess is that she wants some control over her life, even if it's only to say, 'No, that's too private to me.'" My guess is also that she cannot admit to her sister the ambivalence and complexity of her feelings.) So what Ginna doesn't say, what lurks between the lines is as revealing as the words she allows herself to share, like this touching bit of sidestepping and denial:

My parents taught me to share with my sister. I can think of [no jealousy of her]. I think my sister must have been jealous of me sometime. It is only human.
—Ginna, thirty-six, older of two sisters

This was from a housewife about to become a truck driver, ambivalently caught between an older sister and a younger brother:

For some unknown reason, I will never be as close to my sister, understand her or really appreciate her as I should. Because we shared only one common bond, our parents, and because we were brought up differently by this bond, we have too many rocks strewn down the path that stand in the way of our getting to really know each other. We are worlds apart on what to be a woman and a feminist is. I doubt she will catch up, and I know that I won't go back. We are at a standstill.

        —Stephanie, thirty-four, middle of one
          older sister, one younger brother

In some larger families (with at least three sisters), there can, of course, be a disparity in the quality of sister relationships, the bond between a girl or woman and her various sisters being variously closer or more distant, more or less loving, ambivalent or lousy. In some large families, for instance, alliances might be drawn from the earliest years according to age, temperament, shared rooms, friends or education, and later in life according to geography, life-style and the myriad other choices of adulthood: work and politics, marriage and child rearing. In some families, alliances are strategically forged to exclude one or another sibling (scapegoating or making a black sheep out of him or her), and guilt over this may surface way beyond the family crucible and wreak havoc among siblings in later life. Another pattern of alliances is the girl who stays close to all her sisters—except one whose existence is so threatening or disturbing that she must "block it out." Sally, for example, is twenty-four and the middle child of seven siblings ("two different families as far as age goes"): three sisters and a brother older (thirty-eight, thirty-five, thirty-three, thirty) and three sisters younger (twenty-three, eighteen, sixteen). She appraises her varying relationships this way:

Emotionally, I feel we are very close, probably more so with my younger sisters whose age group I am in. I think the [relationships] with my older sisters could be more open, more revealing of inner feelings. . . . My parents tended to give me more attention than the sixth and seventh children, but when my youngest sister was born, I guess they knew this was the last. She took over the spotlight, and I've never been very close to her. I think I blocked out her existence at the age of eight.

        —Sally, middle of seven sisters, one brother

Still another possible disparity is the case where a woman's bond with one sister is so intense that for a particular time (even for years) it absorbs all her energy and attention. Alice, twenty-six and one of four sisters, writes while waiting to hear of the birth of her year-younger sister's first child and explains the transitional but necessary exclusiveness of her attention:

> Generally, I am answering questions only in terms of my sister Lynn, who is closest to me in age. When I think of the word sister, she is my sister who always comes to mind. My other two sisters are eight and twelve years younger than I, and I feel almost more motherly toward them than sisterly, although that is changing as they grow older.
>   —Alice, twenty-six, oldest of four sisters,
>   two brothers

The Questionnaires revealed a complex and interconnected play of influences on the quality of relationships between sisters, an intricate and interwoven pattern of threads tied intimately together in the "sister knot," to use writer Jane Lazarre's phrase in this context. The sister knot is the intrinsic and inescapable bond of blood. In this chapter, I shall separate out and introduce several of the most crucial strands of the sister knot, and the life-stories throughout the rest of the book will dramatize and delve deeper into these themes, untying and retying the bloodlines of the sister knot. And just as the tightness and complexity of a knot occurs not from any one thread, but from the weave, pressure and connectedness of all the strands, so with the sister knot and indeed with the entire family configuration. We may look at one strand, one influence at a time, but our experience of them is simultaneous and many-dimensioned. We may analyze each variable with cool, analytical distance, but inside the family crucible, the heat is on.

One persistent thread that runs through many of the Questionnaires is the general improvement, mellowing, easing of tension between sisters that comes with age and time. Even accounting for the natural and understandable *wish* that things get better (and the common willingness to admit to conflict in the past more readily than in the present), still this thread occurs too often, at too many stages and in too many guises to overlook. Listen to the echoes just in the voices of the sisters introduced so far:

> My sister and I are very close and have been since we entered our teens.
>   —Ellen, twenty-three

My other two sisters are eight and twelve years younger than I, and I feel almost more motherly toward them than sisterly, although that is changing as they grow older.

—Alice, twenty-six

Four years of therapy helped me to see my distorted view of myself and my symbiotic relationship to [my sister]. . . . On returning home now, I see I am one of the few who can treat her as an equal and an adult, because we were so close.

—Sarah, thirty-four

Or this from a woman who took forty years to undo the false images that parents had built of her and her sister:

During the last couple years, I have become more understanding of myself and am growing toward more security within myself and more independence. [My sister] has been very supportive in this effort. . . . We also realized that we had been growing in the same direction while separated.

—Beth, forty-two

From her vantage point of seventy-seven years and her personal history as the eldest of a family of four daughters and a son, Margaret Mead appraised the shifting sands and the mellowing years between sisters in her autobiography, *Blackberry Winter*. There could be no better witness to the squabbling of childhood, the experiments of adolescence, the flowering of work and talents in adulthood, the marriages, childbirths, divorces and deaths both in her own extended family and in the hundreds of families she has studied in other cultures.

Sisters, while they are growing up, tend to be very rivalrous and as young mothers they are given to continual rivalrous comparisons of their several children. But once the children grow older, sisters draw closer together and often in old age, they became each other's chosen and happy companions. In addition to their shared memories of childhood and of their relationships to each other's children, they share memories of the same home, the same homemaking style, and the same small prejudices about housekeeping that carry the echoes of their mother's voice. . . . Generation after generation pairs of sisters have been close friends. In this they exemplify one of the basic characteristics of American kinship relations.[1]

As sisters grow older, taking with them the mark of the family crucible, but not its limits, their personalities sharpen, growing more distinct and individuated. The battleground of direct competition becomes less specific, thus the threat one sister has over the other, less intense. The need for sisterly comfort and support is more keenly felt with the pressures of the years. The death of their parents may also knit sisters closer together, as they turn to each other in the narrowing family circle—and face each other directly rather than through the distorting lens of competition for parental favors. Then, too, with age, the importance, even primacy of blood ties is thrown into high and dramatic contrast, as friendships fade, marriages falter or fall apart, youthful dreams go unrealized. "I once loved my sister when we were young," wrote Bertha, who at fifty-three has seen her estranged older sister for only two hours in the past twenty years, "and would be good to her in her sad loneliness if she would let me." Her Questionnaire described at some length a "sister substitute," a woman friend of her sister's age who was as kind and open as her sister was closed and distant. Nevertheless, regret for the lost, shattered friendship with her sister was the bottom line and the last word. "Blood ties are strong, but others can take their place—almost." In that "almost" hung the full weight of her life's bitterest disappointment.

Most pervasive is the pattern of fluctuation in the quality of relationships between sisters in a given family over time, alternating closeness and distance, rivalry and solidarity, enmity and friendship. (Or, as I have mentioned, a woman's relationships with different sisters might fluctuate during one given period, closer with one sister, more rivalrous with another, ambivalent with a third.) Many women point to a particular developmental period—early teens, breakaway twenties, marriage or having children, divorce, widowhood or older age—as the breakthrough in their relationships with sisters, the time at which they begin building friendships from the debris of earlier rivalries. Some women cite specific experiences in their histories with their sisters, turning points or "critical incidents" (to borrow a phrase from life-cycle psychologist Robert White) that forever changed the emotional life between them. Ellen, the twenty-three-year-old who

liked "being silly" with her twenty-year-old sister, singled out
one such emotionally freighted incident as the "start of a
more woman-to-woman point in our relationship":

> [My sister] was eighteen, and a senior in high school and
> had been going out with (her boyfriend) for about four
> years. I didn't know they were sleeping together at the
> time, but when she missed her period, she told me. I took
> her for a pregnancy test and arranged for an abortion. It
> was a very fast way for her to be shoved into adulthood.
> We rarely talk about it, but it did bring us much closer.

"As I write this, I am waiting to hear of the birth of my
sister's child," wrote Alice, twenty-six, during the charged
atmosphere of the turning point itself. "It made me feel closer
to her to write about what sisterhood is for me." Alice's
Questionnaire spanned the stretch from her own motherly
feelings as the oldest in a farming family of four girls and two
boys to her imagined motherly feelings for her sister's soon-
to-be-born child. Alice, who is divorced and childless herself,
used the Questionnaire to reexamine the fluctuations of feeling for her year-younger sister, whom she now sees only once
or twice a year.

> Up until about three years ago, we were extremely close,
> both emotionally and physically. Then she was married and
> moved away. That marriage ended and at that time of her
> divorce, she turned to me, and we were again very close.
> Her second husband is somewhat possessive and the few
> times I have seen my sister at my parents' home, I have had
> a hard time getting any time alone in which we could
> talk.

She also admitted that she, too, withdrew into the private
world of her marriage, and only since her divorce had she
needed her sister and reached out to her. Against this emotional scrim, she described the play of ambivalence about her
sister's pregnancy (though pointedly never connected it with
her own unmarried and childless state):

> The fact that she was pregnant was hard for us, because I
> wanted to share her feelings with her, and I wasn't able to
> because of the distance between us and the communication
> problem because of her husband. Even though I don't

know yet if I have a niece or a nephew, I feel a great sense
of love for my sister's child. I want the child to understand
how special his or her mother is and what a beautiful
relationship we have shared.

We have shared: the past tense underlined her sense that her
sister's childbirth marked the end of an era in their relationship, a point of change after which the intensity of closeness
between them had not yet been gauged. The yearning love
which she already felt for her sister's child could be, more
symbolically, a yearning for the idyllic love she and her sister
felt as children. That was a cherished time of which her first
memory was "giving her sister a flower and then kissing her."
Those idylls had long since given way to the thousand
changes of growing up, but as she mused about the new
arrival (both the baby and the new stage in her relationship
with her sister), that early tenderness was reawakened.

For some women considering the permutations of change
over time, a "critical incident" signified not the reappraisal or
renegotiation of a relationship, but a stormy break, a bitter
falling-off of friendship. Lottie, twenty-four and the second of
three sisters and a brother, first sketched the rosy period
with her older sister—before the break a year or two before:

> We'd been like best friends. We called and visited con-
> stantly. We also understood each other perfectly and could
> talk about *anything*—no secrets.

For years the relationship had at least the trappings of
intimacy (even got a little incestuous at times): as a little
girl, Lottie scratched her older sister's name on walls, followed carefully, dutifully in her footsteps, "just a few steps
behind," had an affair with a friend of her sister's beau, so
they could "make a beautiful foursome." And then, suddenly,
Lottie jumped radically out of step from her pacesetter:

> Last winter I decided I'd never have another casual affair. I
> could wait five years if I had to, but I was going to abstain
> from sex till an important relationship came along. And it
> did happen, very soon, with a woman.

In the next breath, she admitted her deep-seated need for her
sister's approval—and her deeply felt bitterness when it
wasn't offered:

I was a complete and fulfilled lesbian all spring, and (my sister) seemed to think it was because I'd failed with men and needed to take second best. I resented that so much, I feel we can never really be friends again—at least not for a long time. We've just gone different ways, and we don't have the instant understanding we used to.

Some sister relationships are elastic enough to make room for the invariable differences that crop up with age. Others, like Lottie's, are too fragile, too fraught with unresolved ambivalence, too unbalanced, with the power not shared but clutched in one fist only. When differences occur, these relationships snap under pressure, and each sister is left with a broken piece of something that was precious only when whole.

The quality of a girl's relationship with her parents, how useful that relationship is as a model for what happens with her sisters, and how parents encourage or discourage closeness between sisters—in these ways, parents help shape the quality, intensity and patterns of life between sisters. The play of influence is various, subtle and many-faceted, a delicate matter to predict and elusive to summarize, but several recurrent themes emerged in the Questionnaires and throughout my interviews.

The kind of relationship a girl has with both her parents, but especially with her mother, is, of course, her first model of intimacy. What she learns both consciously and unconsciously from this relationship becomes penciled into the blueprint for structuring and formulating her sibling relationships: what is allowed or taboo, pleasurable or frightening, serious or light, speakable or unspeakable. Many women describe a kind of family emotional texture or pattern, learned from either or both parents and then woven into the fabric of relationships with sisters. A twenty-five-year-old middle of three sisters put it this way:

Luckily for the three of us, we were not compared by our parents, so we didn't compete, were usually proud of one another's accomplishments. . . . Whenever the three of us get together, we enjoy talking over shared times, memories —something as important to my parents and definitely learned from them.

Ellen, the twenty-three-old who was both close and "wacky" with her sister, traced the repetitions of pattern back two generations:

> Because [my mother] is very close to her mom and sisters, she expected and encouraged us three [Ellen, her mother and her sister] to be close. I always was very close with her as far back as I can recall, and my sister has become much closer to her since I left home.

For Ellen, the pattern of sibling closeness was intergenerational and thus, in some ways, doubly reinforced.

For Stephanie, thirty-four and soon to be a truck driver, ambivalently caught between an older sister and younger brother, the ambivalence paralleled and was deeply rooted in her relationship with her mother. "I have a love-hate relationship with her that we both understand," Stephanie wrote about her mother. "The things I hate about her are those that I possess to (I think) a lesser degree, and the things I admire in her I also feel I possess (I hope) to a greater degree." The ambivalence with her sister she summed up this way, "I threaten her with my actions whereas she angers me because of her inaction." But this one was not "a love-hate relationship that . . . both understand." She was willing to face both the troubling and exhilarating similarities she shared with her mother but was not yet ready to acknowledge the similar play of connections with her sister.

"We learn our deepest ways of intimacy with mother," writes Nancy Friday in her thorough exploration of the mother-daughter relationship, *My Mother/My Self*. "Automatically we repeat the pattern with everyone else with whom we become close."[2] Yet the pattern of ambivalence in the "deepest ways of intimacy" which she learned from her mother and describes so eloquently, she neither examines nor confronts in her relationship with her "older sister, Susie." She alludes to her sister in heavily charged asides, dangling like loose threads throughout her book. Writing about her nurse, Anna, she comments: "She preferred me to my sister. I don't know why Anna favored me; perhaps she saw the bond between my mother and sister; maybe it was our similar temperament, but no doubt about it, I was Anna's girl."[3] And then later about her mother's reaction to her decision not to have children: Her husband and she had their roles, she figures, "to be 'different,' not like her neighbors' children, not like my sister, who'd had three children in the first four years of marriage." [4] Whatever her ambivalent feelings about "the bond between [her] mother and sister," about her sister's burgeoning adulthood and motherhood, she never reveals them. With all the complex knots and connections made throughout the book, the thread between her and her sister remains outside the weave, the last taboo.

Some women make the connection easily, seeing in the quality of parental love a model for closeness with their sisters. Laura, for example, twenty-four and the third of four sisters who feel "high and crazy and brave" together, had a particularly strong and influential attachment to her father, which was intensified by her mother's death when Laura was five. The relationship with her father, she felt, underlined and encouraged the unshakable solidarity among her sisters:

> I never felt I had to compete with my sisters for my father's attention or love—he loved each separately and differently. He did often love "his darling daughters" as a group, and that was nice because it gave me a sense of unity, sisterhood, that the four of us together were greater than the sum total.

The "separate and different" quality of this father's love for each of his "darling daughters," his encouraging their unity as "greater than [their] sum total," the honesty between father and each daughter ("Very early on we began talking about sex and marijuana and other things most women don't share with their fathers"), an honesty which was picked up as policy among the sisters—these were the ways he fostered, nurtured, and reinforced the spirit of "high and crazy and brave" closeness among the sisters.

Identical twins Gail and Gwen, among the most luminous of all the respondents, stressed the evenness and openness of their parents' love, which poured equally to the twins and their two older sisters in times of happiness and trouble, success and failure:

> I love my mother dearly. She is one of the kindest, most sincere, loving, giving, honest, unselfish persons I know. [My father] was a very gentle soul, not the type to show his affection publicly, but we all knew he loved us very much by the look in his eyes whenever we tried and

succeeded at something and also whenever we tried and failed. My parents treated all of us about equal, loved us equally, really showed no favoritism.

—Gail, thirty-three

[Our parents] distributed their love and time and money and help evenly among us all. Their positive feelings about all of us certainly gave us positive feelings about each other in terms of caring about each other.

—Gwen, thirty-three

Their parents' love was a bottomless cup which each experienced as bountiful and life-sustaining; it was not measured out in coffee spoons, or calculated and compared on its receipt. This measureless giving of parental love is as delicate a process as passage through the needle's eye. But its realization seems to be the heart of sibling harmony. When the Questionnaires reported no favorites, no comparisons, no pitting of one sister against the other, these most often accompanied the descriptions of relationships between sisters that worked out best.

In glaring antithesis were the family configurations with embattled and embittered sister relationships, families where the complexities were discounted, and parental love was so niggardly that, as one woman put it, sisters "compete for blood from a stone." Here was the frustrating swamp of polarities, festering hostilities, and rivalries intensified by the conflicts of parental confusion. This, for example, about her family swamp, from Nora, twenty-eight, the first woman to answer the Questionnaire and one of the most bitter:

My relationship with my mother was distant. I never felt she loved me consistently or permitted me to have feelings. . . . My father was a very dominating, hyper-energetic man who gave me a lot of contradictory messages about what I should be in the world. . . . My parents influenced my relationship with my sister by not letting us express our feelings, which helped concentrated hostility build up over the years.

The discounting of feelings, the double messages, the scrambling for crumbs of love drove underground the hostilities between Nora and her older sister. When the anger finally emerged, it broke out as violence (Nora tried to smash her sister with a rotting bannister), and when her father squelched that outbreak, she froze her feelings into vengeful, bleak and still-unbroken silence.

Margo and May, twenty-five, were another set of twins, whose voices made a stark and sad contrast with Gail and Gwen and underlined the dilemma that results from enforced parental comparisons:

> [Our parents] set my twin and me at each other's throat. We were constantly forced to compete for "love," attention, space, equality, identity, etc.
>
>   —Margo, twenty-five

> My mother used to characterize Margo as the "smart twin" and May as the "pretty twin." As a result of this constant caricature of ourselves, I'm still trying to prove how smart I am and Margo how attractive she is.
>
>   —May, twenty-five

Though the twins have now wrangled out from under the parental thumb, they still felt the repercussions of the old polarizations in a nagging ambivalence about each other. "I am dissatisfied with our present relationship," wrote May, "as I often feel very anxious and defensive in Margo's presence." Echoed Margo, regretfully, "We still find ourselves hostile to one another often, particularly in competitive sports." In an arena where competition is permissible and circumscribed, the twins allowed themselves to play out the rivalries of their upbringing.

By raising the twins with their identities polarized and categorized, their parents drove a wedge between them. Whether a conscious tool of manipulation (divided, the twins would have been easier to control than united), an inadvertent and innocent "handle" to tell them apart and see them as individuals, or a complex projection of the parents' own conflicts—the result dogged them beyond the family crucible as distrust, competition and a deep-buried fear of incompleteness.

The wedge comes in a variety of other insidious shapes as well. Parents also drive sisters apart by talking about one behind her back to the other, by fomenting rumors or repeating confidences, by making a "son" out of one sister and a cuddly "daughter" out of the other, by holding up one too often and insistently as a model to the other—and even by encouraging sisters to be friends too emphatically, a measure taken with the best apparent intentions that occasionally boomerangs.

One woman, the self-proclaimed "Goody Two-shoes" oldest of three sisters, sketched in the complex corners of the wedge this way:

> My parents desperately wanted us all to love each other a lot, always and equally. Mom also liked to complain about each of us to the others (and get problem-solving help). Constant pressure to be best friends (and feel guilty if we were not) kept us from really being friends. The tête-à-têtes with Mom also strained our confidences with each other (how not to betray a confidence and still pretend to tell Mom something!).

In some families, resisting parental pressures makes a special bond between sisters, a kind of united front against parental demands and intrusions. Remembered Alice, who wrote while her sister was in labor:

> When my parents tried to punish one of us or isolate us from each other, we reacted by forging this kind of united bond. I can remember that sometimes when I was being punished or yelled at, I would cry and run upstairs to the room I shared with my sister. Sometimes she would cry with me and we would hug and comfort each other.

Or from Delia, whose presently shifting relationship with her sister Joyce is described in the introductory quotations to this chapter, "I guess overall my parents brought us closer together, as we gave each other solace from their domineering ways."

In some families, the solace which sisters give each other is specifically a substitute for mother love, which may be physically or psychologically absent. Certainly if a mother has died or if work or illness prevents her from full-time mothering, sisters will turn to each other to replace the lost love, concern and caretaking. But even in families where Mother is an involved and definite presence, sisters may still look to each other to provide what Mother may not be able to offer (or Daughter unable to accept): approval where Mother is disapproving, interest where Mother is remote, companionship where Mother does not have the patience, laughter where

Mother takes life too seriously. Like other surrogates—aunts, grandmothers, teachers, older women friends—sisters may provide an alternative to mother love or an embellishment of it. And the sister relationship need not necessarily detract from the mother-daughter bond, but indeed strengthen it—by relieving Mother of the need to be perfect, the need to be SuperMom and provide her daughter with everything.

Unlike the surrogate figure of aunts or teachers, however, sisters may often share mothering each other in a reciprocal way: the younger sister, in her own way, looking out for the older as much as the older takes care of the younger. A younger sister my comfort an older through a troubled friendship or a broken love affair, a difficult exam or a painful abortion just as an older sister may lend an emotional hand to a younger sister in times of stress. And where in early life, before the separation from Mother, this caretaking may provide an emotional resource or cushion that is additional to mother love, long after the separation from Mother, sisters may still remain deeply emotionally available to each other. As adults, sisters may still be able to provide an extension of "mothering" which is more the mutual and supportive concern of equals.

A footnote to the whole question of parental influence on relationships between sisters: Nearly half the women who answered the Questionnaires said that their parents had no influence on their relationships with sisters—or skipped the question entirely. When I mentioned this to psychotherapist Leah Potts, her reaction was immediate and unsurprised. "Of course! Most parents don't know how to help sisters be sisters." Even in the huge how-to literature for parents on raising children, relatively little space is spent on how to raise siblings to be friends, except for a brief flurry of guidance around the birth of younger siblings and the possibility of sibling rivalry. Dr. Spock devotes ten pages to "Jealousy," but none to helping siblings become friends. (Our language, too, reflects this bias, this oversight: We have words for *parenting*, *mothering* and *fathering*—but nothing for *sistering* or *brothering*.)

As I was puzzling out this question of influence on what life is like between sisters, analyzing both the interconnections and the randomness among parents, daughters and sisters, I stumbled upon a series of clues, superficially haphazard but linked together, the missing piece of the puzzle (italics mine in the four quotes below).

First, these spirited lyrics from feminist folksinger Holly Near's song of remembered adulation for her older sister, now mellowed into easy friendship—"You've Got Me Flying":

> You would run and dance across the field and hay
> I would hide behind to see where you would go to play
> *You were being Isadora*
> *I was being you*
>
> . . . .
>
> Did I know that I'd grow to say?
> You've got me flying, I'm flying. . . .[5]

Then, this observation from Nancy Friday's *My Mother/ My Self*, underlining the connection between mother and daughter, and only inadvertently touching on the connection between mother and mother's sister:

> I can't help wondering how relevant to my mother's decision to remarry was the emergence of all the women in our house into a time of sexuality. It would have been an unconscious pressure, of course, but *timing is so much*. There we were, four women: my mother, Aunt Kate, my sister, and I, each needing her own man, her own identity. *My aunt married within a year of my mother.*[6]

And a call from my sister (within days of my reading Nancy Friday's comment), describing a dream in which she imagined that she was pregnant. Now neither of us has been pregnant, but in the dream my sister told me she thought, *"You had had natural childbirth, so I felt I had to,* even though I was afraid and didn't want to."

And finally, from a published interview with Elizabeth Swados, twenty-seven and maverick director at New York City's Public Theater, this reaction to her mother's suicide: " 'What an unusually spiteful, horrendous act! A parent leaving a legacy that life is no good, that the solutions to problems is to die.' " Then the article continued, "Miss Swados' gloom was deepened by the *death, within a year and a half's time, of three of her mother's sisters.* 'Such a shock,' she said. 'Everyone conked out.' "[7]

The link between these disparate remarks revealed the

missing dimension of influence inside the family crucible and way beyond: the direct and indirect influence of sisters *on each other* at every twist and turn of the life-cycle. In youth and adolescence, the younger sister first seizes on the older one as the revered model, the key to life's mysteries, the image of what's to be and who she's to become. *You were being Isadora, I was being you,* chants Holly Near. Then, getting ready to fly the nest, spread her wings, preparing to build another nest of her own, the sister watches her sister for signs of when it is proper and fitting to make a move and what move is proper to make. *Timing is so much,* observes Nancy Friday. *My aunt married within a year of my mother.* Then, making her way in the world, choosing a path, a life-work, deciding whether, when and how to have kids, again the sister looks to the sister for guidelines. My sister's dream foretells this pattern, years before the fact: *You had had natural childbirth, so I felt I had to.* And finally, through her middle years, she's still picking up hints from her sister (often trading them back and forth) on children and work, leisure and politics, and into her older years, even ultimately to death, which for some makes the last connection: *Within a year and a half's time* of her mother's suicide, *three of her mother's sisters died.* We read often, sad but not surprised, of the husband and wife who die within weeks, months, a year and a half of each other, as if each is the other's connection to this world, and without one the other can't go on. Eerie, but no less believable to see the same primitive connection between sisters, so that one sister's death creates a shock wave reverberating through a family, even devastating it. The other sisters give up their will to live after one of them is gone.

From birth to death, sisters model and pattern their scripts on each other's. They take cues from each other about the way life is or might be, about how to walk, talk, think, dress, about what to fear and what to embrace, about whom to like, whom to scorn, about when to move and how far, what to reach for and why. Inside and outside the family crucible, the patterning is reinforced. "Why can't you be neat/quiet/articulate/creative/helpful/athletic like your sister?" says the parent, repeating a variation of the litany to each of the sisters, so that the yearning for (or rebellion from) modeling is begun at home. "So you're Irmegarde's little sister" says the teacher. "Do you have a crystal voice/round handwriting/line drive/charming giggle like hers?" So that the socialization is further carried on by the schools or by friends, who ask, "Are you as fast and loose/shy and subdued/witty and bright as your sister?" Until eventually the message is internalized and the body is saying, "Be as thin or as curvy/tall or petite/straight-shouldered or stoop-shouldered as your sister," and the mind is repeating, "Walk to the beat of her drummer—or have a good reason why not."

Daughters, of course, take many of the cues for their life-scripts or life-plans directly from their parents, the result of pressures and messages from childhood forward—and contemporary script theorists (such as Eric Berne, Claude Steiner, and Hogie Wyckoff) put analysis of and choice about these cues at the heart of personal growth.[8] But I am also suggesting that daughters also take powerful cues from their other siblings, particularly sisters from sisters, and that any analysis of the fire in the family crucible must also examine these psyche-forging flames.

Naturally, many of the cues sisters pass on to one another are repetitions, adaptations or variations of parental messages. Some are antitheses, and some are culled from different ground entirely, from friends or strangers, television, movies or magazines, dreams or private visions. But whatever the origins of the messages, I think the channels of communication between sister and sister are often more open and accessible, less guarded and defended against than the lines between parent and child. A parent may caution a daughter, "Marry early," or "Keep your virginity for your husband," and the daughter may smile disarmingly and do what she pleases—albeit with conflicts. But if her sister loses her virginity early or marries late, that script is likelier to be followed. While parents play an offstage or backstage role, sisters have the dramatic and constant visibility of peers. At play, at school, at dances—even and especially at home, in the shared rooms of growing up—who could be more influential than the girl her sister sees every day dressing and undressing, laughing and crying, bickering and making up? And what could be more powerful than the last voice she hears before sleep? Sisters' voices also carry the persuasiveness of the contemporary, the hip, while parental style and mores are rooted in the past and always a trifle suspect. (A sister's suggestion to roll up one's jeans à la the French is likely to be taken in stride more quickly than a mother's nervous suggestion that her daughter's skirt is too short.)

It is no coincidence, then, that over and over again in my

interviews and Questionnaires, sisters describe the special, private language they have with each other, usually secret from and undecipherable to parents. It is the language of mutual influence and indoctrination, the language that begins the separation from parents, reinforces the solidarity and bond between sisters and becomes a force in their eventual independence. One symbolic story about the intimate sphere of communication between sisters came from a woman with a sister two years younger:

> When I learned to talk, apparently I spoke some distorted sort of language. My parents could understand only a few of my words for various foods and their names and my grandparents' names. They hoped that my sister would teach me to speak conventionally, but instead, I taught her my language, and no one could understand us but each other, until we learned to speak properly in school.

Their preschool language provided five years of safety for exchanging secrets, intimacies and childhood wisdom that no outsiders could understand or intrude on.

Before they became teen-agers, Carly Simon and her two older sisters, Joanna and Lucy, had a special vocabulary for sex, absolutely secret from their parents, of course, but handy for teaching each other the facts of life—and comparing notes about their smattering of worldly experience. Remembers Joanna Simon, the oldest, "We liked to talk about sex so much that we made up substitute words. One particular thing, for example, was that we loved to talk about having our period. We just thought that was terribly interesting when we were quite young. And we made up a word called 'sponking,' which meant having your period. And to this day, we will say, 'I'm sponking,' and supposedly, nobody knows what that means. And we made up the word 'kettles' for breasts and 'logs' for penises."

Now that they are women of the world and married ladies (Lucy and Carly also each the mother of two), has the secret language and the openness, however rarefied, about sex continued? Joanna answers, "I think a lot of our discussion had to do with curiosity and not really having any sex. We had no sex lives, but we were interested in them. Now we have sex lives, so we don't really have to talk about them. I find that Carly and I will very openly discuss some aspect of sex, but Lucy is really quite up-tight about discussing it with her sisters. I think that during her analysis she made certain discoveries about sharing her feelings with her sisters about this particular thing. She felt that there was something very incestuous about discussing it with us. It frightened her a little."

In some families, as in the Simons', the creation and practice of a private language is intrinsic to childhood and most permissible then. The rarefied form of communication it invites is savored in childhood and into adolescence, but becomes more and more outmoded, even embarrassing as sisters grow up, away from the family and each other, and under the influence and sway of new teachers, friends, lovers. The shared boundaries—and shared rooms—of growing up are naturally supplanted by the distances—actual or emotional—of adult life. When the experience of adult sexuality replaced the Simons' childhood fantasies, the need for the whispered secrets was also replaced. What was appropriate as children, felt inappropriate as married women—at least to Lucy, who separated from her past by marking it taboo: "incestuous."

Of all sisters, twins seem the most likely to deveolp a private language to express their private bond and intimate sphere of communication—and, in many cases, the most likely to keep this connection tight far into adulthood. Asked when she and her twin sister were closest or happiest together, a thirty-one-year-old replied, "When we were babies, because we had our own 'communication system' just between the two of us. No one else could understand what we were saying to each other." When this kind of "communication system" becomes highly sophisticated and linguistically complete, it is called *idioglossia*, or twin speech. Though rarely scientifically documented, a recent case impressed linguists and psychologists: a set of identical seven-year-old twins, Virginia and Grace Kennedy, who understand English, German, sign language and a bit of Spanish, but who for five years have talked to each other only in what appears to be a language of their own. Idioglossia, the experts say, is "usually found in twins who, like Virginia and Grace Kennedy [whose names for each other are "Cabenga" and "Poto"], have grown up in unusually close companionship largely isolated from the influence of other children." And, in fact, the Kennedy twins began developing their private language at age two, when they moved to a rural and isolated community in California, where there was little opportunity to play with other children. While both parents worked, they were primarily cared for by a grandmother who spoke little English. In that sequestered and remote world, the twins turned to each other for support, companionship and confirmation of a shared picture of what life was all about. Their language made the almost tangible connection between them all the more concrete.[9]

For many sisters, the language of deeds speaks even louder than the language of words in the lifelong process of influencing and shaping each other's lives. The younger sister looks at the older sister, going to school while she's still at home, wearing high heels while she's in sneakers, kissing boys while she still makes fun of them, and she sees her fate walking down the road, several paces ahead. Her sister's life becomes an image of what lies ahead for her and how to meet it, tantalizing or scary, illuminating or cloudy. For some women, an older sister's presence is reassuring and validating, as for this woman whose sister is three years older:

> We fought a lot about clothes, hair-pulling and name-calling. But there were times I would listen to all the things she would tell me that were happening in her life. I was just beginning to grow up, and I felt she was already there.

But when an older sister provides an image of not being able to cope, the younger sister understandably becomes all the more fearful about her own possibilities for resourcefulness, as this woman is in the precarious shadow of her older sister:

> I hated her and wished she would go away after she had a nervous breakdown. She made me quite depressed, as I thought it might happen to me when I got her age.

This woman feels such a strong psychodynamic tug to mimic and be like her sister that her struggle is to separate and differentiate from the unsuccessful patterns her sister has set. "I tried to be my older sister" is how another woman put it, "but I didn't succeed." Instead, she internalized her sister's voice as her own worst critic (the way many internalize the voices and commands of their parents), chiding her for not being perfect—and perfectly *like* her older sister. Only now, in her early thirties, is she willing to confront her sister's voice—both within and without—and to begin the complex and delicate process of reclaiming her own identity.

Bisa Williams, youngest sister of playwright Ntozake Shange, describes a critical incident in her separation from the powerful force of her older sister's flamboyant and free-wheeling persona, which the more reserved Bisa did not wish to emulate. Not surprisingly, the incident coincided with a time of greater intimacy than they'd been accustomed to. Bisa crossed the country to spend a summer in California with her older sister, attending a poetry workshop Ntozake taught, living with her and her intense boyfriend and generally falling under her heavy spell. That summer became a time for Bisa to safeguard and stand her own psychic ground. "It was very traumatic at different points, and it was extremely enlightening. It helped me grow tremendously. But I made the decision when I came out to be with her that I didn't want to be her. I don't want to be like her and make the same decisions she has made." On the face of it (and from the outside), Bisa's life has a whole different look and feel than Ntozake's: modest and private, where Ntozake is outspoken and public; a comparative-literature and film student, where Ntozake is an Artist to the flesh and bones, a brilliantly talented writer and effervescent creative spirit; single and living alone, where her sister has been married twice and her scene is free and easy, with fellow artists dropping in every hour of the day and night.

And even though in many corners of her psyche Bisa Williams has detached herself from her older sister's presence, it is hard and painful to make a clean break, just as it's hard to leave home and not return. For her confidante she selected a slightly older woman of the world named Thulani, whom she chose to be a more simpatico model than her tempestuous older sister. She turns to Thulani for words of wisdom on matters of art and love, philosophy and family. It is no coincidence that Thulani is her sister Ntozake's best friend.

Instead of looking up the road apiece, the older sister looks over her shoulder at the younger sister behind her, often gaining on her as they get older and the age gap narrows, more and more her equal with age. For the older sister, the younger one is an image of what she once was, what she has struggled with, what she might have been, what she still could be. The younger sister's influence is often retroactive, reflective. She doesn't so much break ground for the older as tread it in her own idiosyncratic way: a model for how to take the road not taken. The younger looks at the older and her eyes widen with wonder at the infinite possibilities before her. The older looks behind at the younger, even as a parent might (though the narrower gap is more perilous, more threatening), and her eyes mist with memories, nostalgia. She might yearn for her younger self but is also reminded that she has integrated that younger self, that what she sees happening to her sister has already become part of her own weave. A thirty-four-year-old woman celebrates her sister's twentieth birthday with a poem. She reviews the ages and stages of her sister's life, taking advantage of the opportunity to review her own: "sister-babe, sister-child, sister-girl, sister-love." She concludes:

> O sister-woman, whose beauty, brains and strength I bask in,
>   bragging of my sister-daughter, woman-friend,
> I feel as though your birthday is my own.

Fourteen years apart, the younger was born a "sister-daughter" but has emerged a "woman-friend." As the younger one blooms to maturity, the older sister seals their identification. The younger sister is not only a talisman or reminder of where the older has been, but she now has her own weight and presence: She has become an equal. With age and time the roles shift, reorient and realign. The teacher can be taught, the leader can be led. Where there was once imbalance and distance, there is now the possibility of reciprocity and equality. The mimicking and patterning of youth give way to the give-and-take intimacy of adulthood. The family is a piece of music; each sister plays a different theme, a different variation, according to her own vision, tempo, mood, instrumentation. No one hears and understands the echoes, repetitions, nuances and crescendos as her sister does. Holly Near heralds the alliance of adulthood this way:

> You've got me flying, I'm flying
> You inspired a sister song
> All the pain you're feeling
> I will share with you, help you through . . .
> Never knew how good you'd feel my friend to me
> You are family.[10]

4

SISTER ROLES: SISTERS AS LITTLE WOMEN

What books or stories influenced your thinking about sisters?

Little Women. There were very close sister relationships in that novel—much loyalty, forgiveness and love. We all acted out the parts in our own minds, I think: Meg was my older sister, Jane; Jo was the next oldest, Betsy; Beth was the next, Terry; and Amy was me [the youngest].

SHEILA, *Twenty*

Little Women. I was Beth, but always secretly believed I was Jo.

—TERRY, *Twenty-five*

Louisa May Alcott's *Little Women.* Funny, I can't think of any others.

—BETSY, *Twenty-seven*

Little Women IS UNDOUBTEDLY THE MOST POPULAR AND powerful model women have for thinking about sisters: a charmed story which for generations has transcended the limitations of its sentimentality. It is a parable of sisterhood, of multiple roles with family unity, of squabbling and conflict with family harmony, as this chapter will explore. For years a paean about sisters in the popular consciousness, *Little Women* has recently been reexamined and reclaimed by feminists as "a militant vision of permanent sisterhood," which we read "engulfed in the [March family's] lives as a fifth sister."[1] It is still as intrinsic to the mythology of most American girlhoods as slumber parties, dress-up clothes and fantasies of Mr. Right. I myself had a brief prenatal existence as Amy, then Beth (even have a silver baby spoon monogrammed to that effect), until my parents finally settled on the name Elizabeth. Then, as if by predestination, I dreamed and swooned my way through every volume Louisa May Alcott ever wrote—and waited patiently in every rain storm for the professor of my dreams (like Jo's Professor Bhaer) to appear beside me, offering his umbrella and his lifelong dedication and protection.

Of course, it is Jo who is EveryGirl's heroine: the spirited, lovably sharp-tongued renegade and tomboy, stand-in "brother" in a household of femininity, and stand-in for the author as well. "Jo was the miracle," Columbia University professor

73

Carolyn Heilbrun has observed. "She may have been the single female model continuously available after 1860 to girls dreaming beyond the confines of their constrictions to independence."[2] But if Jo is the most alluring model for girls who grow up to be liberated women, still each of the sisters has her appeal, her niche, her role in the family and in the pantheon of models for identification:

> Margaret, the eldest of the four, was sixteen, and very pretty, being plump and fair, with . . . a sweet mouth and white hands, of which she was rather vain. Fifteen year old Jo was very tall, thin, and brown, and reminded one of a colt; for she never seemed to know what to do with her limbs, which were very much in her way. . . . [She had] the uncomfortable appearance of a girl who was rapidly shooting up into a woman, and didn't like it. Elizabeth—or Beth, as everyone called her—was a rosy, smooth-haired, bright-eyed girl of thirteen, with a shy manner, a timid voice, and a peaceful expression, which was seldom disturbed. Her father called her "Little Tranquillity." . . . Amy, though the youngest, was a most important person—in her own opinion at least. A regular snow maiden, with blue eyes and yellow hair curling on her shoulders, pale and slender, and always carrying herself like a young lady mindful of her manners.[3]

Spaced close together in years, so each follows on the other's heels, like footsteps, each of the March sisters nevertheless has her own turf. They are neatly separated according to looks, temperaments and talents. Meg, the oldest, is the surrogate mother and born teacher; Jo, the rebel, bookworm and writer; Beth, the angel, long-sufferer and divine pianist; Amy, the slightly spoiled brat, ravishing beauty and budding artist. Alcott subtitled the book *Meg, Jo, Beth, and Amy*, for it does tell the sagas of the sisters' separate lives and of how they intertwine. So part of its magical appeal for girls grasping onto the first thin reeds of an identity is the clarity and definition of the sisters' individual roles, a neat novelistic order imposed on what seems the chaos and haphazardness of growing up.

But even deeper than that, and, I think, more seductive to starry-eyed readers, lies the fundamental core of unity in the March family, the solidarity of an essentially female household where Father has gone to war, and "Marmee" becomes the head of the household. The all-female family is unified against the war and against poverty constantly sniffing at the door like an animal about to pounce, and the life-sustaining energy springs from the mother and sisters. The novel is titled *Little Women*, after all, to underline the unity of the sisters —both within the family and without—and, years ahead of its time, becomes a kind of parable of matriarchal power and of sisterhood. Even in the face of conflict, jealousy, pettiness, anger and despair, there is still the possibility of "loyalty, forgiveness, and love."

Alcott's fiction faithfully imitates life, and then life turns around and faithfully imitates fiction. Of the many families of sisters who identify with *Little Women*, twenty-four-year-old Laura, introduced in the last chapter, makes most explicit the coexistence of multiple sister roles with a deeper sense of family unity. First she describes the creation of the four sisters' roles:

> I felt my father tracked us some. Harriet [now thirty-one] is the artist, Carla [twenty-six] the beauty and brain, me the rebel and pioneer, Tracy [twenty-two] the baby girl and friend of animals. Carla and I got the strongest message we could conquer the world, do anything we wanted. Harriet got the strongest message that in order to have Daddy's love, she must please him and do what he wants. Tracy got the message that she doesn't really have to get anything together, because Daddy will take care of her. I got the strongest message from Daddy's college and fighting self that the world is not as good as it should be, and by fighting it, it can be changed.

But despite the careful division of roles, this is the family whose father also loves "his darling daughters" as a group and that gives them "a sense of unity, sisterhood that the four of us together were greater than the sum total." The "darling daughters," the Amazonian "Little Women" have learned and now know that unified they are more powerful than diversified, together they are a force to be reckoned with.

When this lesson is learned too late, the roles that define the sisters also divide them. Terry, introduced in the opening of this chapter, was earmarked "Beth," while her secret self, "Jo," cried to get out. She testifies to the awkwardness and polarization of roles without the unifying sense of family and spirit of sisterhood:

> I'm the middle daughter in that I seemed to have no specialty. Sheila was the baby, Jane, the older, responsible

trailblazer. Betsy was the precocious, brilliant, talented [one]. I was sort of pretty and nice, middling child in every way.

Like the roles of "good" and "bad" children, and the myriad variations of opposites, multiple roles in families of sisters develop for a complex of reasons both predictable and unpredictable, both constructive and destructive. In some families, as in Terry's, roles are programmed from the dictates of birth order, with the eldest the "responsible" surrogate-mother figure, the youngest the "baby," and the two in the middle fighting over the emotional goodies in between (one the apparent winner with "brilliant" and "talented," the other "pretty and nice"—and a self-defined loser).

Parental allegiances, identification or neglect may also contribute to carving out sibling roles. There may be a father or mother stand-in or foreman carrying out parental wishes among the siblings. Or different children may respond to or express differing parental messages, characteristics or fantasies, or instinctively ally with one parent or the other. "I got the strongest message from Daddy's college and fighting self," pinpoints Laura of the four Amazonian "Little Women." And presumably her sisters' most freighted messages came from other selves and stages in her father's development. One woman I interviewed, mother of a brood of daughters, speculated that she and her husband pinned their adult ambitions (for professional success, stability and wealth) on their oldest girls and their fantasies and wishes from their own childhoods (for freedom, adventure, mischief and high times) on their younger children. So the older girls turned out to be responsible, respectable career women, and the younger ones are rebels and devil-may-care scamps—and their parents cherish the achievers and the rascals with equally open arms.

Physical characteristics as well as psychological ones may also shape family roles. The one dark-haired in a family of towheads is usually the likely contender for black sheep—as is the fat child among slender, the bumbler among athletes. (The invalid in a family of healthy siblings, however, is more likely to be the candidate for special attention than for additional privation.) In one family of five black sisters whose ages range from twenty to forty, roles and family factions, from their own report, organize predominantly around subtle gradations in skin color: The oldest and fourth sisters are the darkest-skinned and most black-identified; the second and fifth sisters are the lightest-skinned and most allied with a largely white culture; and the middle sister, who is also lightish-skinned, straddles the line between generations, inclinations and cultural orientations of her sisters.

The balance and distribution of the sexes also stamps its influence on family roles. Even today, with social options radically reorganizing, the presence of brothers as well as sisters is likely to shortchange the possibilities for the sisters without unduly limiting the choices for the brothers. If, for instance, family money can float only one Student or Traveler or Adventurer, it is still first likely to be a brother. An only boy in a family of girls often presents a special case, a unique influence on the balance of family roles. Alfred Adler sketched it rather bleakly:

> An only boy brought up in a family of girls has a hard time before him. He is in a wholly feminine environment. Most of the day the father is absent. . . . Feeling that he is different, he grows up isolated. This is especially true where the womenfolk make a joint attack on him. They think they must all educate him or they want to prove that he has no reason to be conceited. There is a good deal of antagonism and rivalry. . . . He may fight strongly against [the female] atmosphere and lay great stress on his masculinity. He will then always be on his guard not to be dominated by women.[4]

Engulfed by femininity or aggressive about his masculinity, shining star or sharp disappointment, family pet or key target for rivalry (the first, of course, an easy cover for the second)—for better or worse, the only brother among sisters makes his presence keenly felt.

In many large, all-girl families, "surrogate son" is one common role slipped into consciously or not by a daughter sensitive to a father's search for a son. The Josephine (like Alcott's heroine) who chooses to call herself Jo, the Phyllis who metamorphoses into Billy—they are girls who renounce their femininity to win parental love, sibling distinction, or simply a more socially valued identity than the one they were born into.

Wanting to be "Daddy's girl" is another catalyst to finding a role of one's own in a large family. That, coupled with the laterborn sister's panic that the highly coveted and seductive roles have already been filled, may drive the most benign daughter to Machiavellian strategies. Third sister Carly Simon (whose parents fully expected a son—to be called Carl) gives a wry but touching account of her finagling to carve out a niche that would be noticeable to Daddy, livable for her, and perceptibly different from her sisters:

See, my older sister was definitely one way, she was born that way and she was allowed to be that way—always sophisticated, always very poised and theatrical. And Lucy was another way, shy and angelic and sweet and soft and adorable. I remember thinking, literally, that I had to make a conscious decision about it: to decide who I had to be.

The ingenue had been filled. The sophisticate had been filled. So I chose my role. [She offers a wide, crazy smile.] The comedian hadn't been filled yet. By the time I came along, I think the novelty had worn off for my father—the third girl child, you know—and when I was born he was going through some turmoil in his work and wasn't able to be close to me.

I think my mother knew early on that I wasn't terribly interesting to him; she used to give me *tips on how to win him*. She'd say, "Go into his room, honey, and make a funny face!"[5]

In *The Large Family System*, James Bossard and Eleanor Boll study one hundred large families (with six siblings or more) of mixed sexes and of various ethnic and religious backgrounds and come up with an intricate hypothesis of role specialization within the large family. "In the small family," they point out, "first selections and assignments [of roles] are made by adults, chiefly the parents, whereas in large families they tend to be made by the other siblings." The siblings seize on differences in "traits, aptitudes, interests and/or idiosyncrasies as a way of distinguishing one from another,"[6] like keeping track of variations of color and marking to tell apart a litter of kittens. From reports from sixty-four informants, Bossard and Boll list eight general types that often recur in large families:

1. The responsible one: the one that is looked up to, the one that assumes direction or supervision of the other siblings, or renders service to them. . . . The most clearly and frequently identified of all these responsible siblings is the oldest or older daughter who become in varying degrees a second mother to the younger children.

2. The popular, sociable, well-liked sibling. . . . He or she proceeds to gain recognition through personal charm rather than personal power.

3. The socially ambitious . . . "social butterfly."

4. The studious . . . [who] apparently sought and found recognition within the family and outside by doing well in

school, or withdrew from sibling activities to find surcease in books.

5. The self-centered isolate . . . [in some cases, shows] a withdrawal from the family and an organization of life on an away-from-home basis.

6. The irresponsible one . . . [who] simply sit[s] back, as it were, and withdraw[s] from the responsibilities which the others accept.

7. The physically weak or ill.

8. The "spoiled" . . . most often this is the last-born child, although there are cases . . . where it is the second youngest.[7]

Finally, they offer this interpretation of the eight types, which serves, in part, as background to my own family portraits later in this chapter. They consider the eight roles in order of frequency of identification, "keeping in mind always the constancy of the individual child's drive for recognition and status":

The first ones to appear develop patterns of responsibility because they are first and are followed by younger and more helpless siblings. The next ones, finding this role pre-empted, seek recognition by making themselves agreeable. They do not seek to wrest control from the older children; they compete with it or supplement it with their personal charms. The next children, finding these two roles pre-empted, turn from the family to the community. They become social-minded and socially ambitious. Those that follow in turn have to turn to a new avenue of achievement. These turn to the schools. They become the scholars, the studious ones, the sophisticates, the intellectuals. The next child withdraws from competition. This is the family isolate. Or he may not withdraw his presence, only his sense of responsibility—these are the irresponsible ones, who participate but let the others hold the bag. . . . The physically defective, the sickly, and those who pretend to be— they have their excuse for relative failure to find their roles, if they wish to use it. Finally, at the end of the line is the terminal child, either pampered into relative ineffectiveness or wearing the "magic boots" to overtake the older ones.[8]

Roles can be useful shorthand, both differentiating the family members inside the family, and labeling them outside as participants in a sophisticated social system. Still, a role is not the whole book, only a book jacket toted around by a salesman and shown off, while reading and digesting the contents of the book would require more subtlety and commitment. A friend tells you of a family of four sisters, a classic composition of the variables: three blondes and a brunette, WASP, privileged, socially gracious and presentable. The oldest is maternal, secretive and intellectual, the wit, observer and peacemaker. The second is the only dark one and the strongest; and in the eyes of the others she's the most spoiled, in her own eyes the misfit. The third is the clown, stretches her face in a thousand guises, androgynous, Daddy's girl, wishes she'd been his son. And the fourth is the beauty, the baby, the tap dancer, dancing her way into the others' hearts, dancing for approval, for money, for love. You think that you see them, think from their labels that you know them, portraits in a *tableau vivant*. Then you hear from your friend that one of them has killed herself or one of them has suddenly married a European prince twenty-five years her senior, and you are baffled, stymied—which one? Knowing the family's roles does not necessarily get you underneath the family's skin.

Roles may be labeled as early as the nursery and continue to peg a family of sisters till old age—with a dozen shifts and exchanges, blowups and turnabouts in between. The family misfit may use her freaky energy to become a chillingly funny comedian, or the porcelain doll of the family may smash her role and join the SLA. "Being cast in a family role," Robert White observes, "tends to promote growth in certain directions and restrict it in others." His carefully balanced appraisal takes for granted that any understanding of family roles still accounts for only part of the story:

> If on certain occasions a child is shy and the parents begin to think of him as the shy one, every meeting with a stranger will be affected by the cues emanating from these expectations, so that the trait of shyness is pregressively strengthened. In like fashion, family role expectations can strengthen qualities of a more desirable kind: confidence, poise, friendliness and consideration for others are all more easily developed in an atmosphere that presupposes their existence. The restrictive aspect of roles derives from what they implicitly exclude. It may be difficult for the court jester to get his family to take him seriously, for the hard-headed practical one to stray into whim and idle fancy. . . . When roles in the family are narrowly defined, stereotyped, and crudely used for control—"you are a person who does these things but does not do those things"—they can have a decidedly restrictive effect on growth. When they have greater breadth and softness of outline, so that not all behavior is forced into them, their effect can be highly supportive.[9]

Evelyn, Flo, Grace, Joy and Faye Kennedy: five black sisters who call themselves "the Other Kennedys" with glee and guffaws and tongue-in-cheek outrageousness, which is how they do just about everything, from appearing dry-eyed at the funeral of the mother they were absolutely crazy about to bickering about Idi Amin while being filmed for "60 Minutes" to cutting off communication if one rubs the other the wrong way to loving each other feverishly, shamelessly down to the marrow of their funny bones. Five sisters who span generations, political persuasions, cosmic orientations and psychological qualifications. Evelyn, sixty-four, is the oldest, the most conservative and most reclusive. "Lynn would always be the last to do anything, 'cause she was scared," says one of her sisters. "Because of her fright, she was always holding back, and she would always get stuck with worse things than we would get stuck with," like "nursing our mother through her coma before she died of cancer." Grace, at sixty, is a shade less conservative but equally reclusive. Roughly twenty-five years younger (though neither will reveal her exact age, so as not to embarrass the other) are Joy, the former model, glamour girl and social climber, and Faye, the ever-ingratiating, mellow-spirited family baby. And unclassifiable, either in the family hierarchy or in any other system on the planet, is Flo Kennedy, sixty-two, the foulmouthed, huge-hearted, feminist-activist attorney, writer, founder of the Feminist Party, media manipulator and gadfly extraordinaire on the bulging underbelly of the capitalist cow. "A lot of people think I'm crazy," Flo Kennedy has quipped in her inimitably quotable style. "Maybe you do, too, but I never stop to wonder why I'm not like other people. The mystery to me is why more people aren't like me."

"When we were growing up, we were always on," Flo chuckles, one feverish, frantic summer morning. "We loved being conspicuous. We thought it was the greatest fun in the world to be as conspicuous as we could be. It was like a form of show business. We'd dress like twins, and everybody would ask us, Were we twins? And they would get us mixed up, and we would laugh."

Even in her own New York City office apartment, which smells of an idiosyncratic mixture of grease and Jean Naté, Flo Kennedy is as conspicuous, as gorgeously outrageous as the blood-pink orchid tucked behind the ear of Billie Holiday (whom Flo once represented). Slightly stoop-shouldered, and a salt-and-pepper Afro wrapped in a salt-and-pepper turban, she pads and zooms around her cluttered rooms with the grace and energy of a jungle animal, flashing her gold rings and chains and a charm which reads "THE WORLD SUCKS" and zips from constantly ringing phones to constantly buzzing doorbells to a sweet-potato-and-marshmallow pudding she's preparing for a party that night for feminist comedians Harrison and Tyler. Her raspy, nonstop patter flashes equally cheerfully with "mother-fucker" and "sweetheart," both profanity and endearment offered with absolute sincerity, pure put-on, so she seems at once like a zany grandmother and a huggable child. She is a live wire of sexual energy and also curiously asexual, neither typically feminine nor masculine but a hybrid of the flashiest of each.

She thrives on frenzy, interruption and tangent, adores making waves and making headlines, in which she is joined by the two younger sisters, Joy and Faye, while the two others scorn the limelight in favor of the cozy privacy of their homes in New Jersey and their jobs selling at a department store. The Kennedys have been dubbed the Black Brontës, and indeed three of them have written books: Flo Kennedy's *Abortion Rap* (with Diane Schulder), *Pathology of Oppression*, and recent rocking autobiography, *Color Me Flo*; Joy Kennedy's spoofy *The Neurotic Woman's Guide to Nonfulfillment, or How Not To Get a Man*; and Faye Kennedy Daly's thriller, *Good-bye, Diane*, taking off from the same grisly murder story as *Looking for Mr. Goodbar*.

But as a literary trio, their scene is more the stage than the salon, more the scat-singing, knock-'em-dead energy of the Pointer Sisters than the reclusive self-absorption of the Brontës. From "60 Minutes" to *Jet* magazine, from political benefits to a star-studded Town Hall celebration for Flo's sixtieth (with her own "Feminists' Prayer": "Our Mother, Which art in Heaven/Sister shall be Thy name"), the sheer chutzpah of their sisters act tends to overwhelm both the medium and the message.

The limelight-loving branch of the family and the low-profilers somehow manage to remain on good terms, partly, as Flo explains, "Because we don't try to be ritualistic about seeing each other. We would argue if we saw each other a lot, but we're smart, so we don't." So there's equilibrium even in helter-skelter, offhand but unquestioned unity even in diversity, and a bedrock of family confidence and good spirits traceable to their earliest years. As kids, Flo remembers, they were taught "Anybody that doesn't like you just doesn't have any taste. So we were so crazy about ourselves, that we sort of like each other."

The Kennedy sisters were raised in Kansas City by an adored mother whom they called Zella, adventurous and ambitious ("snobbish in a peasant sort of way") and an adored father whom they called "Daddy," conservative and daughter-doting. Daddy ran a taxi business, so the family had a car at its disposal and, as Flo colors it, "seemed very prosperous, certainly to ourselves. We continued to have a sense of superiority that was predicated on not very much, but yet we had it. There was none of this lolling around in the ghetto. So we never felt oppressed personally. But we were politically aware of oppression, you see, and when you can distinguish between political oppression and personal oppression, you are able to be more political."

Not-taking-shit was a family trait, a glittering but dependable part of their family inheritance, bequeathed to them the way parents in other families leave their children a country estate or a trust fund. Once, goes the story about Daddy, the Ku Klux Klan came to his door, shouting that it was a white neighborhood and he'd have to get out. So Daddy got his gun and shouted back, "The first foot that hits the step belongs to the man I shoot." And that smartly drove the Klan away, never to come back. And once, goes the story about Zella, when she was doing domestic work during the Depression, an employer accused her of stealing something. So she stripped to her sanitary cloth and shook it in the boss's face, saying, "Now you can see I have nothing of yours."

"So, in other words," Flo Kennedy sums up with a proud and eccentric grin, "that indignant ability to say 'Kiss my ass' came from both of them. And it's that kind of spirit on which my policies are based." That ability to say "Kiss my ass" flashes through the family like hot lava through rocks. It runs deeper than politics, deeper than the issues on which the Kennedy sisters seldom see eye to eye. Even Evelyn, "the mouse of the family," laughs Flo without malice, once sat down next to a white guy on a bus in Missouri, and when he started to get up, shouted him down with "Sit back down there, you son of a bitch." "Kiss my ass" is their code of survival, binding them together as women and as black women in a world that has not been notoriously friendly to either. If *Little Women* is the myth, they are at times its heroines, at times its antiheroines, loyal and loving, irreverent and smart-ass. "Grace always got along with people superficially but with no flare-ups," remembers Faye Kennedy Daly from her vantage point as family baby. "Flo and Joy were the fighters. Evelyn was peaceful. And I was kind of sucking around after Joy." Today, Faye is a denim-jumpsuit-clad New York City parole officer, who drives a Mercedes and is married to a spunky Irishman. Grinning the family grin, utterly and engagingly smitten with itself, she sums up the family politics: "We get along real good, except for the times we're not talking to each other."

The sisters agree on some of the things about each other, each other's roles, triumphs or Achilles' heels. They agree on the fierceness of Joy's temper, Evelyn's conservatism and Flo's outrageousness. They agree that none of them want children and all of them fantasize about having more money. But the lines between them are soft and the edges are frayed like a favorite old pair of pants and there's a live-and-let-live tolerance of each other's quirky differences.

"See, my mother really prepared us to be very loose with one another," Flo explains as she plops the marshmallows on her sweet-potato pudding. "She would make five salads—one with lettuce, one with tomato with no eggs—you know, she adjusted to each person's liking. So, in other words, we are definitely inclined to respect each other's differences. It's very interesting to me that my sisters are different, because it makes me know better how other people are. They absolutely do not relate to any of this bullshit that I'm into. But if I got arrested, they'd mortgage their houses for my bail. They don't support my policies, but they support me, see."

The Unterbergs: another clan, another large family of five little women, two little men (and three who died young). Their heyday was another era, the era when Our Crowd worked its way from the cul-de-sacs of eastern Europe and Russia to the ghettos of the Lower East Side and from there, by wit and work and will and worry, to a place not only fit for their children, but lavish and elegant and more than a little rarefied. My grandmother Sylvia was the eldest, born in 1888, then Mabel, two years later, and Doris, two years after her. These three were born to the Victorian era, went to finishing school, rode sidesaddle and learned to paint on china. In the middle of the family came a girl who died an infant and the first boy, David. And then, eleven, twelve and fourteen years after Sylvia, another three: Lilian, Clarence (known to one and all as Dutch, ostensibly from the pale blond locks of childhood) and Adele; and finally, two still-born babies.

The Unterbergs were two families within a family with their own hierarchy of command, their own byzantine roles and allegiances, pairings and partings of the way, shifts of grace and fortune over the passage of time. By the time I knew them, they had crossed into the magic kingdom the child calls "old" (all except David, who had died a few years after I was born; and Adele, who married and moved to a "foreign country"—Cleveland—and died after childbirth at twenty-six, and who was only a precious, stinging memory, a legend). When I knew them, the youngest was fifty, and they were all settled in their niches, settled in their ways. Even to the child's eye, they were at once eminently classifiable, yet defied classification, with that uncanny streak of the unpredictable that is the child's fascination and fear and the novelist's delight, and, I believe, the quality that left them perpetually on their toes in each other's presence and always a little uneasy, too. It was as if the years spent growing up together didn't quite add up to the adults celebrating Friday-night Sabbaths or sharing the holidays or weddings or funerals or bumping into each other on the crosstown bus. One sister would have a violent burst of temper, or one would up and do something batty, or two would flare into an intense vendetta, and the others would try to piece the eccentricity into the pattern, into the family history, yet still be baffled by it. But there is the story of family life: just when we think we have our families ready for literature they become stranger and more incalculable, unfathomable than fiction.

The men of the Unterberg clan were imposing—and the one who survives is to this day—but no one doubted that the power of the family for as far back as anyone could or cared to remember rested in the hands of the women, a matriarchy of word, manner and deed. It was a matriarchy held together not by mustering against war and poverty, like Alcott's March family, or by the nose-thumbing at outsiders and oppression, like the Kennedy family, but by a dedication to Judaism (and a fury against its detractors) so fierce as to be, at times, unrecognizable as religion.

Sylvia, the eldest daughter, the eldest sister, my grandmother, was the first matriarch of her generation, and every inch of her spoke it, from the tip of her silvery chignon, washed by a hairdresser once a week, to the tip of her made-to-order shoes. She had grown to be a young woman in a household where she was used to her word being law, which made her not the easiest of mothers, or the cuddliest of grandmothers. When she stood at dusk to light and bless the Sabbath candles, her back was as straight as the backs of the mahogany chairs around the table. But she had a vulnerable side to her, for once she had weighed nearly two hundred pounds and in some nook of her psyche never forgot it. She was deeply frightened of being alone. "If I were to have three wishes," she once confessed to one of her sisters, "they would be to drive, to cook and to have a sense of humor."

Two years after Sylvia came Mabel, who clearly had eyed Sylvia's progress in figure and purpose and grown gracefully in the opposite direction. Where Sylvia was ramrod-straight and utterly down-to-earth, Mabel has always been gentle, lyrical and otherworldly. (Once she gave me a broken kerosene lamp because she was taken with the design on the glass, and another time a single earring which she thought would make a pretty pin.) She was most generous with her time and wisdom, took me to the Cloisters when I was little and taught me the names of every flower in the garden.

Where Sylvia prayed every Saturday morning in a spartan synagogue, simple enough to be a Friends' meetinghouse, Mabel's synagogue was ornate and ritualistic, the oldest and grandest in New York; the men and women sat separately, swaying and praying to the music. Mabel has violet eyes that in her youth were her pride and her family's and now seem always on the verge of tears. She wears dresses as delicate as strudel dough, hats as rich as *Schlag*. She has already made a gift of one of her costumes to the Museum of the City of New York, and sometimes has seemed a walking museum piece herself, striding through Central Park at dusk, her hat dwarfing her face and her long skirts billowing in the wind. In Martha's Vineyard, where she spent every summer for the last thirty years, she was a fearless hitchhiker. Now, at eighty-nine, the edges of her past and present have blurred. But for thirty years in Martha's Vineyard she could be seen by the side of the road in her bathing suit and enormous hat, wandering until she thumbed a ride.

Doris came next in line and was not as extreme a personality as either of her predecessors, neither an autocrat like Sylvia nor a romantic like Mabel. She was short and compact, the family tomboy, who until she died whiled away summer afternoons watching baseball games with the men. She had a cap of neat curls and a walk that spoke the family determination, when she strode across town to synagogue first thing every Saturday morning and sat down dutifully next to Sylvia, whether or not they were on speaking terms. She was sweet and generous, softened by a sadness from youth, for, as I found out after she died, her heart was broken at a tender age, when she lost her fiancé at war. Doris was the family historian and chronicler, and kept the family scrapbook with its proud but yellowing photographs and letters, wedding announcements and anniversary menus. She had the turn of mind to remember precisely who married whom, what they wore and what was served, and, like all the sisters, referred to most married women (even the elderly ones) by their maiden names. I would swear on the family Bible that all the sisters called themselves Unterbergs in spite of and throughout their marriages.

Lilian was the fourth sister I got to know, and as one of the "second generation" of siblings, she still prides herself on being more modern and forward-thinking than the others, and is treated like a pal and comrade by her thirty-year-old granddaughter. Lilian was the first of the sisters to go to college, the first and only to go to work and the least observant of Jewish ritual and custom, though loyal, as they all were, to Israel, as if it were another relative. Still, she has never pushed the limits of the family anywhere near the breaking point and today, at eighty, is a freckled and be-speckled, gracious, suburban lady.

For more than thirty years, Dutch has been the only surviving Unterberg male, and he has swelled to bear this mantle. He has spent his life growing rich and powerful on Wall Street, and to me he personifies Wall Street, a towering figure in three-piece suits, solid as the building which houses the Stock Exchange, with a voice so deep and cavernous it could make the Dow Jones rise or fall with a single bellow.

Once, as a child, I went to his legendary lollipop party at his New Jersey summer house. There, sure enough, was a huge oak tree, its branches dripping with lollipops, yellow and red, green and orange, hundreds of them. It was a frightening sight, seeing a fantasy come to life like that, as powerful and unnerving as if an immigrant were to see money growing on a tree. For years after that, whenever I saw Uncle Dutch, I got a sinking feeling in my stomach, just as I do when I see certain foods I used to crave but ate too much of all at once, pumpkin pie and Clark bars, to name two.

"Frankly," roared Uncle Dutch when I told him I was writing about the Unterberg sisters, "I only liked two of them."

Of the five of them, Lilian is the one best able to tell the tale, and one summer afternoon we sit talking about it for hours in her apartment, which is neat and tidy as her father's fingernails, with especially spotless bathrooms, separate for husband and wife, as were the bathrooms of all the Unterberg sisters and their husbands.

"Just recently I was talking to my brother Clarence," she begins, while we have tea and brownies. "And we both felt that our father was both father and mother to us. He was most devoted. He was the one who tucked us in at night and seemed very concerned about us, and after we had children of our own, he visited each of us in turn after he left his office." Israel Unterberg, her father, was an immigrant who spent his first nights in America on a cutting board in a shirt factory and grew to make a fortune in shirts and with his wife, Bella, to become a pillar of Jewish philanthropy.

"When my mother's oldest child was nineteen," remembers Lilian, who was eight at the time, "she felt that she had finished with childbearing. Being a very spiritual person, she went to her rabbi and said, 'Now I would like to do something for my community.' " His suggestion, in turn, gave birth to her idea for the Young Women's Hebrew Association (YWHA), a home-away-from-home where young Jewish working women could keep the Jewish rituals. "So we were turned over to a governess," Lilian continues. "The house was very well staffed. Sylvia, the nineteen-year-old sister, ran the household, did the marketing, gave the orders, and when she got married, the next in order stepped in. Fortunately, it never got to be my turn. Sylvia felt being the oldest was a great, great responsibility, and unfortunately she made us feel that, too, because we really had to pay her due deference."

The children felt their mother's absence with a mixture of pride and resentment, a more modern complaint than might be expected at the turn of the century. Dutch claims to remember his mother "only with a hat on," and Lilian admits no particular "closeness of feeling for her." Once her mother sadly inquired, "Why is it that I can advise two hundred fifty girls at the Young Women's Hebrew Association, and my own daughter makes up her mind without consulting me?"

Lilian closes her eyes, as if to bring the answer into focus.

She does this throughout our conversation, to punctuate, to force the distant nearer. "I think I was always independent, and I really can't explain why. I always wanted to make up my own mind. And I was the rebel in the family."

It was not a family that looked kindly on rebels, this authoritarian family where "our parents' word was law,' where Father decreed that none of the sisters should borrow each other's clothes, where two separate dinners were served every night on two different floors of the five-story brownstone, one for the older set and the parents and one for the younger, where order and stability, cleanliness and industry prevailed, and even in the summer Father made the children write down a program of activities, hour by hour.

"Father," says Lilian, "gave us a great sense of—" She breaks off, and as she searches for the right word, she folds her hand into a fist and pushes it toward me, gently but absolutely firmly, as if pushing through a far denser substance than air. "Drive," she finishes. Then she tells the story of her first job, and the first and only job ever held by an Unterberg sister.

"My father came home one day from a meeting at Federation [of Jewish Philanthropies] and said, 'There's an opening there. Why don't you go down and see the executive director?' " So she went for the interview, was offered the job and came back swashbuckling.

" 'He had some nerve! You should hear what he offered me! Here I am with years of training.' " For she had studied at Columbia Business School.

"Well?" said her father.

"I told him what I'd work for, and he said he'd pay me what I asked!" And at that, Israel Unterberg threw his head back and roared. Since "he wasn't the laughing type," his daughter thought, "He must be very proud that I'm getting what I think I deserve!"

She worked for Federation for a year, forty-eight hours in four-and-a-half days (Friday, the Sabbath, was a short day), and one day the boss called her to his office with the promise of a promotion. "I am sitting there idly and looking at his desk, and across his desk I see a letter with a very familiar handwriting. So I turn it around and enclosed is a check for the exact amount of my salary—signed by my father." The hand which was recently folded into a fist fidgets in her lap. "I resigned then and there." Nor did "Izzy" ever apologize "That was just not part of the relationship."

So the sisters were taught "drive" by their father, who also subtly undermined it, and some of them subverted their own ambitions into the powerful careers of their husbands and other channeled it into charitable (hence acceptable) service to the community. But for the two sons, the path to success was paved in gold from the cradle.

"After four daughters, at long last a boy arrived—David," Lilian recounts. "And you know, that's what every Jewish family wants. My father told me again and again that it never mattered to him what sex the children were, as long as they were healthy. But the first time my mother ever got a gift when a child was born was when her son was born, and I have the watch that she got to show you, and it's a very beautiful one." Dominated by his sisters, "ridden by them," Lilian thinks, David maintained his sweetness and his sense of humor as he grew up. He was also the apple of his mother's eye. "You know, boys are supposed to be closest to their mother," Lilian muses. "And there was really a love affair there."

And as for Dutch, whom his father called "Boysie," he was sent to Columbia University and then to Europe to study banking. When he returned, he landed squarely on his feet on Wall Street, where he grew to manhood and to found an investment firm flourishing to this day. Now at seventy-eight, he is the financial sage and elder statesman of the family; Boysie has become a patriarch treading in his father's footsteps.

"Sibling rivalry was a luxury we didn't have in Authoritarian families," Aunt Lilian wrote me in a letter of afterthoughts, months after our visit. "Or maybe there were too many of us to provide competition for our parents' favor." But even the child's eye dispels her theory, remembering the subterranean bickering and posturing at family holiday gatherings: who laid the better table, who had the more devoted cook, who'd made the better match, who'd made the better pudding. All this, mind you, only buzzing beneath the surface, for all that was visible was the linen tablecloth, smooth as a peaceful brow, and the Sabbath candles in the silver candlesticks, and the *challah* loaf, squatting round as a hen, and the voices lifted in the shared prayers of ages past.

The first Sabbath that her daughter Adele spent in that "foreign country"—Cleveland, Bella Unterberg wrote her a letter that now rests proud and yellow in the family scrapbook. "I shall say to myself," wrote the mother, the matriarch, my great-grandmother, "our little Adele is building up a Jewish home, aglow with the Sabbath spirit. Can that be far away? The same light, the same grace." The same light, and same grace that threaded from mother to daughter, from sister to sister and bound them in a Jewish sisterhood of their own. It was a sisterhood which was dazzling when it shone with genuine family feeling and only disconcerting when it shed light but no warmth.

5

SISTER RIVALRY

The biggest thing I wanted from age three to eighteen was a horse. My parents said we couldn't afford one, which was bullshit. Anyway, when my sister came to the horse-crazy stage, my parents thought they'd lost me to drugs and sex (I was a virgin), and got her a horse to divert her. This seems silly, but it's a big problem—a holdover from the past. I felt my parents didn't love me, etc. I grew really distant from them. My sister, besides having a horse, was *the* object of their affection. I'm most jealous that my parents and my sister can express affection for each other so easily.

—BARBARA, *Twenty-eight*

I can't think of any way in which I am *jealous* of Jean, but there are many qualities she has that *I* wish *I* had. She is tall, and I am short. She is calm, and I am nervous. She has periods of anxiety, like anybody, but they pass. My anxiety is my normal state, and I have periods of calm! She knows how to relax. Also, she is at peace in her relationship with her husband, while I have had many different relationships that never brought me *any* peace. I think Jean has better luck with being happy and content, and I wish I could learn to do that, too. I think, too, that she is a great beauty and that I am pretty frumpy in comparison. It could be a source of jealousy, but instead I just feel so happy that she is beautiful.

—MARGE, *Thirty, about Jean, Twenty-five*

THERE IS NO SET OF SISTERS ALIVE, MYSELF AND MINE IN-
cluded, despite our unflappable closeness, who have not, at
one time or another, felt the bitter, belittling and bedeviling
sting of sibling rivalry. It may be submerged, denied, pro-
jected, rationalized or repressed for a time, only to reemerge
when and where least expected, its power as unpredictable,
as many-headed and often as ineradicable as a mythic beast's.
It may first appear flailing with the rashness, the impetuous-
ness of childhood: the two-year-old who smears her excre-
ment over the walls the day her mother returns from the hospital with a little sister; the five-year-old who lops off her
baby sister's curls in a fit of self-serving rage. Or it may surface later in childhood with a stomp of the foot over territoriality, what's mine versus what's yours, who allies with
whom in the hills and plains of the family. "Who do you love
more?" is the sisters' nervous and wheedling plaint to the
parents during this period, and the hackles rise at even
imagined slurs, the merest whisper that *she* is preferred to *me*.
What is your worst jealousy of your sister? asked the Questionnaire. "The time we forgot whose turn it was to go to the
store with Mother," pinpoints the eleven-year-old twin, who,
as one of thirteen children, keeps careful tab on such things,
and she "got to go instead of me."

When rivalry seethes into adolescence, or if, with pimples
and periods, it emerges for the first time, it needles the

tenderness of this time, the ego bruising easily in its hurry, its insistence to be unique. Who am I? versus Who are you? is the itch under the skin this time, and Which parent's footsteps do we follow in? "We each had very different parts of my father," remembers Jane Lazarre, who wrote the highly acclaimed and deeply personal *Mother Knot*. Her tug-of-war with her younger sister, Emily, for their father's affection was the more desperate because their mother had died when Jane was seven, Emily, four. Now they are thirty-six and thirty-three, a writer and a potter with two children each and the best of friends. But as adolescents they were bitterest rivals. For the division of their father's psychological booty gave Jane the intellectual goodies, Emily, the emotional ones. "My father identified with me intellectually and educated me politically," remembers Jane, whereas, "He was very protective of my sister. She looked a lot like him, and I think he saw her as being like him. I think that she got most of the intense Oedipal sexuality, which is probably what I am most jealous of. Each one was jealous of what the other had," she concludes.

Years later, Emily's memory is an unprompted echo: "I think there were a lot of things that my father gave Jane which I missed out on. For instance, I would have loved the intellectual companionship, the political theory. By the time I was old enough to be interested and would say to him, 'What's the difference between communism and socialism?' he would say, 'Ask Jane.'

"But in fact, I wanted that contact with him. The contact I was getting was that I was the good, easy child who was open to a lot of love and emotional warmth, whereas his relationship with Jane was much more complicated. So she saw me as getting what I wanted, and I saw her as getting what she wanted."

Still locked in the embrace of the family romance, the adolescent sisters define their rivalry in terms of competition for the gold cup of parental love. It is never perceived as a cup which runneth over, rather a finite vessel from which the more one sister drinks, the less is left for the others. The growing sisters are always thirsty, and they blame and bait each other for it.

As they get older, if the rivalry persists, the sphere of competition widens. The vying and sparring for parental love becomes translated (or sublimated) into jockeying for the world's favors. Who has more? and Who has achieved more? is the yardstick which measures the rivalry of adulthood. Imagine two sisters, in the middle of their lives, whose life choices propelled them in opposite directions. One at fifty-three, married, with six children, a rambling old house in the suburbs and the privacy and insularity it suggests; the other, forty-five, single, independent, child-free, preeminently public and political. Recalls Gloria Steinem, the younger, "[My sister] said to me once that she was glad that I hadn't married and had children, because then I would have been able to have both things at the same time, and that would have made her jealous." To have "both things at the same time" would have rocked the precarious balance of power, upset the ledger, which listed "hearth and home" under Susanne's column, "public domain," under Gloria's.

If rivalry haunts sisters until old age, it appears with a testiness, a pettiness that is almost a caricature of childhood spats. Such is the circularity of the life-cycle that the voices of older women, measuring tit for tat, echo the little girls' hassling for territoriality, of mine versus yours. "Our mother always said, your hair has to be perfect! So when my sister comes over, I care about how I look, my hair, my dress," admits a sixty-year-old woman. "Days later, I'll ask her, 'Why don't you comment on my new dress?' And she'll answer, 'I just can't. Why didn't you ever mention my new coat?' " If she's not your sister, it could almost be a grim joke, but her own sister is not laughing. "When I go to her house, I make sure my hair is perfect. Won't that ever stop?" The voice is plaintive, and after fifty-seven years, the sting is deep.

There is another set of sisters, also sixty and fifty-seven. These sisters have spent their whole lives in the same city, talk on the phone every day, sometimes twice, nurse each other through *tsouris*, grief and anger. Both are married with several children each, yet they claim to have more fun on vacations together than traveling with their husbands. Neither wants to be the last to die, because neither could imagine living without her sister.

Rivalrous and inseparable, fiercely competitive and supportive until death: these antithetical pairs are, of course, the same set of sisters. Beneath the petty squabbles of later years lies the bedrock of certainty that their bond has also lasted, stretched and tugged, but never snapped, while friendships have been forged and broken, acquaintances made and drifted

away from. Their lifelong rivalry is intrinsic to their lifelong
chiseling of separate identities and, paradoxically, the fuel of
their individuality.

For just as the central tug between mothers and daughters
is the need for dependence versus the pull toward independence, the pull between sisters is the realization of similarity
versus the need for difference. On the one hand is the
comfort and familiarity of being similar: looking the same,
speaking with the same voices, liking the same things. On the
other hand—and partly in defense against the sameness,
which, after all, could be only an accident of birth—is a
deep-rooted need to be different: developing different values
and styles, talents and friends, strengths and foibles. So the
rivalry enhances the process of differentiation and individuation, and in a profound sense is therefore not a barrier to
friendship but, in many cases, a necessary and natural part of
it. In the bickering between the eleven-year-old twins is the
complement to their puppylike affection, in the adolescent
jockeying between Jane and Emily Lazarre the root of their
dedication to each other now that they're mothers, in the
fastidious boundaries between the Steinems the seeds of their
fierce loyalty. Without conflict, no solidarity; "Without con-
traries," as Blake has put it, "no progression."

Life-cycle psychologist Robert White sums up the complex
fluctuations of hostility and solidarity between siblings this
way:

> Typically brothers and sisters play different parts in each others'
> lives at different times. For example, in childhood, a girl may
> view her older sister as a rival; when puberty approaches, the
> sister becomes an admirable guide to the adolescent world;
> shortly thereafter, when both are receiving boys' attentions, the
> sister may again become an unwelcome competitor. The in-
> fluence of any given sibling, taken over time, may consist of a
> complex pattern of benefits and harms.[1]

With patience, luck and the will to change, the quarrels of
the early years fertilize the soil in which friendship takes root.
From the psychological jousting between sisters in the early
family arena emerge the first tentative boundaries of their
personalities. As these personalities become less tentative,
more clearly separate and settled, the threat of acknowledging the common bonds lessens, and the potential for friendship blossoms. Over the years, sisters generally draw closer,
knitting together their differences out of common threads,

much as children, as they grow up, close the gaps with their parents. At last they acknowledge the similarities that surface with time, rather than stubbornly insisting on the differences and divisions. The process of becoming friends with a sister may take a lifetime, but its reward is the comfort of her companionship in old age. "Above all," Margaret Mead has written in her autobiography, *Blackberry Winter,* "perhaps, sisters who have grown up close to one another know how their day-dreams have been interwoven with their life experiences."[2]

Once upon a time there were three sisters. To be precise, they were stepsisters, for one was the daughter of her father's first marriage to the sweetest woman in the world, and the other two were daughters of their father's second wife, the proudest and haughtiest woman in the world. Each of the sisters followed in her own mother's footsteps. The first was goodness and gentleness incarnate, the other two were uppity, vengeful and self-absorbed. The first was made to do all the dirty work for the family, and she did it with patience and without complaints. When at last she rested, she crouched in the chimney corner with the cinders, and thus became known as Cinderella.

Now it happened that the king's son gave a ball for everyone who was anyone, and Cinderella's stepsisters flounced off to it, elaborately dressed and coiffed because of Cinderella's labors with their hair and gowns. Cinderella was left behind in tears, bemoaning her fate, when magically a fairy godmother appeared. With a stroke of her wand, she transformed a pumpkin from the garden into a coach, six mice and a rat into horses and a coachman, and Cinderella's tattered rags into a splendiferous gown. Then she gave Cinderella a pair of pretty glass slippers and hastened her to the ball—with the warning, not uncommon between mothers and daughters, that she return before midnight.

The mysterious guest was the sensation of the ball, confounding her stepsisters and winning the prince's heart. Three nights Cinderella twirled in the prince's arms until the stroke of midnight, and on the third, in her hurry, she lost a glass slipper on the stairs. The prince found it, and, swooning with love, announced a few days later he would marry the lady who fit the slipper.

When the prince's courier came to the house of the three sisters, Cinderella's stepsisters tried in vain to cram their feet into the slipper. Finally, and to hoots of derisive laughter,

Cinderella gave a try, and of course made a graceful and easy fit. At that moment, her fairy godmother reappeared, and once again transformed Cinderella from rags to riches. Her stepsisters at last recognized her, and fearing for their vicious necks, they threw themselves at her mercy. She forgave them with all her heart, and after her marriage to the prince, she brought them to live with her at the palace and married them off to two lords of the court. There, no doubt, they lived happily ever after.[3]

"By all accounts, 'Cinderella' is the best-known fairy tale, and probably also the best-liked," reports Bruno Bettelheim, in his comprehensive and illuminating study of fairy tales, *The Uses of Enchantment*.[4] Of the same seven hundred recorded versions dating back to ninth-century China, Perrault's tale, just retold, is among the most well-known in this country. It was originally bowdlerized for presentation in the seventeenth-century French court and, centuries later, sentimentalized by Walt Disney. Also popular is the harsher version of the Brothers Grimm, translated into English in 1826, minus the happily-ever-after ending.[5]

What accounts for "Cinderella's" popularity, both with children and the parents who tell it to them, is the undisguised fulfillment of wishes, the virtue rewarded, the magical transformation from rags to riches and the tidy ending, where strife is resolved and happiness reigns. But deeper than that is the subconscious picture the story portrays. Explains Bettelheim:

> The psychological issues touched upon in the story are so covertly alluded to that the child does not become consciously aware of them. In his unconscious, however, the child responds to these significant details which refer to matters and experiences from which he consciously has separated himself, but which nevertheless continue to create vast problems for him.[6]

Even for listeners too young to name its themes, "Cinderella" is an accessible and provocative portrait of the roots of sibling rivalry and its configurations within the family. It is a chronicle of the connections between parent and daughter, between sister and sister—the complexities of the family romance. The Cinderella motif reminds the readers that what happens between sisters from the first stirrings of their relationship and ever after cannot be separated from what happens between parent and child. I have chosen "Cinderella" as a psychological paradigm because it illuminates both primitively and profoundly many of the pieces in the puzzle of sister relationships. The most complicated piece begins our inquiry: the triangle of mother, father and daughters.

As "Cinderella" opens, the lines of allegiance and the sides of good and evil are starkly drawn. In one corner (the ash-ridden one, of course) sits the exemplary Cinderella, daughter of "the sweetest woman in the world," who has died before the story beings. Opposite Cinderella stands the evil stepmother and the two stepsisters, her henchwomen, who, as Bettelheim notes, "are so closely identified with each other that one gets the feeling that they are one unit split into different figures."[7] In the apex of the triangle, curiously passive (especially in Perrault's version) though pivotal, is the father for whose love both sides fervently and shamelessly compete. The heart of the fable thus becomes the Oedipal triangle at its most intense.

In a more complex symbolic transformation, sibling rivalry replaces the Oedipal rivalry with the mother as the center of the plot. Cinderella's wish to eliminate Mother is completely repressed; instead, the churning welter of Oedipal emotions is displaced onto the relationships with the stepsisters—and appears to ignite and aggravate the pettiness, nastiness and bitterness, in short, the feelings we call sibling rivalry. Again and again, the rivalry we will see between sisters is, at least in part, an expression of the rivalry girls experience with their mothers, in a more manageable, less threatening form. As Rachel succinctly observed in the opening chapter, reviewing her family constellation to prepare for having a family of her own, "I think I had a lot of jealousy of my mother, which I couldn't express, so I took it out on a littler version of my mother—my sister."

In a case study of a neurotic woman patient, psychoanalyst Karen Horney further corroborates the connections between sibling rivalry and the Oedipal triangle:

It transpired that . . . a sister had been born (when patient X was five or six years old) and that she had felt herself supplanted by this sister in her father's affections. As deeper strata were revealed, it became clear that behind the jealousy of her sister there lay a furious jealousy of her mother, which related in the first instance to her mother's many pregnancies. "Mother *always* had the babies," she once said indignantly. More strongly repressed were two further roots (by no means equally important) of her feeling that her father was faithless to her.

The one was sexual jealousy of her mother dating from her witnessing parental coitus. . . . A repetition compulsion in this patient spoke in language no less clear: The typical experience of her love life was that she first of all fell in love with a father-substitute and then found him faithless. In connection with occurrences of this sort the final root of the complex became plainly evident; I allude to her feelings of guilt. . . . It was possible to trace very clearly the way in which the feelings of guilt, especially those that resulted from strong impulses to do away with her mother . . . had produced in her an expectation of calamity, which of course referred above all to the relation with her father.[8]

The Cinderella story covers this dense material in symbolic form, for the vagaries of the plot, as Bettelheim and psychoanalysts Ben Rubenstein and Donald M. Marcus (among others) have pointed out, parallel the Oedipal development of a girl.[9] Her first love attachment is her mother, "the sweetest woman in the world," the all-giving, undemanding, nurturing "good mother," who disappears (or, in the fairy tale, conveniently dies) before the next stage begins. In this next stage, the girl's primary attachment turns to her father, and her mother and siblings, particularly female ones, are perceived as rivals for her father's affection. Cinderella's dirty treatment by her stepmother and stepsisters can be explained analytically as a projection of her own rivalrous, dirty feelings toward them. (Calling the mother and sisters "step-" is the fairy-tale convention to indicate, as Cinderella would perceive it, the split between the good mother of the earliest years and the cruel, demanding mother and sibling rivals of the next stage.)

As the Oedipal period ends, the girl feels isolated and all alone; this stage finds Cinderella sobbing at home, while her more powerful and independent (if narcissistic) sisters break away, the proverbial older sisters enjoying the titillations of the ball. But if all goes well during puberty (romantically symbolized by the prince's ball), the girl once again reestablishes a relationship with her mother (the "good mother" who reappears as the magical godmother in the story) and begins to identify with her. "Little Cinderella gets her every wish," is Donald Marcus's conclusion in his psychoanalytic study of "The Cinderella Motif: Fairy-Tale and Defense," "an Oedipal victory and unlimited access to a good, giving mother."[10] By the time the story ends, Cinderella has also broken free of the Oedipal triangle in time to fall in love and marry. Her growing up and away from the family has been a delicate, often painful experience. But our heroine, who is delicate and agile enough to dance in glass slippers, also has the dexterity to disentangle from the Oedipal morass.[11] "Cinderella has to work through her deep Oedipal disappointments to return to a successful life at the story's end," notes Bettelheim, "no longer a child, but a young maiden ready for marriage."[12]

Bettelheim also argues that, in Erikson's life-cycle model of "phase-specific psychosocial crises," Cinderella has navigated through basic trust (her relationship with the original good mother); autonomy (accepting and making the best of her humble role); initiative (in some versions, planting a twig and watering it with tears and prayers); industry (her labors); and finally identity (insisting that the prince accept her as "Cinderella" as well as his princess-to-be). According to Erikson's scheme, only after these crises are resolved is Cinderella ready for intimacy with another.[13] I would also add, only then is it possible for Cinderella to forgive her sisters and accept them as friends and equals, living together in the palace, three married women and their noble husbands, happily ever after. Such is one possible sibling script, viewed through rose-colored glasses, perhaps, of the depth of sibling rivalry and the sweet promises of reconciliation.

Not all sibling scripts, however, are as promising, and in some versions of "Cinderella," the sisters live far from happily ever after. In the Grimms' tale, for instance, "When [Cinderella's] wedding was going to take place, the two false sisters came and wanted to curry favor with her and take part in her good fortune."[14] But the split between the sisters is too deep, the sisters' mistreatment of Cinderella too severe, and instead of favor or reconciliation, the stepsisters are punished. Their eyes are plucked out by doves, who in the Grimms' story are symbolically linked with Cinderella's godmother. Blindness is chillingly correct retribution for the sisters, for they could never see their sister's worth or accept her love. Their blindness (like the self-inflicted blindness of Oedipus in another myth of the family romance) becomes an immortal symbol of their shame.

In still earlier versions of "Cinderella," the knot of Oedipal entanglement is tied squarely between Cinderella and her father, rather than displaced onto the rivalry between Cinderella and her sisters. The Oedipal fire burns overtly instead of covertly, and, most significant, the father's complicity for instigating it is out in the open. Psychoanalyst Helene Deutsch has commented on the recurrence of the Cinderella phenomenon between father and daughters, particularly when there are three daughters. A seductive relationship to the father, she has observed,

> is often provoked by him and the psychologic motive for maintaining it often lies in him. Sometimes he wants the daughter to replace the son he never had or who was a failure, and to inherit his spiritual values; often the man's love for his mother is transferred to his daughter. . . . Interestingly enough, such a relationship often obtains with the third daughter, especially if she is also the youngest. It is as though the father's relationship to the daughter has got rid of its dangers and freed itself from the fear of incest with two older daughters. The third one—Cinderella—seems to be particularly suitable for the father's love choice because of her helplessness and apparent innocuousness. The need to save the little daughter from aggressions of the mother and the older sisters certainly plays a great part here.[15] [Italics mine.]

In some versions of "Cinderella," as Bettelheim reports, Cinderella runs away from a father who actually wants to marry her.[16] In still other versions, the father tries to exact a declaration of love from his daughter, which falls short of his maniacal expectations, and becomes cause to banish her. Thus the third—and purest—daughter finds herself in the Cinderella position. Marian R. Cox, a Victorian codifier of Cinderella tales, dubbed this version the "King Lear Judgment,"[17] and indeed, King Lear can be read as a haunting sequel to the Cinderella story.

King Lear is a morality play about what happens when the Oedipal entanglements of youth curse a family into adulthood and old age. Lear is the tragic figure of a father who wants too much from his daughters. He is the too well-intentioned parent, who in his eagerness (and his own hunger for love) divides his family, even as he divides his kingdom, driving sister from sister—and from him. "Lear not only loves his daughters," observes psychoanalyst Arpad Pauncz, in his "Psychopathology of King Lear," "but he is also in love with them, especially the youngest one."[18] When, as the play begins, the old king offers to divide his kingdom among his three daughters, dependent on their avowals of devotion to him, his offer is a "kind of love-suit for the favor of his daughters." The devotion he petitions seems more libidinous than filial.

"Which of you shall we say doth love us most?" is the king's ominous request, and within it are the seeds of the strife of the entire play. However buried his conscious intentions, he offers the lordly cup of parental love and manipulates the thirsty, hungry sisters to squabble for sips. The flattery for which he fishes sets the sisters against each other, vying for good, better, best, against the limits of truth and the bonds of blood.

The two older sisters caricature themselves as they speak. Goneril, the eldest, rises to the bait first. "I love you more than word can wield the Matter," she simpers, ". . . As much as child e'er lov'd, or father found; / A love that makes breath poor, and speech unable. . . ." Her speech is not unable enough, dripping with flattery and hyperbole, and too-rich icing on an already sweet cake. Regan, the second sister, attempts to go her one better, hooked into the sibling competition that by now has its own momentum. "I find she names my very deed of love; / Only she comes too short. . . ." Theirs is the superficiality, the narcissism and the social-climbing at all costs of Cinderella's evil stepsisters.

When Cordelia, the youngest, speaks, she refuses to get sucked into the competition. "I cannot heave / My heart into my mouth," she said, "I love your Majesty / According to my bond; no more nor less." Cordelia alone recognizes the impossibility of her father's demand and the havoc it implies for family relationships. She is really the only member of the family to respect its bonds. Her father stretches the bonds to the breaking point, and her sisters willingly comply, because to them the bonds are as meaningless and vapid as the hot air of their empty praises.

What follows Cordelia's banishment for speaking the truth is the tragedy of the breakdown of the bonds between parent and child, sister and sister. And in the neat strictures with which the Elizabethans order chaos, with macrocosm mirroring microcosm, the breakdown within the family is paralleled by the collapse of the state and the rumbles of disintegration of the universe itself. Vengeful acts, murders, rivalries for lovers, storms on the heath and the "tempest in [Lear's] mind"—the chain of disasters makes of *King Lear* more devastating a morality play on the subject of bonds between sisters than the Grimms' swift, sightless end to the evil step-sisters.[19]

Once upon a time there are two sisters and a brother, Violet, Lucy and Will, Jr. Violet and Lucy are close, perhaps too close in age, twenty-nine and twenty-seven; Will, Jr., the youngest and the only son, named of course after his father and his father's father, was born years later, and now, at twenty, is just beginning to come into his own, though he retains the round, pale, babied face of his protected boyhood. He and Lucy, the middle sister, have the same honey-colored hair, the same freckles and the same toothy grins, so that they manage to look like summer all year round. Sometimes strangers mistake them for twins, despite the seven years between them, a mistake Lucy chooses to consider a compliment, and Will an embarrassment. Violet, the eldest, never looks like summer; even in the dead heat of August, her pale skin has a wintery cast to it. Her blond hair hangs long and lifeless around her, like a protective and magical cloak; her hair was long years before that look was fashionable and many, many years afterwards. In every picture of the family Christmas reunion, Violet, though front and center, seems somehow a creature apart, her skin more ashen, her eyes more grave and vacant, her hair more extraterrestrial than the others. "She usually gets very ripped for Christmas" is Ludy's explanation. But there is more to it than that. In a family that is out of the sketchbook of Norman Rockwell, Violet is the character drawn by Edward Gorey.

Their mother is pure corn pone, once Agriculture Queen at a midwestern university, now in her late fifties, blond and sunny as her second children, the type who calls her brood "the whole fam damily." But she has some bite to her, even a sudden, surprising streak of the bizarre. On a family Christmas card, she is sweetly draped around her husband on a cozy armchair, wearing a long plaid skirt, a frilly white blouse—and a mask of Dracula. She is fond of chiding her children, "Just you wait, I'll dance on your graves."

Their father is staid, warm and powerful. He is also one of the most famous men in America, a sort of father figure to the whole country.

They are the kind of family that is photographed, even publicized to give other families a model of hope, photographed in their spotless, gingham-checked kitchen, on the seas or the slopes, at a star-studded public gala. "It had been a long time since the family had been together," glowed an article about them in one of the women's magazines, "and it brought back loving memories of previous years [they] had cruised these same islands—the five [of them] stretched out on the deck, hands touching, heads on shoulders. 'Here we are again,' ([Will] used to say, 'a happy little family group.' "

I happen to hear another side of the story—perhaps because I knew the family when I was young, or perhaps because Lucy and I were once on "The Howdy Doody Show" together, or perhaps because we both have freckles and look young for our years, and because women who look even modestly alike occasionally have the sympathies of sisters. Whatever the reason, after a letter and several phone calls of arrangements, I find myself sitting in a joint on Sunset Boulevard, sharing a waffle and sipping champagne and orange juice with Lucy, who has lived in Hollywood for the past three years, one of a bevy of would-be's, struggling to break into pictures. I haven't seen her for fifteen years (since the days when she'd come to class protesting, "My dog ate my homework"). But I kept up with her haphazardly through the old girls' grapevine and through random clips my father faithfully sent me of her cameo appearances in one film or another, and from that I'd managed to piece together a razzle-dazzle picture of her Hollywood, starlet life.

In the giddy rush of the champagne, she spills out the outlines of fifteen years of events: the several schools she'd gone to before graduating from one, the brief college career at college where her father "knew someone," the early marriage to a man who dreamed of land and chickens (I'd read about their wedding in the heyday of hippie weddings, with vows that ended, "as long as we both shall dig it"), the move to California, the messy divorce (after they didn't dig it). As it turned out, the Holly Golightly life of the glamorous starlet was, in fact, "three years of bit parts," and it was getting harder and harder to tell the casting agents she was eighteen.

Only later does she realize that in the long, detailed spiel of events she has left out "all the emotions and love affairs," all the rich, dense, buried complexities between one external event and the next. That is the first hint of how life was negotiated in the "happy little family group." The second hint hits me between the eyes, when we get back to her place.

She has made excuses for it the last hour of brunch, while I demur politely. When we arrive, the excuses turn out to be understated. On the stoop of the tiny stucco bungalow, a mangy mutt huddles on a pile of piss-stained sheets, a world-weary Cerberus, guarding the door to an indescribably subterranean chaos. There are so many layers upon layers of debris that objects are barely distinguishable from each other, seem to have merged into a new manner of mass, papers upon bits of machinery upon books upon hideous plants upon dirty dishes. There is only one brave stab at beauty on the premises. In the bathroom, where the toilet has black rings inside it, someone has tacked to a cabinet a little postcard of a flower.

Here, in the shadow side of the gingham checks of her mother's magazine-spread kitchen, in the sordid underbelly of the "happy little family group," she unwinds the family saga. It is a kind of Cinderella story gone sour, a tale of a good sister (who is not so very good), an evil sister (more pitiful than evil), and a brother caught willy-nilly in between. All of them want to be the apple of their father's eye, the sparkly center of attention at the prince's ball. But even in Hollywood, there is rarely a prince's ball.

"I was always the 'good child,'" Lucy begins, settling among the debris into a backless sofa and hoisting her long blue-jean skirt to get comfortable. "That was very much a ploy on my part, but of course I didn't realize it at the time, which is the greatest defense of all." The "good sister" was Mama's favorite, wide-eyed and innocent and just a little passive. Rebellion she postponed till her twenties (what she now calls the "'My parents are terrible, they fucked me up, and anyway, I was probably adopted' stuff"). But her good-little-girlness was not without ulterior motives. When Violet scratched her face (in the heat of the fights at the center of their relationship, until long after they should have known better), Lucy would make sure her face was good and red before she appeared before her parents, sobbing, "Poor little me, I didn't do anything to deserve this."

Violet, meanwhile, with her endless fighting and scrapping (not just with Lucy, but bitterly, furiously with her imperturbable parents), her running away, her drinking and smoking in the girls' room at school, her early discovery of black stockings and drugs, fit snugly into the role of "bad sister." She was the bad seed in the corn pone, the stepsister in the All-American family unit. Over the years, the family came up with rationales for it, but no reasons. "I write off most of my sister's problems and behavior as, well, she's crazy," offers Lucy. "It's some kind of hormone imbalance that can happen to anybody, like multiple sclerosis." She tries to make a joke of it, but cannot manage a laugh. In another mood, she adds,

"It's like some Martian came down and zapped her and changed her into something else." Later, she sounds more sympathetic, as if she has finally convinced herself of the family line. "She can't deal with the outside world. She has no strength, no mechanisms for coping with problems. We all worry about her, and feel very sorry for her." Her words echo with her mother's and a faint crackle of incredulity.

As far back as Lucy can remember, her relationship with Violet has been a patternless dance, with Violet unpredictably leading, fits and starts of closeness and distance, sympathy and rivalry as red and angry as the scratches Violet slashed on her face. Close as children ("I have heard," says Lucy), the first schism came at puberty, when Violet started hanging around with her own smoking, boozing, black-stockinged circle of friends. "She got totally vicious toward me and used to beat me up all the time. It would be inappropriately provoked, like if she thought I was on the phone too long, she'd come at me with fists flying." In retrospect, Lucy's reaction to the attacks is even more poignant, more chilling. "I would curl up in a little ball, and wouldn't ever fight back. I idolized her for years, and wanted very much for her to be my big sister. I really wanted that closeness I always thought that sisters had. I realize now that most of them don't, anyway." She says it to console herself, the way women who've been unhappily married for years console themselves that other women's husbands are more difficult than their own.

There were intermittent moments of closeness—Violet turning her on to acid, Violet's unexpected and intimate letter from Hawaii, saying that she'd gotten married—later to divorce and marry again. But the closeness was always clouded by Violet's outbursts of violence and rage. Within this maelstrom of rivalry brewed another squall—the competition between them for Will's affection. The late child (born when Violet was nine, Lucy seven), the only son, a placid boy who preferred his histrionics "on his own time, in his own head," rather than center stage, Will became a kind of living psychological prize for his sisters to vie for. For years, Violet appeared the victor. She and Will formed a tight allegiance, cemented by drug-taking and their similar freaky, febrile imaginations. "He always worshiped her," remembers Lucy, "and then one day she beat up on me in front of him, for apparently no reason. He was horror-struck. That was really a kind of turning point, his realizing she wasn't everything he thought she was." The "good sister" has the grace to finish with a candid smile. "I'm sure I milked that to the hilt."

Didn't anyone in the family dare face what was going on? "All five of us," Lucy answers in the matter-of-fact tones adopted to neutralize the sting, "are closed off in our emotions in one way or another. Mom was once a Christian Scientist, and she still feels not only in physical but also in emotional areas that if you have a problem, you deal with it. It's not anybody else's business, and it's not anybody else's problem." Was it Christian Science or ostrichlike denial? Or was it that nobody wanted to get to the root of the matter?

For all the sibling bickering and uncontrollable spasms of violence were really a plea to the warm, staid and powerful father who was busy being a father figure to the country. The carefully staged rivalry for Will, Jr.'s, affection was the handiest substitute for the competition for the father who was not around. Even absent, he had an enormous hold on the family, and winning or losing his approval could make or break an ego or a heart. His intellectual opinion, especially, was the final word in the family, and only once can Lucy remember knowing more about a subject than he did. It was a conversation about dolphins, a subject she'd studied in depth, but even though she caught him in a mistake, she couldn't bring herself to mention it.

"I had thought of myself as a failure for so many years," she reflects about her relationship with her father, "I had always assumed that I'd let Dad down, and I had always assumed that he agreed with me. Like many children of famous parents, I constantly compared myself to this illustrious man who happened to be my father, and I always came up short. But I kept hoping that someday I would find a way to win his respect." Not until one recent conversation, when he paid her the compliment of suggesting she follow in the footsteps of his career, did she realize she might have had his respect all along.

Sharing a father with the rest of the country made sharing him at home all the more difficult, even desperate, and one of the few moments of truth, even compassion between Violet and Lucy was a conversation, several Thanksgivings ago, about their father. "We started talking about the way we really felt about each other and our relationship with our father and problems we had with men that were similar," recounts Lucy, wide-eyed and apocalyptic. "It was the first time I can remember since we were young that we had had that kind of open, sisterly conversation. Violet said, 'I was so jealous of you, when we were growing up,' which was a total shock to me, 'cause I was always so jealous of her." As they talked, they put together two pieces of a puzzle, two pieces that each had been holding on to for dear life, for as long as they had been sisters. "We started finding out that we were jealous for *exactly the same reasons*. Each one felt the other was prettier and more intelligent and closer to the rest of the family. And we were both very jealous of each other's relationship to our brother. I always felt he worshipped her so much and she always felt he worshipped me so much. We had exactly the same feelings, right down the line." It was the kind of puzzle, once put together, that inalterably shifted the boundaries between them, and suddenly they were breaking through taboos, talking about their disastrous histories with men and sex and, specifically, the secret they had never shared. "She asked me if I had ever had an orgasm, and I said, 'Well, I think maybe once or twice,' and she said, 'You have, really? Wow!'" They felt as if they were in a dream, running down a long hall, clearing the cobwebs out of closets. And at the end of the hall was a meadow, full of high wet grasses and rich mud, and the meadow meant acknowledging their common ground, their common destiny, past and future, even though many, far too many times after that conversation, they were entrenched on opposite sides again, fists flying.

The next Christmas, they were at their parents' house again, the air as usual thick with expectations, poses of filial devotion and sibling rivalry. Lucy walked upstairs with a glass of milk in her hand, and Violet swerved around the corner, toward her. Instinctively, Lucy jumped back, anticipating Violet's attack. Then, for the first time in her life, she thought, Goddamn, why are you flinching from her? She grabbed her sister tight by the arm and shouted, "Don't you dare beat up on me anymore." By then each had the other by the hair, and each made a kind of struggle, but Lucy maintained the upper hand. "I'm just not fucking going to take this from you anymore. You punch me, and I'm punching you back." Later, it was tricky to pinpoint exactly why and how she'd done it (the Thanksgiving conversation? her year of therapy? age and intolerance?). But her manner obviously didn't merit challenge, and Violet finally huffed off.

As Lucy mopped up the milk with paper towels, her
mother walked by, and Lucy told her she had spilled the
milk. Her mother eyed the milk all over the walls and ceiling
and the scratches on her daughter's face. "Violet beat up on
you, didn't she?"

"Not really, and it really doesn't concern anybody but me
and Violet." It was one of those moments when the patterns
of the family could almost perceptibly be heard changing.
Then her mother said okay, and helped her favorite daughter,
still honey-haired but no longer innocent, clean up the spilt
milk. At the time, Lucy was twenty-six, Violet twenty-eight.
That was last year, and there have been no physical fights
since.

Once, this most recent Christmas, when Lucy, Violet and
her husband, Steve, were reunited, the sisters came perilously close. Lucy happened to take Steve's side of a question,
and suddenly Violet was at them, accusing them of ganging
up against her. The accusation carried with it the bitter
memory of the Oedipal triangle, the struggle that was still
unresolved. And before Lucy could even try to laugh it off,
Violet was screaming at her with the unleashed rage of the
primal curse, "I hope I never see you again. In fact, I hope
your plane crashes. I've always hoped that. I've always hoped
that you would die." As she ran out of the house, running
with the fever of one who fears God might strike her for her
words, she hurled behind her the *coup de grâce*, "I'm leaving
so Lucy and Steve can get married, and I hope they live
happily ever after." Lucy, who has never particularly liked
Steve, and Steve, who has never particularly liked Lucy, were
left with their jaws drooping.

Since that brush fire, there has been an unspoken but
unarmed truce between them, until the revised set of boundaries can be drawn. They live on opposite sides of the country,
leading curiously parallel borderline lives, both in the shadow
of their father's fame, waiting for their own ship to come in.
Lucy, the "actress," has had, by her own admission, "three
years of bit parts and not one piece of film to show anybody."
Violet, the "published poet and editor" of a prestigious
literary journal (says the article in the women's magazine),
house-sits a sailboat with her husband, does sporadic volun-
teer editing—and once, many years ago, published a poem in
a magazine for college girls. Will, Jr., is soon to graduate

from college and is said to show promise in his father's field. Lucy seems to think he is likeliest of the three to make it.

"We all have a very deep commitment to the family," Lucy admits, her voice wearing a little thin from the intense day of talking. "My family right or wrong, you stick by them no matter what they're going through, because they're blood. To a certain extent, I buy that. To a certain extent, I don't. I still feel, yes, you have to stick by them, because they're your family. But I don't feel any longer that you have to like them."

As we're finishing, the phone rings and, as happens at least once or twice a week, it is her mother, calling from across the country, calling with news or chiding or gossip, a lifeline to hold the family together. This time the news is not good. Violet's best friend has killed herself, hurled herself from the top of a building, and Violet is in despair. "I hope she doesn't do anything drastic," says her mother, spent and confused, three thousand miles away. "I hope so, too," says her favorite daughter, her confidante, her conspirator. And then they drop the subject and go on to talk about the blouse Mother just sent, because it is too hard to face that there really isn't a happily-ever-after.

6

SISTERS AS OPPOSITES

She always wanted straight hair, and I always wanted curly.

—ANDREA, *Twenty-three*

WE HAVE ALL MET (PERHAPS ARE ONE OF A PAIR OURSELVES) the sisters who do not appear to be related, whose looks or characters, whose careers or politics, whose marriages or life-choices are so divergent, so antithetical, so opposite that the sisters do not on the face of things appear to be connected by birth, blood or environment. One might be blond and lithe, straight-haired and fair, the other, stolid, olive-skinned and darkly curly. Or one may be prim and prudish, the model of propriety (even the monarch of an empire), while the other is fast and loose, reckless and free (even thumbs her nose at convention and idles on resort islands with a notoriously younger man). Or they may be Beauty and the Brain, or Beauty and the Beast, or one whose name is a household word, whose face is as recognizable as one's own, and the other who is destined to obscurity in the shadow of her sister's fame. One may be staunchly Democratic, the other rabidly Republican, or one flamboyantly heterosexual, the other militantly gay, or one may march for abortion-on-demand while the other rages for the Right To Life. One may marry a millionaire, the other a ne'er-do-well; one may mother a brood of children, the other have her tubes tied and mother none. And once we know that two (or four or seven) women are related, we mark their opposition and struggle to make sense of it, searching for the common tie; we insist on

117

digging beneath the antitheses of the surface to find the common bond of blood.

The theme of sisters-in-opposition has intrigued story-tellers as far back as the Bible and as recently as today's best-seller list, and this chapter will explore several versions of the theme in stories and fairy tales and then bring it to life with a contemporary story of sisters-in-opposition, Gloria Steinem and Susanne Steinem Patch. The biblical forefathers clearly realized how common this pattern was in family life as well as its richness for moral instruction, when they depicted Leah and Rachel, sisters who became Jacob's wives, one "beautiful and well-favored," the other modest, but first-favored by the Lord with children. Or Mary and Martha, sisters of Lazarus whom Jesus raised from the dead: Mary left their house to anoint the feet of Jesus with precious oils, Martha stayed at home toiling over supper—two sisters, two attitudes, two paths, one toward the world, one by the hearth. (And, of course, among notoriously antithetical biblical brothers are numbered Cain and Abel, Jacob and Esau, whose paths diverged with mythic *Sturm und Drang*.)

Polarization between two sisters as well as between two brothers is also a recurrent and powerful theme in fairy tales, and examining its implications is what Jung calls "thinking by metaphor." "The spell of the fairy-tale poetry," he has written, "which is felt even by the adult, is explained by the fact that some of the old theories are still alive in our unconscious minds."[1] Two particular patterns of sibling polarization blaze through fairy tales and may still burn in our unconscious minds when we face the sibling relationships of our adult lives.

One is the story of "Snow-White and Rose-Red," a pair of sisters who are gently and harmoniously opposite: "Rose-Red would run and jump about the meadows, seeking flowers and catching butterflies, while Snow-White sat at home, helping her mother to keep house, or reading to her if there was nothing else to do."[2] Like Mary and Martha, they, too, represent the two paths, the seeker and the stay-at-home, the wanderer from home and mother and the mother's helper, her psychic extension. But despite their polarities, they are inseparable, "lov[e] each other so dearly that they always walk hand in hand when they [go] out together"—and swear never to separate. Their mother equally accepts their divergent identities and seeds their common ground, telling them, "What each girl has, she must share with the other."[3]

Among the symbolic trials and tribulations of the story: The sisters befriend a bear, save a nasty dwarf three times from calamities, until finally the bear kills the dwarf, breaks a spell and turns into a golden-clad prince. The happily-ever-after ending is the marriage of Snow-White to the prince and of Rose-Red to his brother. In this variety of fairy tale, the sisters, though their identities are disparate, live harmoniously side by side from girlhood through marriage and happily ever after.

A more common pattern is the group of stories which Bruno Bettelheim calls "Tales of Two Brothers" (which also include, though less often, two sisters). In this genre, the two brothers are chafing opposites who cannot live sympathetically, but are destined to follow their separate stars, their divergent routes—though in many cases they will assist each other's journeys and be reunited at the story's end. In the Brothers Grimm story "The Two Brothers," the two are rich and poor, the first a goldsmith with an evil heart, the second an honest broom-maker. Enhancing the symbolic dimensions of the story, the good brother has identical twin sons, who, like their father and uncle, also lead dissimilar lives. But after one is turned to stone by a witch, his brother rescues him, and the twin brothers are finally reunited. However, their father, the good brother, remains defeated by life and never reconciles with his brother.

For Bettelheim, "The Two Brothers" is a symbolic parable of the dichotomy of our psyche: "the two figures symbolize opposite aspects of our nature, impelling us to act in contrary ways . . . the striving for independence and self-assertion, and the opposite tendency to remain safely home, tied to the parents."[4] About the resolution of the Grimms' tale, he observes:

[The good brother] loses his sons because he fails to comprehend the evil propensities of our nature—represented by his brother—and hence is helpless to free himself of its consequences. The twin brothers, by contrast, after having lived very different lives, come to each other's rescue, which symbolizes achieving inner integration, and hence can have a "happy" life.[5]

"Thinking by metaphor," as Bettelheim does, makes the two brothers (or two sisters, as the case may be) into a representation of the dualities of the psyche. But the fairy tales also invite a more literal interpretation: the Grimms' "Snow-

White and Rose-Red" and "The Two Brothers" are prototypes
of the patterns of sibling pairs most commonly found in
families. Snow-White and Rose-Red are the harmonious opposites, each expressing and following her individual inclinations, but sharing common ground and common destiny. The
Two Brothers are the chafing and competitive opposites, who
neither understand nor accept each other's alternate routes—
and die poorer in spirit because they neither face nor resolve
their differences.

Beyond the Bible and fairy tales, permutations of these
themes are also commonplaces in the development of the
novel. Women novelists, especially, use them both to weave
the fabric of family life and to probe the polarities between
sisters as a kind of dialectic of women's choices, women's
roles and destinies. In her sweeping and incisive retrospective
of women writers, *Literary Women*, Ellen Moers points
out that

> the sisters-in-opposition theme . . . not surprisingly is pervasive
> in women's literature, at least from *Sense and Sensibility* to
> *Middlemarch*. Its most neurotic variation can be found in Har-
> riet Martineau's *Deerbrook;* its most dramatically symbolic
> presentation in *Lelia,* where George Sand opposes a sister
> courtesan to her intellectually frigid heroine.[6]

This theme of sisters-in-opposition is so deeply pervasive
that the broad outlines of its polarities are portrayed with as
much passion and ambivalence from one century to the next.
In *Middlemarch*, George Eliot juxtaposed Dorothea and Celia Brooke: Dorothea "remarkably clever" while her sister
had "more common sense"; Dorothea "enamored of intensity
and greatness,"[7] brilliant and creative, searching and pushing
at society's limits, Celia modest and conventional, a home-
body with an armful of babies, her path what one critic called
"the chastening normality of the happy, comfortable life."[8]
Nor is the polarity neatly resolved, because at the novel's end,
Dorothea succumbs to a kind of chastening normality of her
own when she chooses Will Ladislaw and the confines of
domestic life.

A century later, in *Fear of Flying*, Erica Jong transforms
these juxtapositions with the idiosyncrasies of her times. This
time, the sisters are Isadora White Wing, the literary and
lusty adventuress, still afraid of flying, though her lovers litter

the corners of the globe, and her sister, Randy, very settled, very married and continuously very pregnant—while her husband tries to make a pass at Isadora. Nor does this novel resolve the ambivalence in a neat knot. The novel ends with an open question: Will Isadora go back to her husband and a future of marriage and babies or will she opt for the footloose and fancy-free life of an independent woman? One hundred years later and the choices are startling in their similarity.

And other novelists continue the argument: Gail Godwin's stepsisters in *The Odd Woman* (the one single, intellectual and restless, the other self-righteously married and unquestioning) or Judith Rossner's strangely intermeshed whore-and-madonna sisters in *Looking for Mr. Goodbar*. The debate that rages in the society also storms in the novel. It is clearly not only about the choices from sister to sister, but also about the choices *within* each sister's mind and heart, the puzzling out of the polarities within a woman's nature. And it is not only about the roles within the family, but also about the options without. For both within the family and without, our sisters hold up our mirrors: our images of who we are and of who we can dare to become.

The polarities that may dog two sisters till old age may begin as early as the nursery, when one baby is labeled "the easy one" and the other "the difficult one" and be reinforced at a thousand junctures along the way by parents and teachers, friends and strangers and, of course, eventually by the sisters themselves. Psychologist Robert White believes that informal roles like "good child" and "bad child"

> come into existence because they serve some purpose in the family social system, helping at least to describe the members, define their relations, and make things somewhat more predictable. They continue as long as they serve this purpose and perhaps, out of inertia, for some time beyond; but if the pattern becomes too frustrating for one member, or if it ceases to perform its function for the group, informal role assignments may change or fade out.[9]

"Good child" and "bad child," as White points out, are never absolutes, but relative according to definitions that vary from family to family. But "good" generally decodes as "adult-oriented," sharing adult values and fulfilling parental expectations, while "bad" usually means the rebel, the angry or resistant child and often the one who turns to peers for identification and the road to independence. White explains the complex origins of the "good" and "bad" roles:

> Anything that makes parents like or dislike a child can contribute to the process. Temperamental traits that make caring for the child easy or hard may start maternal preferences early in life, as may personal appearance or resemblance to other members of the family. . . . The favored child will have his liking for the role progressively strengthened by parental approval. The other child, becoming aware that his sibling is the favorite and seeing no way to outstrip him in goodness, finds less and less to be gained by sacrificing his desires to parental expectations.[10]

So the "good" and "bad" children lock each other into their polarities, and the family roles, which originated to give order, shading and distinction to family life, eventually cramp the children's growth and any possibility for closeness. Raised only *in comparison to* each other, rather than encouraged toward the limitless possibilities of each, each child clutches tightly to an identity which seems to have reality only *in opposition to* the other's.

Subtle reinforcements from parents as well as parental projections of their own conflicts or inner antitheses can create a maze of polarities in their offspring, beyond the classic split between "good" child and "bad." In some families, mother and father each ally with a different daughter; often it is the one who is physically and temperamentally most akin and whose personality can best be molded as a flattering reflection. The polarization between the sisters that results can be deeply disturbing, as this thirty-year-old woman describes:

> My sister and I are practically polar opposites, which I find very frustrating. Although we love each other, we do not like each other and were we not related, would probably not want to know each other. She is very up-tight, rigid and outwardly cold, although I know her feelings run very deep—she just doesn't show them. In this way, she is very much like my father, and emotionally (and physically as well), I am more like my mother.

Not only are the sisters distanced from each other by their allegiances to and modeling after different parents, but their differences are further fanned by overt and covert parental messages:

> I was always the "smart" one, and she was always the "pretty" one, and I can remember my parents saying this. As a result, I still feel like the ugly twelve-year-old I was, and my sister has grave doubts about her intelligence. In reality, I am very attractive and she is relatively bright— she is not quick, but is a real plugger.

By raising these sisters in opposition to each other and allowing each only half the psychological goodies (either "smart" or "pretty," but not both), their parents held a kind of crippling emotional hold over them. Each sister was only acceptable if incomplete, if only half a person; to have or be *everything* was too threatening, too guilt-provoking (so to this day the "smart" sister still sees herself as the "ugly," but presumably lovable, twelve-year-old and defines her "pretty" sister as only "relatively bright"). Just as their parents may well have felt incomplete within themselves or each without the other, they conveyed to their daughters that each of the daughters also had something missing—which the parents were more than willing to provide in return for an expanded sense of worth and importance.

In some families, parents' labeling differences, naming roles and underlining polarities begin in childhood with the best intentions, and only as the sisters mature do they recognize and squirm under the no-longer-loving constraints. A twenty-five-year-old who is the youngest of two sisters shrewdly delineates their antitheses as they were growing up:

> When my sister and I were growing up, our mother was determined to give us separate identities, even though she dressed us alike as children and always encouraged us to think of ourselves as a "team." The way she made us "different" was to give each of our characteristic "differences" a label. For example, I was The Smart One. My sister was The Popular One. I was The Pretty One; my sister, The One With Personality. I was The Bookworm; she, The Athletic One. I, The Funny One; she, The One With Talent. In this way, we were supposed to see that we had "separate but equal" identities. We were supposed to see that we were perfectly balanced in our good points, our talents. For while I could play the piano well and couldn't

skate, my sister could skate well and couldn't play the piano. We were supposed to see that we were perfectly balanced in our bad points, as well. I was unfriendly (the Cold One), but level-headed (The Cool One); my sister was personable (The Warm One), but temperamental (The One With Temper). This is how we gained our visions of ourselves—each in comparison with the other.

With maturity came the inevitable break from the family and from the tyranny of the family's labels, which the daughter bends over backward to understand, even while disengaging from them:

While I understand my mother's wish to separate us in our minds, and I acknowledge that her labels were based on legitimate inclinations in both of us, I think the results of her method were unhealthy competition and frozen role-playing. For it was a long time before my sister and I began to question the labels we were given. For many years, we simply accepted them as assumptions and acted on them. I, for example, was The Cold One, and I acted as such. Later, I found that I was not The Cold One. But I had lived for many years as if I was. We both had become entrapped within our labels, fearing to cross over into the other's "territorial labels." And we both found that we were different, even from our labels. I discovered that I enjoyed athletics, and my sister learned that she was very smart.

But after she has dramatically outlined the rigid polarities and after she has described the process of rebellion from them, she acknowledges her mother's plan as "right in theory." She grows distant, philosophical (the "you" subtly replaces the "I"), and her words are understandably self-justifying, but also heartfelt:

It is very important to promote division or separate visions among sisters, especially in adolescence. For if you are a sister whose appearance and voice and actions are often mistaken for another sister's, you are very annoyed, very frustrated. You want to think of yourself and be thought of as a separate person. My separation as a person from my sister was a painful experience but a necessary one. And my mother's endorsement at that period in my life helped me through it.

Beneath the analysis, the inner debate continues to sizzle: the pervasiveness of similarity versus the deep need for difference, the passion to separate versus the deep need for closeness. For sisters who are raised as opposites, the debate is all the more intense, their responses all the more sharply chiseled.

For some sisters (whose myth follows the Snow-White and Rose-Red archetype), the definition-in-opposition provides a reassuring psychological cushion. The clearly defined perimeters of each sister's personality become ironically liberating for the other. I can fully follow my destiny, one sister might feel, while my sister follows hers—and our arenas of expertise (as well as our failures) need never threaten or overlap. Between these sisters, the opposition becomes a complementarity, the yin and the yang of a comfortably unified whole:

> We are so different, almost opposites. Once in high school I wrote of the two of us, comparing us to Hesse's Narcissus and Goldmund. She is blond, the china figurine, beautiful and respectable, golden and refined. I, in contrast, am the wood carving, weathered, earthly as opposed to her celestialness. We have always and will always defend each other, and we share the feeling that despite our disparate life-styles, we do understand each other in a very special and basic way.

For the earthly sister, the celestial one is an exhilarating alter ego, allowing her to experience vicariously the other world, allowing her to touch and express the buried part of her own psyche. And for the celestial one, the earthly sister provides necessary grounding and steadiness. "Poor Margaret, I do understand," Queen Elizabeth is said to have remarked to a friend about Princess Margaret's dalliances. "It is easy to tolerate in one's sister those emotions we must suppress in ourselves."[11] Behind the model of propriety, the wild and woolly self is crying to get out; Margaret expresses that fantasy self for the Queen and allows the regal surface to remain properly cool and unruffled.

But for other polarized pairs (whose archetypes could be called the Grimms' "Two Brothers"), the antitheses are not complementary but instead highlight and intensify the rivalry between the two. I want to be or have that, one sister might feel, but my sister is or has it, so I cannot. One sister's world becomes circumscribed by the other's—occasionally dangerously so. A recent story in *The New York Times* told of two teen-age sisters in love with members of two rival Brooklyn gangs. The two young women live only blocks apart, but neither can cross the street that separates the terrain of one gang from the other. By projecting their differences onto their lovers, the sisters have made that street into both a literal and metaphorical dividing line. And they look at it with a grisly fatality that again is both real and charged with psychological fantasy. "We're both going to get hurt," says the older sister. "One of us is going to end up dead."[12]

For sisters hamstrung by their differences, one sister's presence deprives the other of an authentic sense of herself. For these sisters, the fierceness of the differences masks both the fear of the nagging similarities beneath and the fear that neither has ever truly separated from the other or understood herself. These are the differences that can haunt sisters to the grave, thwarting each other's growth and choices at every stage, for these sisters never come to know themselves, except in opposition to, in the widening and engulfing shadow of the other.

The Steinem sisters: two outlooks, two paths, two worlds. The firstborn, now fifty-three, is motherly and homey, pleased wife and rapt mother of six kids with a roomy house in the suburbs and an orange Volkswagen bus parked in front. The secondborn, now forty-five, is worldly and glamorous (once, as a budding free-lancer, she posed as a *Playboy* bunny to write an exposé), single and child-free, independent, activist, perpetually on the move between political conferences and conventions, lectures and meetings.

But they have the same roots, the same jaw and the same mouth, the corners slightly turned down in repose, wide and toothy in laughter, with flashes of the same cool, ironic sense of humor.

Both went to Smith College, lived in the same dormitory, majored in government, eight years apart. But now one is private and absorbed with her family, keeps the holidays and car pools, brags of her husband's mind and her teen-age son's beer-can collection and keeps an eye on her aging mother in the apartment annexed to her house. The other is public and ardently political, a pivotal figure in the Women's Movement, from her feminist conviction of freedom of choice and opportunity for all women to her frankness about her abortion and her personal stance against marriage. One is primarily an unknown, a Mrs. listed in the phone book under her husband's name. The other is quintessentially a Ms., and her name is part of history.

Their views on politics and sexuality, feminism and family dramatically diverge. But when they speak, they speak with the same voice, the same midwestern accent, the same rhythms and inflections.

Gloria Steinem and Susanne Steinem Patch attribute their differences to age, to their differing relationships with their parents, to the different circumstances of their childhoods. They nod at their similarities only in passing. "We really are not typical," insists Gloria Steinem on the phone. "Our stories would not be that helpful to others, because we're so far apart in age, more like mother and daughter than most sisters." But one of the lessons of sisterhood is that no story is really atypical, every pattern more pervasive than we assumed, every thread part of the common weave. However glaring, however sharply etched the differences between the Steinem sisters, they are echoed over and over in other families, of other backgrounds and visions, other ages and stages of consciousness: sisters who are following their independent dreams and tending their own boundaries, the limits of their separate psyches, while scrupulously trying not to threaten or tread on each other's terrain. And where the differences are obvious, the similarities, the overlaps tell another part of the story, a missing, but necessary link.

Susanne and Robert Patch and their six hearty children live in an old and rambling house on a quiet, tree-lined street in suburban Maryland, not the most elegant house on the block by a long shot, but comfortably lived-in by their brood, a daughter and five sons, aged fourteen to twenty-three, including a set of nineteen-year-old twins. I visit on a muggy June morning, and the children drift in and out and hover in the background with a cackling parrot and a tiny yelping dog. It is exactly the family of six that Susanne and Robert Patch (she, one of two sisters, he, one of two brothers) envisioned when they married more than twenty years ago: livelier, if not cheaper by the half dozen.

Susanne Patch greets me, wearing a blue cotton housedress covered with polkadots, and cotton slippers. She is a large woman with a wide face, showing the years, the raising of a family; her face is crowned with a blond chignon. She resembles her sister only in hints around the jaw, the set of her mouth. At first she is reserved, but poised, well mannered the way Smith girls of the Forties were raised to be, and carefully introduces me to her children as "Miss." We settle into comfy, well-worn chairs by the fireplace (with an All-American eagle watching us from over a mirror), and Susanne toys with a mosaic egg while she speaks. "You're asking me questions some of which I've never thought about before," she says, but still her answers are expansive, if controlled, thoughtful, if at times self-protectively naïve, bright, if a little old-fashioned, old-worldly. As she talks, I scan the living room, listening between the lines. In the corner is an unassuming cabinet which houses an extraordinary collection of animals made of semiprecious gems: a jade alligator with a jasper tongue, a dormouse with sapphire eyes and golden whiskers, an obsidian hedgehog. A gem menagerie: totems of a vision yet to be revealed.

And on the mantelpiece, under the spread-winged eagle and next to her oldest daughter's freshly minted Smith diploma, is a black-and-white photograph of her sister, framed in red: intense, unsmiling, even in black and white, it is a riveting presence peering over our shoulders.

The morning of my meeting with Gloria Steinem is the morning after *Ms.* magazine's fifth birthday. As a founding editor of the magazine, Steinem is central to the celebration, a boat cruise to the Statue of Liberty and back (the symbolism not lost on the merrymakers), with dancing to the Deadly Nightshade. There is also plenty of justifiable rejoicing that *Ms.* has not only had five years of success in an era when most new magazines have floundered, but has also become a feminist institution, a record of the critical breakthroughs of the past five years of the Women's Movement, and a clearing-house for brainstorms for the future.

It also happens to be only a day or two after the Supreme Court ruling against abortion-on-demand (predicted weeks before in *Ms.*'s fifth-birthday issue), the ruling which requires the government to pay only for abortions necessary for the physical or mental health of the mother. It is, in other words, a ruling against the poor, a devastating defeat for the Women's Movement. So contradictions hang in the air: The dearly earned high spirits of the fifth birthday mix with the sober reality of the Supreme Court ruling and its message of how much more must be gained.

Gloria Steinem lives at the center of this web of contradic-

tions, symbolically linked with both the victories of the
Women's Movement and its setbacks, beleaguered from the
right and the left by those who fear she is too radical and
those who insist she is not radical enough. So her mood is not
surprising when she arrives late and apologetic to her *Ms.*
office (where I'm waiting, staring at the button in her collection that announces, "I'M LEARNING TO SAY NO AND NOT FEEL
GUILTY"). She is exhilarated, but a little weary, downing her
take-out breakfast as we talk, washing it down with a handful
of Vitamin C, sustenance for endurance stashed by her desk.
She looks casually elegant and ageless as ever, tall and
willowy, her shoulders hunched slightly forward as if once
long ago she wanted to hide her height. She's wearing a
simple white T-shirt with clouds floating on the front, and
tailored jeans, and her hair hangs long and loose and slightly
streaked with blond, with the earpieces of her tinted blue
shades tucked over her hair and behind her ears, her signature.

It is of course her almost tangible glamour, her apparently
effortless and ageless good looks that the media have latched
onto, that have graced magazine covers and beamed below
newspaper headlines since the Women's Movement first became news—a figurehead of the kind of woman who could be
(or marry) anyone . . . and has chosen to be a feminist,
marry no one and cast her lot with her sisters. Today, at her
paper-laden desk, popping Vitamin C and slightly frayed
around the edges, she is intense and not too often smiling, as
she puzzles out the complexities of her family history. She is
thoughtful and questioning about herself, analytical where
her sister is anecdotal. She also has a native ability to involve
herself in other people's lives, other people's stories. "Gloria
is just like she's always been," says her sister in a moment of
pride. "Very friendly and very interested in what *you're*
doing. She doesn't talk about herself. She's interested in other
people." So while we talk, people flock in and out of her
office, other editors and writers, the male receptionist, even
the office toddler, daugher of one of the production people.
They chat about the birthday party, about politics, about
food, about where to find a good divorce lawyer. She focuses
her attention on each of them, lightly, seriously, taking the
interruptions in stride, cherishing them, without losing her
train of thought, just as her sister handles her children
trooping in and out, making requests of her, coping with the

interruptions and reveling in them at the same time. As Susanne has chosen her family unit, Gloria has chosen this family, this vision, this extended set of sisters.

"I always used to be convinced I was found," says Gloria Steinem, only half-joking behind the blue-tinted shades. "And I found, interviewing people, that they have this conviction either because they hope it's true or because they fear it's true. I've wanted it to be true. It wasn't that I was afraid to be adopted. It's that I hoped—not because I didn't love my parents, but because I seemed so different from them—that this would explain everything."

Beneath this fantasy lie the realities of the two different families in which Susanne and Gloria were raised. The family Susanne was born into was, for a while anyway, in its heyday of order, stability and rosy promise for the future. Mother, Ruth Steinem, was a "top editor" on a Toledo newspaper who quit work for Susanne's first year, then went back to work and left her by day in her grandmother's care. Father, Leo Steinem, was "a very gregarious person," his older daughter remembers, "who was interested in the entertainment business," did newspaper photography, worked for an advertising agency and helped manage his father's real estate. In the summer, the family ran a resort in Michigan: "forty acres of land and our own tennis court." Gloria's image of her sister's early years: "She went to nursery school and took naps and had an ordered childhood."

But when Susanne was about six, the order was shattered, and the ephemeral glimmer of All-American family life was snuffed out. In the chronicle of her childhood, Susanne Patch chooses not to mention this detail, but Gloria describes it as pivotal: "My mother had what was then referred to as a nervous breakdown. She was hospitalized for quite some time, and became gradually less independent. She felt she had to choose between taking care of my sister and working. And there were other pressures. So by the time I came along, my first six years were very different from [Susanne's]. My parents were almost ten years older. My mother was *only* at home, having loved being a newspaper reporter. And we traveled a lot by that time. Every winter we would get ourselves into a little house trailer and go buying and selling antiques on our way to Florida or California."

For her parents' sake and her own, Susanne prayed on her knees for a little sister to flesh out the family picture. But by the time Gloria was nine and Susanne had left for Smith, their parents were separated. Gloria and her mother were left to reclaim and rehabilitate the family home in Toledo, and a curious kind of role-reversal occurred. For eight years, the younger daughter was "essentially taking care of my mother. We were like equals, and sometimes I did become her mother."

Meanwhile, Gloria retained an affectionate if distant feeling about her father. He emerges from her description as a significantly different man from her sister's father: not politely "interested in the entertainment business," but "a show-business person," not unstable, but rather appealingly madcap. "He was sort of this charming, irresponsible person who took me to the movies and came and went, which I kind of liked because it was like having a playmate. I have a suspicion that my sister disapproved of my father more than I did. I think she resented that he wasn't more of a stable figure and a providing figure. And I always felt that there may be a weight question there, because my father was extraordinarily heavy. And I think that my sister feels that living with him, by herself, all alone, while my mother was in this mental hospital was the beginning of her weight problem and she resents that."

She tells this matter-of-factly, not without sympathy but with a distance that comes from having processed the old stories, having put the past behind her. But for her sister, the past is as contemporary and as daily as her mother, who lives next door, her father who, years after he died in an automobile accident, appeared to her in a fragment of a stranger's face at the door, in dreams where he would say, "You thought that I had died, but I really didn't." So there are more taboos in Susanne's side of the story, more lapses of memory, less ease with taking leaps, making the connections between past and present, between family then and now. While for Gloria the interpretation is succinct and relatively free of emotional freight.

"It must be a hard thing for a child to change from order to chaos, or from chaos to order, right? Well, I started out with chaos, so it wasn't as hard on me as it was for my sister. I didn't have to live through that change. Susanne has, she had, I don't know if it's still true, a vision of a kind of very close and affectionate family life, that, I think, was in part a reaction to the instability of our upbringing. Not that our parents didn't love us. They did, but we moved around a lot, and it was a very unconventional childhood, which I think my sister felt deeply. I didn't mind it. I sort of liked it."

Liked it enough to repeat the unconventionality when she came of age, with what she has called "a series of little marriages" to such heavyweights as Mike Nichols, Ted Sorensen and Rafer Johnson and to found an unconventional family of her own at *Ms.* When her sister approached thirty, she found herself a mate, a quiet, but dependable patent lawyer named Bob Patch. She still boasts about him with a kind of newlywed wide-eyedness. "I guess I resolved the first dilemma of you're always supposed to look up to and defer to your husband, by finding a husband who, I thought, was in fact intellectually smarter than I was." And the two settled down to the serious business of building what Gloria calls their own "One Man's Family."

Appraising her family, watching them with fondness and a touch of irony over the years, Gloria puts her finger on the common note that each member sounds with private instruments. "I think we all share a terrific sentimentality that attaches itself to different things. In my mother, it's mysticism. In my sister, it's children. In my father, it was money. If he talked about someone who made a lot of money, tears would go down his face. And in me, it's a kind of utopian idea of how people could behave toward each other, which doesn't attach itself to family. In fact, somehow it seems less possible with family. But still, it is kind of soft, sentimental, easily tapped. . . ." Her thoughts trail off into the visions of this family sentiment, some of them private and secretive as dreams, some public and accessible as history.

There is this story, for instance, that Susanne remembers as keenly as if it happened last season. But it was more than twenty-five years ago, Gloria's senior year in high school, when she moved from Toledo to Washington, D.C., and spent the year with her older sister and her roommates (who first forced Susanne to give away her giant Chow in exchange for the inconvenience of boarding her sister). Susanne and the roommates, then in their late twenties, mother-henned young Gloria, while she got into the high school scene, dating and finally pledging a sorority. Susanne took the ritual seriously and remembers it vividly: "It wasn't entirely the characteristic sort of hazing, because one of the requirements was to give a party for everyone in the sorority, which we gave at our house. And part of the hazing which was very hurtful to Gloria, and, because I identified with her, very hurtful to

me, was that when the girls left, they all went up to her and
said it was the worst party they had ever been to. And I
remember the anguish of that occasion for both of us."
Twenty-five years later, when I repeat the story to Gloria, she
laughs it off with a shrug. "I don't remember that. But if they
did that, everybody knew it was part of the hazing." Then her
eyes sparkle, as if she has caught the family sentimentality in
the act of unmasking itself. "But, you see, that's classic in a
way. I'm very gullible, but my sister is even more gullible. She
would believe it and be hurt by it."

"I always wanted to have some kind of work that could be
picked up and put down," Susanne Patch explains, walking
over to the gem menagerie in the corner of the living room
and lovingly handing me each of the perfect, precious animals to examine. She is the proud mother hen, the rapt
admirer as she points out each detail, each miracle of crafts-
manship: the alligator's jasper tongue, the dormouse's beady
sapphire eyes, his tiny golden whiskers. Since her childhood,
when she kept a collection of colored pebbles in cigar boxes,
precious stones have been her hobby and, for a while, her
trade. A geology major at Smith, she was hired by an
association of jewelry stores to go on the road with educa-
tional diamond exhibits to different stores around the country, including Barry Goldwater's family's in Phoenix. "Half a
million dollars' worth of diamonds," she says, and her eyes
glisten at the memory.

Most recently, she has written a book for the Smithsonian called *Blue Mystery: The Story of the Hope Diamond*, an elegantly produced and gracefully, if rhaposdically
written volume. Unlike her gemstone animals, which are
perfect and precious, but possessable, the Hope Diamond is,
of course, defined by its very unobtainability. (When its final
owner, jeweler Harry Winston, gave it to the Smithsonian in
1958, it was insured in transit for a cool million dollars.) A
symbol of elusiveness and power, it is laden with infinite,
many-faceted and flawless possibilities. "Perhaps the Hope
Diamond, like the complex and powerful people who have
been driven to possess it, can never be completely known,"
she writes, stunned with awe, in her preface. She describes
"the most exciting moment for me," when museum authorities
allowed the diamond to be removed from its mounting, and
Susanne traced the diamond with a pencil and found her
drawing matched a lapidary's from 1812. "A tiny fragment of

midnight sky, fallen to earth and still aglow with star gleam,"
she quotes as the epigraph to her book. Between the lines,
barely subdued, is an almost mystical attraction, and I think
of the tears falling down her father's face when he talked
about someone with a lot of money.

Like the mother of the Roman tribunes whose sons were
her jewels, Susanne Patch's six children are her crowning
glory. She is at once down-to-earth and dewy-eyed about
them. Recalling her six childbirths in eight years, she beams
offhandedly, "Oh, I usually have the children so that Bob
can have an early breakfast and a late lunch." And about
raising the brood of five sons and a daughter, her casual
comment is "As far as bringing up boys is concerned, in some
ways it's not as different from bringing up girls as I had
thought. I find now at this age, at least, that the first one up is
the best dressed, because they all borrow each other's
clothes." But when I ask her the angriest she's ever been at
Gloria, the casualness dissolves: It is the recent time when
Gloria was *almost* late to her niece's Smith graduation. In
fact, Gloria was *not* late and, in fact, is a loving and devoted
aunt, who stayed with the older kids while Susanne was in the
hospital with the younger ones, who swung them exuberantly
in the air when they were children, and who is known in the
family as the perfect gift-giver. But still, when the sanctity of
her daughter's graduation was threatened, Susanne's protective hackles rose. After twenty-two years, and several changes
of work and focus, being a mother is still where she lives.
When Gloria confided to Susanne recently that she was
injured by a writer's political attack against her, she brought
the point home by asking, "How would you feel if somebody
wrote a book that said you weren't a good mother?"

After the birth of her first child, twenty-two years ago,
Susanne wrote Gloria a rapturous letter describing the experience in detail. Remembers Susanne, "Gloria wrote back and
said that after reading my letter, she could hardly wait to
have a baby." But while the younger Steinem imagined she
was waiting, history intervened. Now she sits in her office
with the dozens of political buttons pinned to the bulletin
board behind her, and the clouds floating on her T-shirt, and
describes her illumination as a feminist, "maybe about sixty-
seven, sixty-eight, sixty-nine—much too late." Though she
has told this story hundreds of times before, her voice is
strong, the eyes behind the tinted glasses are absolutely clear,
and the passion does not sound rehearsed: "I was not differ-

ent from most women, I guess. I just felt very excluded and angry and humiliated in a lot of situations, and I didn't understand why. So I kept denying it and saying, 'I'm not discriminated against.' And then, suddenly, women were beginning to talk about their lives and have public speak-outs on abortion. It was like a blinding truth. I thought, That's my life, and nobody has ever talked about it before." That was during her free-lance years in New York when, she admits now, she was "trying to be the one girl journalist in a group of men and not write about my own experience. Suddenly all this truth-telling just made me understand that there was a reason why we felt all these angers and humiliations, and there was a reason why I kept identifying with the wrong groups—working with the farm workers or something that I wasn't supposed to be doing as a graduate of Smith. Having worked hard to boost into the middle class, I still identified down instead of up, much to the horror of other people. The politics of it and the emotion of it just suddenly came."

So the path she chose also chose her with the *Click!* between the personal and the political that *Ms.* has since made its name documenting. And the sentimentality that she calls her family birthright attached itself to a vision of a utopian society with egalitarianism as its most radical goal. "If Women's Lib wins, perhaps we all do," she dared to imagine almost ten years ago, in an essay in *Time* called "What It Would Be Like If Women Win."

Today when I ask her whether her sister's having children made her eager for her own, her answer has been carefully weighed, so that if it had ever been too heavy to handle, it is manageable by now: "Sometimes I have a distinct thought that she's done it for me, so I don't have to. And having children can be done in as many different ways as any human task can be done, but my sister's children and her household are very—well, it's the classic model. She gave up all outside interests in order to have the children, so it became less tempting to me."

The delicate divisions between the sisters have, over the years, proved a relief to them both. Had Gloria married and had children—that, Susanne once admitted, would have nettled. But as it was, Gloria remembers, "It seemed to her more that we had chosen different ways, and it was okay."

Different choices, different ways, different visions: so the differences in the choices make them less threatening on either side. The differences in the ways give the thrill of the vicarious to each. "Sometimes I have a distinct thought that she's done it for me, so I don't have to," says Gloria about her sister's children, and says Susanne, about her sister's friends and allies, "I think that some women are friendlier and more open [to me] than they would be if they didn't know that Gloria was my sister." And the differences in the visions make for complementarity, each filling in the other's loopholes, the corners overlooked in each other's psyche. So the pattern between them is more aptly the live-and-let-live harmony of "Snow-White and Rose-Red" than the angry, vengeful opposition of "The Two Brothers."

Of course, issues have cropped up over the years which challenge the boundaries, the carefully etched psychic demarcations—occasionally changing them altogether. Not surprisingly, the watershed issues have been political, some with *Ms.* as the focal point, others directly between the sisters, and often the red flag is children-home-and-family, the sphere in which Susanne Steinem Patch has so long defined herself.

"Have you ever been shocked by your sister's political views?" I ask Susanne, and her answer carefully shifts the focus of disagreement to *Ms.*: "Oh, I think I find it difficult to accept some of the things that *Ms.* has printed on Children's Lib, on the freedom of children to make all their decisions as soon as they're able to articulate them. It seems to me that maybe it's because I'm not a child at the moment. Maybe if I were a child, I would agree wholeheartedly. But as an adult, it seems to me that there is a certain order and form that older people try to give children's lives, so that they are able to use liberty wisely, so it's not just a completely laissez-faire relationship."

Obviously child rearing is serious business to Susanne Patch, and after twenty years of childbirth-training classes, PTA meetings, car pools and probably hundreds of hours mediating between scuffling children, she is not about to renege responsibility to the newfangled rights of children.

As delicate as that subject is, one of her sister's crusades is a more sensitive matter entirely. Indeed, the gaps in the two sisters' sides of the story make it seem something of a blind spot in Susanne's line of vision. Gloria tells her version this way: "I remember when *Ms.* first started, we had a petition of women who came forward and said, 'I've had an abortion,' and I signed this petition because I had, indeed, had an abortion, and I didn't feel I could ask other people to sign it, if I didn't sign it. I warned my sister and my mother in advance, and my mother doesn't believe it to this day. My mother said, 'Every starlet says they've had an abortion, just to get publicity,' which sort of hurt me, because the motivation of wanting to get publicity is a hurtful one."

But Gloria says that Susanne "believed it, but said with surprise that she didn't know that I had ever even slept with anybody. And I said, 'What did you assume was my relationship with these various men who would come to Christmas dinner over the years?'" That was five years ago, "at a rather advanced age," adds Gloria, with her tongue tucked in her cheek, and is a clue to how boundaries can also become walls, monitored by silence and never-mentioned's.

Susanne's opinion on abortion, at least as a political issue, remains a few dozen shades more ambivalent than her sister's. The twists and turns of her sentences speak the ambiguity as much as her words: "I find it very difficult to say I'm for or against abortion. Because it just doesn't seem to me that one can say it that way. But if it ever came down to, Do I think the government should interfere and decide whether or not something of this kind should be done? Or do I think that it's strictly up to the woman and her family and her doctor? then I can say, Yes, I don't think the government should impose itself in this sort of an affair. But it's certainly a decision I would be eternally grateful never to have to make." Nor is it a decision she has ever had to make. But when I ask her how she felt when Gloria had an abortion, her answer is firm: "I didn't know she had one and don't now know the truth that she did."

"You haven't talked with her about it?" I press.

"No," she says, and the tone that she uses says that the matter is closed. Later it is the same tone in which she gives her opinion of homosexual relationships between women—"An awful waste." This is the tone that guards the boundaries; it is the blind spot in the heat of confrontation.

But lately, the boundaries between the sisters are realigning, and the tone between them has changed accordingly. In the background while Susanne talks is the persistent thumping of her daughter typing out a paper for her. It is the sound of a new era for Susanne Patch, for after twenty years of more or less undivided attention for her family, she is going to law school. The change was heralded with the acceptance to Antioch framed and posted on the front door; the family was polled and found agreeable; and for the better part of the two weeks just before classes, Mother (like all beginning students) lived with an inner-city family to begin to acclimate herself and her family to the turnabout to come.

At first, understandably, when every premise of her life was about to be transformed, she was "paralyzed with a sort of What have I done? What am I doing? feeling." But now, nearing the end of her program, she is deeply satisfied with the changes that have occurred, not the least in her relationship with Gloria. "I am now learning about and becoming active in so many areas that concern her," realizes Susanne, "that we have more to talk about than we had before." Gloria defines this change even more basically—from relatives to friends: "[Susanne's] going to law school has brought her into a world which I understand better than the world which she has been in for the last twenty years or so. So recently when we've had contact, it's been about subjects we mutually care about, rather than just, How are the kids? Her experiences in law school make a political difference, too. She sees a wide political variety of people there, and they seem less odd than they used to."

The *Clicks!* between the personal and political that started for Gloria Steinem as the only girl journalist in a city full of ambitious men have lately been registering for Susanne, too. The acquaintance who assumed Susanne's "friend the psychiatrist" was a man, the tourists at the Smithsonian who scorned the women docents in favor of the men: Each realization building on the next makes the incriminating case. Today, she boasts proudly that her law-school class is half women. Still, she is a long way from joining a lesbian separatist commune or even from using her legal training in a political context (her post-law-school ambitions center on combining her new skill with her interest in gems, perhaps through the Federal Trade Commission, which regulates the jewelry industry). Though her incipient feminism and change-of-life focus have built a new bridge to her sister, Susanne is still candid about a fundamental difference in their orientation: "I can appreciate how Gloria feels, [because] she is thinking about all women. Whereas, frankly, I think about what my own situation is."

For the Steinems, as for many of their sisters in the Women's Movement, the past years have been a time of transition. They've defined themselves for years as totally different, polar opposites, and that definition provided protective boundaries, the safety of padding around identities delicate as gemstone carvings. Their precisely drawn differences

spared them jealousy and comparison—as well as the closeness born from knowing each other under the skin. But as the
rigidity of their differences has mellowed, however gradually
and, at times, awkwardly, long-ignored similarities have also
had room to surface. And with the realization of sameness,
long-buried jealousy and competition have emerged from
underground.

"I admire Gloria, and I'm proud of her, and I'm happy
with her for the things that she's doing," says Susanne slowly
and cautiously, treading on freshly seeded ground. "But of
the things that she's done, there's only one thing that she's
done that I think I'm envious of. And that is her selection as
a Woodrow Wilson fellow at the Smithsonian. It's funding for
a year of independent research, which would be appealing to
me." In a time when Susanne has at last acknowledged her
own ambitiousness and worldliness, the fellowship is a symbol
of a shared dream that her sister has already realized.

As the sisters allow their similarities to break through their
differences, like wild flowers through rocks, they become
more vulnerable to each other, with more danger for hurt,
but also more possibility for closeness. Gloria Steinem evalu-
ates the awakening similarities between her sister and herself
in the recent years of awakening consciousness: "My sister
and I have the same voice. People mistake us for each other
over the phone. Same midwestern voice and hands and
jaw—you know we have some resemblance. I had a lot of
problems—I have a lot of problems with being unable to deal
with conflict, with being overly vulnerable, with a lot of
things I saw in my sister to a greater degree. So that probably
in the past that would have caused me to reject my relationship with my sister, because I was a little afraid I would
become more something I didn't want to be. And now I'm
more likely to understand what it is that made both of us that
way. I mean we weren't crazy to feel like victims. We were
victims. So I accept it in both of us, instead of trying to deny
it in me and therefore to deny the version of it I see in
her.

From polarized differences to a gradual dawning of similarities, first the realization of being victims together, of
shared oppression, gradually the dawning of common
strength, shared power—their process of becoming sisters
within the family also mirrors the process of sisterhood
without.

7

SISTERS IN LOVE: THE SHARED LANGUAGE OF SEXUALITY

One recapitulates with lovers the relationships with one's sisters, if one loves women. Almost every relationship I have is either my older sister or my younger sister. You see, I have an elder sister five years older and a younger sister five years younger. I guess if somebody were all that much older or younger, it might not work, but I can stretch it. I hardly know anybody my age, having lived in the Women's Movement where everybody's always younger to a tedious degree.

—KATE MILLET, *Forty-four*

"YOU ARE NOT BORN A WOMAN, YOU BECOME ONE," SIMONE de Beauvoir has observed, and sisters are crucial to this awakening, companions at each station of the journey, teachers, models, initiators, points of comparison and departure. *Little Woman* is not only a parable of sisterhood, but also a classic saga of the artful and ingenious socialization of sisters by sisters, from one hearth to the next, from first kiss and first crush to first wedding and children. When eldest sister and surrogate mother Meg admonishes "Josephine" that she should "leave off boyish tricks,"[1] and remember she's a young lady, Meg sets the stage and tone and first of dozens of lessons and confrontations of sisterhood that the novel will breathe to life. And Jo, who at first is rakishly whistling and devilishly tossing off slang, by the end of the novel has mellowed around the edges, and, like Meg before her, leaves the cozy circle of sisters to get married. Her spirits no less fiery, her will no less strong, the tomboy has become a little woman. Her sisters' teaching and teasing, gossiping and confiding are integral to this transformation as Jo is crucial to theirs. Meg, Jo, Beth and Amy are not only disparate individuals discovering sisterhood, they are also four adolescents floundering toward womanhood. The story of this blooming and stumbling, alternately nurturing and tripping over each other is as complex and interwoven as the braids Meg wears on her wedding day.

I have explored earlier the shared, private and, in some cases, primitive language between sisters which expresses their interwoven scripts, the stories of their growing up (the younger looking to the older for images of who she might become, the older glancing over her shoulder for reminders of who she has been or could have been, or may, in some psychic corner, still be). But even more striking than the babbling language of childhood, indecipherable to parents and outsiders, or the secret vocabulary of adolescence, or the rare and rarefied idioglossia between twins, is the powerful and direct language of the body. This is the language which transmits and translates the images and lessons sisters present to each other about their sexual identities as women: from first bra and first kiss to menstruation and masturbation, from the "first time" and the gropings of early sex to love affairs with men (or women—or both) and marriage and having children.

On my bulletin board while I write this is a little sketch by Judith Shahn from the *New Yorker* of an older sister with a tidy single braid down her back, carefully braiding her younger sister's hair, the strands over and under, under and over, a perfect replica of her own. They are, of course, not the March sisters, but could be distant relatives in another era. The older sister is about twelve, balanced on the brink of womanhood; the younger must be six and is still a little girl. Their profiles echo and repeat each other's: not just the neat braid, sturdy as an umbilical cord, but the eyes and noses, pert as punctuation marks, and the identically ladylike outfits. The artist has caught and preserved their precise moment of connection and identification. Soon these sisters will go their separate ways, the matching dresses of girlhood discarded for something more eccentric, more stylish, more expressive of the first fluttering of individuality. But for now, this juncture at twelve and six, the language of the body speaks the shared messages of growing up without words.

Psychologists have always been interested in the cathexis between mother and daughter, in mother's primal influence on her daughter's earliest sexual identity. Recently, feminists have reopened this question, once again sorting out its dimensions and probing its implications for women's changing roles and identities as they yearn for a closeness with other women that seems rooted in an acceptance of the relationship with mother. In Nancy Friday's *My Mother/My Self*, early symbiosis between mother and daughter and the lifetime's worth of subsequent separation is defined as the central issue of "The Daughter's Search for Identity," stamping its influence for better or worse on a woman's relationships with friends, husbands and lovers.

And in *Of Woman Born*, poet Adrienne Rich's profound study of "Motherhood as Experience and Institution," she, too, focuses on the centrality of the early mother-daughter bond to all later female development. Citing Margaret Mead's observation of the "deep biochemical affinities between mother and child,"[2] Rich suggests that

> probably there is nothing in human nature more resonant with charges than the flow of energy between two biologically alike bodies, one of which has lain in amniotic bliss inside the other, one of which has labored to give birth to the other. The materials are here for the deepest mutuality and the most painful estrangement.[3]

The same year Adrienne Rich published her book about mothers and daughters, she also wrote a poem about sisters called "Sibling Mysteries." She included it, appropriately, in the collection *The Dream of a Common Language*, and referred to her sister and herself as "translations into different dialects/of a text still being written in the original." The poem puzzles out her history of distance and closeness, of treachery and affinity, with her sister and concludes by placing their relationship in the context of the family and showing the primacy of the sister bond. She takes the image of marriage, the image of deepest intimacy, and stretches it for her own purpose:

> The daughters never were
> true brides of the father
>
> the daughters were to begin with
> brides of the mother
>
> then brides of each other
> under a different law
>
> Let me hold and tell you.[4]

What Rich touches upon in "Sibling Mysteries," but what has usually been ignored—and what I wish to emphasize here—is the magnetic influence of sisters on each other's emerging sexuality, each other's identity as a woman, each other's relationships with friends, lovers, husbands and children.

As Rich writes of mother and daughter, sisters are also "two biologically alike bodies," with "the flow of energy" between them "resonant with charges." Sisters, of course, have never nestled, one inside the other, in "amniotic bliss" (although twins have lain together, side by side, in the amniotic sea where often begins their most profound connection). But still, from babyhood through adolescence, most sisters are intimately physically linked, bathing, dressing, cuddling, eating, playing, fighting, exploring, sleeping or at least, rooming together, so that the physical boundaries between them are flexible and shared. Recalls one thirty-year-old woman: "When I was about fifteen, my older sister had an illegal abortion, a real butcher job, and they thought she was dying, so I came home from boarding school. I spent a lot of time with her when she was delirious, holding her hand and stroking her, and the thing I remember very much is the physical closeness. I still feel the effects of that in my life, of what it meant to have another human being where physical boundaries were not really there. Our bodies were very much each other's in a close way."

Between mother and daughter, the deep-felt, lifelong issue is symbiosis and separation: the daughter's quest for independence versus her need to stay close to mother, the mother's wish to keep daughter close versus her growing ability to let go. Between sister and sister, the central struggle is the comforting yet threatening realization of similarity versus the threatening yet comforting need for difference, the fascination with the mirror versus the lure of the opposite, adventure and the unknown. Now clearly the *pas de deux* of mother and daughter and of sister and sister are unextricably linked in the dance that family therapist Salvador Minuchin calls "individuation and mutuality" (and linked all the more intimately if mother should die young and sister slip awkwardly, nervously into her mothering shoes).

In her dense and lyrical first novel, *The Grab*, Maria Katzenbach traces the intersecting patterns among three sisters and their mother, who has just died, as the sisters follow a family tradition and gather in their mother's mansion to "grab" for her possessions. Of the language of the body shared between mother and daughter, between sister and sister, Katzenbach writes, "The words pass into bodies as resemblances, as family traits, the mind of Mother trading places with the bodies of the daughters. Perceived only as a whispering language, she moves from the space outside into them. As one might speak without hearing the words, these words rise up into the daughters."[5]

Because sisters are peers, not unequals, because they share the daily intimacies and proximities of eating, playing and sleeping and because their relationship is not traditionally fraught with should's and shouldn't's (the soldiers of parental command), the channels between sister and sister are more easily viable, less guarded and defended against than the byways between mother and daughter. A sister rushes in where Mother might fear to tread, daring to dare her sister beyond the confines of the family, toward the wide world, reaching for the moon. Erica Jong cheers and coaxes and cajoles her younger sister in "For Claudia, Against Narrowness":

> Sweetheart, baby sister,
> you'll die anyway
> & so will I . . .
> As long as you're at it,
> die wide.
> Follow your belly to the green pasture.
> Lie down in the sun's dapple.
> Life is not as dangerous
> as mother said.
> It is more dangerous,
> more wide.[6]

The messages exchanged between sister and sister—in bodies, words and deeds—follow the pattern of sameness versus difference, similarity versus differentiation: Should I copy my sister's choices or diverge from them? Should my body, lovers, lovemaking, marriage, children be like hers or different? Some girls take pleasure in following in a sister's footsteps or walking shoulder to shoulder along the path to womanhood, finding comfort in the news that her sister has lost her virginity and lived to tell the tale or that she, too, is nervous about nonmonogamy. "I think that my sister has sort of looked to me to determine what was right in terms of sexuality. She has come to accept aspects of sexuality which I had accepted or practiced," writes a twenty-six-year-old about her year-younger sister. And "what was all right" for the younger was to do exactly what the older had done: Between these two, similarity became a refuge in the stormy uncertainty of sexual choices.

For other girls, the thrill of blossoming sexuality is in its differences from Sister's choices: The wild woman rebels against a more properly socialized sister (the "good girl" versus "bad girl" phenomenon), the younger competes with the older by scrambling first to the altar or having the first baby. For these sisters, the assertion of independence, the flaunting of a unique sexual identity lies in veering in an opposite direction, scooping up the goodies first. Nowhere does this competition rear its head more fiercely than in the obsessive comparison, weighing and measuring of bodies, looks and clothes.

What is the angriest you've ever been at your sister? I asked, and again and again, the answer was "When she borrowed/stole/ruined my clothes." That is, when she dared slip into my carefully planned persona, color-coordinated to complement my skin and hair—and tried to palm it off as her own. My great-grandfather tried to stamp out the fire among his five daughters by declaring they could not borrow each other's clothes, as if strict manners could eradicate the jockeying for identity. But still, beneath their own clothes, their bodies continued to burn. *What is your worst jealousy of your sister?* I asked, and over and over again came the answer, an eerie refrain from sister to sister and family to family, "She's thinner than me," or "She can eat all the carbohydrates she wants and not gain a pound, and I go on Weight Watchers and don't lose a pound," or worst, and most self-pitying of all, "Once I was thinner than all my sisters, and now I'm the heaviest of all." What society teaches all women, sisters internalize in the family circle. Their bodies become the focal point, both real and metaphorical: To be acceptable, says each woman, each sister, I must be thin, thinner *than her*, another woman, another sister. In the sparring over clothes, in the competition over bodies is the push-pull dilemma of sisters' sexual choices: the threat and enticement of similarity (Will she become me if she wears my clothes?) versus the fear and attraction of difference (If she is thinner, will she be better?).

These questions hover in the background like recurrent dreams as sisters negotiate the passage from girlhood to womanhood, turning to each other, both younger and older, for initiation and indoctrination, advice and consent. At each rite of passage our sisters are with us, noting and comparing notes: from my own sister, still a little girl, comforting me with tea and heating pads during the throes of my early menstrual cramps (and shuddering that someday such a fate could be hers); to her coaching my walk in my first pair of heels; to my chatting about John Cage with her first serious boyfriend, or watching her do the hustle at the soiree before graduation. Rarely is the taboo as strong at these junctures as between mother and daughter (mother hiding her sexual self from daughter, daughter returning the courtesy, the lie to mother). But always between sisters, there is the push-pull between like and not-like, between what Salvador Minuchin calls "enmeshed" boundaries (diffuse with lines of identification blurred) and "disengaged" boundaries (rigid with distant lines of communication.)[7] Somewhere in between lie the "clear" boundaries that make for more harmonious family relationships, and it may take a lifetime to get them settled.

Among the pushing and pulling between like and not-like, there is the woman who meticulously documents the peaks and valleys of love and hate between her and her sister, and then admits that the very first time each of them made love, she did it in the other's bed. Or the older sister who is convinced that sex was a far bigger deal for her than for her younger sister, involving more conflicts, doubts and inner recriminations—and then remembers when, at thirteen, as she was dressing for her first date, her little sister "scribbled all over my copy of *Jane Eyre,* kicked the cat in the stomach to make her throw up all over the book and then threw it in the bathtub." Without a word spoken, the younger made sure she made absolutely clear her position on her sister's spreading of wings. Her sense of loss and her dread of her own sexual future were intimately connected with her sister's passage, too murky to understand, too frightening to put into words. And there is also the woman mentioned earlier in this chapter, who is so physically close with her sisters that boundaries are just not there, so demonstrative and physically affectionate with her sisters that husbands and lovers feel excluded—and yet she also admits that each is a little nervous about her own sexuality, and none of the five sisters has ever masturbated. Even in a framework of easy intimacy, there may still be a sexual taboo. "When you compare boys and girls and men and women," points out Harvard psychologist George Goethals, "there is a paradox in the notion of access and disclosure in showing affection. Physical contact between grown men is taboo, whereas women don't get up-tight about 'grooming,' or even sleeping together. However mutual masturbation between girls is rare, though it's a common practice for boys and brothers."

Sometimes the sexual boundaries between sisters are so subtle that no one is aware of them until they are transgressed. The youngest sister in a large working-class family names as "the angriest she's ever been" the time her sisteen-year-old sister went to the hospital for appendictis—and came home with a newborn baby. So complete was the younger's ignorance about the facts of life and so thick her defenses against reality that she refused to face the widening gap and widening belly between them. Today, years later and light-years closer, they are relaxed and jocular about it, time easing the sting of that rite of passage for both of them. And an oldest of three vivacious black sisters boasts that she is the family's much trusted "sexual adviser and confidante." Then her youngest sister recounts with a shudder the time her sister decided to initiate her into the ways of men, brought home two of them—and proceeded to monopolize their attentions, physical and otherwise, all evening. "If you want to act like a whore, that's your business," screamed the disoriented younger sister the next day, for her eyes had been opened wider than she could tolerate. "You don't have to get an attitude," came the supercilious reply. Stony silence, intense hassling to test each other's limits, and finally, through to the other side. "By the end of the day we were cool, and more tightly bound to each other, I think," the younger realized, putting her finger on the sister knot, the intertwining of sameness and difference, the wish to follow in the ways of a sister's world and the fear of it.

Because the transition from one family to the next is a pivotal and tender one, because it means a new relationship between parent and child and sister and sister, because allegiances shift and boundaries redefine, marriage is a highly charged theme in many novels about sisters. And a sister's wedding—both as event and symbol—becomes a central image in many of them. The weddings range from the traditional—Meg March's predictably modest and teary-eyed ceremony in *Little Women* ("the sweetest chapter in the romance of womanhood")—to the contemporary and jaded—Louise's tension-laced wedding to a man she turns out to scorn in Margaret Drabble's *A Summer Bird-Cage,* a novel of two sisters' interwoven loss of innocence ("Louise even said once," realizes the open-eyed younger sister as the novel ends, "that in marrying Stephen she was trying to stop me overtaking her"). And in D. H. Lawrence's passionate *Women in Love*, intimately entwined sisters, Ursula and Gudrun, meet their lovers at another woman's wedding and spend the novel re-entwining and redefining intimacies with each other and with their lovers—while their lovers, who also yearn to be brothers, go through their own ritualistic paces of closeness and distance, involvement and separation.

In the symbolic texture of the wedding lies a hint of the changes between the sisters to come: the easiness or estrangement, influence or betrayal. For years the sisters have exchanged messages in the whispered secrets that are the girls' language of sexuality. The wedding symbolizes the leap to another world with another language, the shared language of husbands, children and lovers.

Bring men into the family picture, into the close-knit, emotionally charged world of sisters, and naturally the dynamics change. Boyfriends, lovers, husbands—they may be intruders or rivals, friends or newfound brothers. They may alter the bond between sisters in a way threatening (or supportive) to the sisters—or to the men. "My marriage has not affected my relationship with my sister to any great extent," insists a twenty-nine-year-old woman in a response typical of one pattern, but her relationship with her sister "has affected my marriage in that I am closer to my sister than I am to my husband." Worries another, "My sister being married kind of blocks communication, as though her self and sexuality is settled and mine has never been." Or from a third, one of a particularly close, large, all-girl family: "There's a way that we really feel that no man can really take care of any of us, or not the way that we take care of each other. There's something missing [in each of the sister's marriages] that we have to offer each other."

From the man's point of view, loving a pair of sisters has been titillation and obsession in art, pornography and life. From David Hamilton's lush photo-essay of the demiclad and prepubescent *Sisters* to purely exploitative shlock novels like *Lesbian Twins* or *Lust Sisters*, the fantasy of making love to sisters has the erotic charge that is part lure and part taboo. From Charles Dickens to François Truffaut, men have fallen for sisters and transformed their attraction in their art. Truffaut's great loves were sister actresses and intimate opposites Catherine Deneuve and Françoise Dorléac (about her relationship with Françoise Dorléac, who was tragically and violently killed in an auto accident, Catherine Deneuve once told a reporter, "You will never truly know me until you understand my sister,"8 so interlocked were their psyches). And the sisters motif runs through several of the films Truffaut made after Dorléac's death.

The paradoxical lure and taboo of loving and marrying sisters has surrounded this custom in different ages and cultures. In England, until 1907, it was illegal for a man to marry his deceased wife's sister, and as Margaret Mead pointed out in an interview shortly before she died, a great deal of drama ensued because "she was the most natural person to marry." In many cultures it is still a common custom for a man to marry sisters, either several at once ("one of the commonest forms of polygamy") or one after another (termed *sororite*). Mead mentioned that even in our own culture, such marriages are not unusual (indeed, Mead's own brother married his wife's sister after his wife died). But except, perhaps, in cases like that one, where the first wife never saw her husband's attention turn to her sister, sisters' involvement with the same man may become so threatening that in most families I interviewed the sisters themselves declared it taboo. Joanna Simon, Carly's oldest sister, called the biggest mistake she ever made stealing away one of sister Lucy's boyfriends—and then dropping him immediately when the sport was over. Relationships with the same man might, for the sisters, begin as adolescent competition and for the man as a kicky fantasy (a strange sort of Oedipal triumph since the only other man who usually has both sisters' love is their father). But too often such relationships end in deceit, manipulation and hopelessly "enmeshed" boundaries.

Sally and Molly are a pair of twins from a Catholic, working-class family who, at thirty-five, describe themselves as "alike, yet very different, night and day." Sally, says Molly, in the language of paradox characteristic of the twins, is "very open and aboveboard with her emotions, while I keep everything inside. But in public, I'm outgoing and she's shy. In private, I'm more secretive and she's more honest." They are not identical, and Molly has taken a fine-tooth comb through their similarities and differences, as if labeling the differences exactly will stay the threat of too-engulfing similarity. "We have the same eyes. We are very close to the same size, though she has thinner bones than me, and I outweigh her. Neither of us is fat, but I'm rounder and she's lankier.

She's bowlegged. I have a large rear end. She's terribly busty. I'm pretty busty."

Their history of competition (that exact calibration between "terribly" and "pretty" busty) starts with the games of childhood (who could run, punch, crochet faster), continues through the one-upsmanship in a strict Catholic boarding school, and runs through the present like an icy stream. But after thirty-odd years, their bodies are numbed to the shock of the cold. As with many twins, their enmeshment is so deeply pervasive that it has become second nature. "I can be thinking of her, and she'll call me," offers Molly about that fine psychic tuning common to twins, so that one might break a limb and the other feel a phantom pain. "Or we'll be walking along talking and come up with the same sentence. I can't put my finger on it, but it's there. We're so close though so different." They take their overlaps—of anger and attraction, husbands and lovers—so much for granted that they both tell their story kind of deadpan and only once in a while punctuate it (and betray its unruffled surface) with a rough, nervous laugh, crackling in the monotone like a flare on a deserted highway.

"We're very evenly matched," says Sally. "I feel I'm stronger but she would say the opposite." Echoes Molly, "She would describe me as being very cold and her as warm. But at first, it seems like vice versa." Say both of them, "We're always competing—at bowling, pool and men." Their shared history with men began at age sixteen. "I was engaged to be married to a guy," Molly remembers with a kind of childlike, surreal glee, "and I caught Sally out with him, so in retaliation, I married his roommate who had been her date a few times." The next year, Sally also married, and several years after that, after Molly's first marriage had inevitably run its course, Molly married for a second time—the brother of her sister's husband. Then the plot thickened, as the boundaries between sisters merged beyond recognition, and there began the adult years of feints and parries, fallings in and out of favor (both between the twins and between each twin and her own husband). "My husband was down on Sally," Molly explains, "but after we'd have a fight, he'd go to her. At the same time, he was critical of her moral standards. She did run around. But so did he. It turned out they ran around together."

From the rest of the evidence, her feelings about her sister's husband are no more or less surprising than the rest of her story. "I accepted him as a brother," she says without missing a beat. Then she pauses, and the laugh flares out, flashing a warning. "There was one time I got so sick of them playing around together that I went off to a motel with her husband and found out how the other half lived."

Deadpan again, she sits back and takes the long look at the situation. "Basically we would both appeal to the same man but for different reasons. Sally would be earthy, sexy, open about showing emotions. Very few men have called me sexy. I think of myself as reserved. But when I'm one-on-one with a man, I'm a lot worse." She laughs the nervous, flaring laugh. "We've shared the same man in the same bed, so I know I'm worse."

What is the happiest or closest she's ever been with her sister? There is a long, long pause, in which she is not so much thinking about which example to give as about how to make its context believable. "We've always fought so much," she answers. And then, unduly emphatic, as if she has not really convinced herself of her own paradoxes: "We *are* close. I guess the closest was when we worked at the coffee shop together. We were feuding under the skin, but of course we're happy feuding. It brings out the worst in both of us. It's a very natural state of affairs."

"My sister, Emily Lazarre, has always been both mother and daughter to me," writes Jane Lazarre about the tightly bound sister knot in the acknowledgments of *The Mother Knot,* her exploration of the strands connecting being a daughter (whose mother dies young) and becoming a mother herself. "It is through my lifelong love for [Emily] that I have begun to understand motherhood, sisterhood and friendship."

Echoes Emily with a similar rush of feeling, "Definitely, ever since we have been children, Jane's life has opened pathways for mine." And then, more soberly: "It has taken me a good five years in therapy—and not that its over—to really come to terms with my own strengths and weaknesses, and to sort of accept who I am in terms of myself and not in terms of Jane."

Jane and Emily Lazarre are now thirty-six and thirty-three, married and mothers of their own families. When their mother died, they were seven and four, a seven wise beyond her years and a lost and innocent four. Not having a mother was and still is "one of the main psychological underpinnings" of their lives, "an unending theme." Today, with their father gone, too, they call each other their "only family" and have recently traded back their married names for their family name, Lazarre, as if to underline that first and foremost connection. Between them, the language of sexuality—of menstruation and bodies learning to be women, of marriage, childbirth and mothering—was and is complexly shared and profoundly intertwined, made all the more intense because their early bonding replaced the loss of mothering. On Salvador Minuchin's continuum from "disengagement" to "enmeshment," Jane and Emily Lazarre are squarely enmeshed. Their enmeshment appears in the fluidity of boundaries between them, an intricate sharing and overlapping of mothering and daughtering, similarities and differences, strengths and weaknesses.

The echoes and exchanges are spoken in their voices, looks and mannerisms, their husbands and children, their houses and art (Jane a writer in New York, Emily a potter in Berkeley). On the phone, their voices are interchangeable and have been known to fool even their husbands on occasion. In person, Jane is dark, short and *zaftig* with brooding, deep-set eyes and a mobile, expressive face. Her energy is intense, both sensual and intellectual, grounded in her body's form and function, and in her rapid juggling of ideas. Emily is taller and thinner with lanky limbs and blue eyes and mustard-colored hair. Her energy is cooler, more remote, not so seething around the edges. She is less at home with words, by her own admission, her energy and ideas lodged in the quick play of her potter's fingers. But as both point out, their mannerisms are the same: the wide, lush smile, the gesturing hands, the thoughtfulness.

"We have always been anxious about the subtlety of our similarities," wrote Jane in an unpublished story called "A Family Likeness." "Perhaps that is why [Emily] has moved so far away." But even on opposite sides of the country, their places echo each other's: Jane's high-rise apartment on New York's Upper West Side, where she lives with her lawyer husband, Douglas, and sons, Adam, who's seven, and Corey who's four; Emily's white clapboard house in Berkeley, which she shares with her husband, Mickey, daughter, Sara, who's also four, and infant, Simon. But though the New York City kids skateboard in a concrete courtyard and the Berkeley kids play on their quiet, shady street, inside, their houses are a similar mix of funk and clutter, books and family photographs, and everywhere the stamp and signature of kids: kids' art, toys, diapers, and, at Emily's, a Swingomatic with a *dreydel* hung over it to catch the baby's eye when the thrill of rocking wears off.

"I hate to mythologize people in families into separate corners," begins Jane, untwining the strands of similarity and difference between her sister and herself, tracing them to their family roots, "but it is true nevertheless that in my family as a child, I was the difficult one, the loud, intense, troublesome one that everybody worried about, and my sister was the one who was always supposed to support me and to find ways of building bridges between me and my father." Adds Emily about the same patterns of polarities, "My father looked at her more as an intellectual companion and to me he looked more for emotional and caring kinds of love. I was his baby, more or less, and his relationship with me was less complicated."

Father was intellectual and political to the quick, a Communist and political organizer during the years his daughters were growing up; Mother, as Jane remembers her, was "a very elegant, sophisticated, successful businesswoman." It was one of those families split down the middle in looks and allegiances, what Jane calls the "dark and light function in some families," she and her mother the dark ones, Emily and her father the light. As Jane sees it, "My sister was just like my father, and I was like my mother, and had been identified with her all the time." Though Emily has only the haziest memories of her mother, Jane remembers her vividly and sings her children the lullabies her mother sang to her, with perfect recall of the words and melody. "Let me call you sweetheart, I'm in love with you/Let me hear you whisper that you love your mommy, too."

"When our mother died," recalls Jane about the event that shattered the family harmony, "Emily was just four and I was just seven. I know now, because my children are four and seven, that there is a great big difference between a seven-year-old and a four-year-old. A seven-year-old is capable of consciousness, while a four-year-old isn't. So I really took on very much a mother role to her, and she constantly asked me for it. She always said, 'You're my mother.'" Her mother's death made Jane's identification with her go haywire. Between searching for her lost mother and mothering her lost sister, the boundaries of her self were frayed to the breaking point. "By the time I was seventeen, when I went into analysis, I was not your basic ordinary neurotic. I was really not sure whether I was [my mother] or myself, and I really believed her to be alive. My own boundaries were very unclear."

Emily's experience of her mother's death was not on the surface quite so disorienting. Noting the divided lines of allegiance between the two parents and two daughters, Emily observes, "When my mother died, it seemed on the outside more like Jane's parent was dying, and my parent was alive. Of course, as a child who lost her mother, I didn't feel that way." Meanwhile, Jane, the seven-year-old, older and wiser than her years, and later, Jane, the seventeen-year-old, her boundaries shaky and shifting, rushed to replace the nurturing her mother had abandoned.

"We both had a lot of nightmares and lot of insomnia after my mother died," recalls Jane. "I used to sleep with Emily a lot and hold her when she couldn't sleep. If she ever had any problem in school, she would always come running to my classroom, and I would physically take care of her. And I would always advise her about things that I had gone through before she had: sex and menstruation, she asked me about, masturbation—anything that had to do with sexuality." The comforting, both physical and emotional, the advising, the ground-breaking between one stage and the next—tasks usually shared among all the women in a family—were shouldered entirely by Jane. She calls it having "that parental magic" and felt it both as a burden and thrill. Meanwhile, the lines between the sisters' sexual experiences became so muted that at times Emily felt that if hers weren't exactly the same as Jane's, they hadn't really happened (a phenomenon that another woman, intimately acquinted with and influenced by her sister's sex life, called "having my sister's orgasms").

"Jane was very protective of me," remembers Emily, "in the sense that she would share her experience with me. Very often, then, as I added those three years to my life, I would repeat certain things. I'd think they were okay since she did them. Sometimes I'd feel that her experiences were the valid ones, and mine weren't, because they weren't the same." Their identification was so thorough ("even," notes Emily, "similar body types, internally, in terms of menstruation and development") that the younger sister was shocked when her first childbirth was not just like her sister's but, in fact, much easier.

The intricacies of the knot between Jane and Emily growing up, the enmeshed strands of mother and daughter, sister and sister were tied all the more tightly when the sisters married and became mothers. They both candidly admit (relishing, after years of analysis, how the pieces of the puzzle interlock) that each married a man reminiscent of her sister, "a man that complements each of us and what we're used to," says Emily. Jane's appraisal is carefully wrought, like one of those black-and-white drawings that is an optical illusion: you look at it once and see an ornate white goblet, look again and it's two black silhouettes, staring at each other. "My sister's husband is very like me emotionally, and my husband is very much like my sister. Now this isn't a complete parallel, obviously, because they're men and we're women. But there are many ways in which there are these crossovers. In some sense, we married each other. When [the couples] are together, there's often tension, because although there's a very good relationship between brothers-in-law and sisters and a lot of respect and love, there's also sometimes a resentment acted out"—a kind of sibling rivalry between in-laws.

"I've been thinking lately that you always love people, including your children, on some level because of your mother, father and siblings," Jane muses, while Adam fidgets next to her, gets bored, is firmly chided by his mother to entertain himself, unearths his skateboard and is off. "I always call Adam Emily, for example." Then she tells this story, a symbolic square in the quilt of family mythology, and the centerpiece of her story "A Family Likeness." "Once Emily was here for a Christmas vacation when Adam was about three. As he was waking up one morning, I went into his room and lay down on the second bed in his room, and we talked about ten minutes. All of a sudden he looked at me and said, 'Oh, I thought you were Emily,' which is very strange because obviously I'm his mother. But it was also obvious that unconsciously he had totally identified us."

So the enmeshed strands between the sisters are passed along to the children, and the knot is retied once again—and yet again, as the sisters thread the lines to their own children and each other's. "In the beginning," remembers Emily about her sister's first child, "I very much saw Adam as my sibling. I had a lot of jealousies about the way Jane related to him and handled him. She would talk about what his hands looked like and how soft they were, and I remembered thinking to myself, Oh, she used to say that about my hands." But over the years, Emily's jealousy has mellowed into a deep attachment for both her nephews—and a special thread of identification with Jane's second son, Corey. "I feel a similar way about him that I feel about my second child, and maybe the way I feel about myself," she realizes, nursing and burping and cuddling Simon in her arms, "that he's a little bit more vulnerable, a little bit more sensitive, not in terms of other people's feelings, but in terms of his own."

For Jane, too, the birth of her children sounded old resonances with her sister, which at times she heard with sorrow, at times with joy. When Adam was born, she felt sharpest of all the displacement of her husband's affection to their son. "I felt what many men say they feel—jealous of the child. On the one hand, I was demanding that Douglas take a lot of care of him, on the other, I would resent him. Resenting it is a mild term. I was torn apart by loss. I think that the older, more deeply rooted resonance of that was the feeling of my sister having robbed me of my father, when she was born and as she grew. That was one reason why I constantly called Adam Emily. I really felt him as a usurper." Then she adds the paradox that is the crux of their sister knot. "But I also felt him as the intensely desired being that I felt my sister."

Just as Emily keeps a special corner of her heart for Jane's second child, Jane saves that cranny for Emily's firstborn, Sara. "As if the gods had planned it that way, she looks just like me, or at least everyone says that. I see it a little bit, but I think she looks like all three of us, Emily, Mickey and me. She's either like me or she's like Mickey—very temperamental, very intense. Naturally my sister finds that very difficult to deal with."

And just as when she and Emily were children, Jane spread her mothering wing over her sister, when they became mothers, the pattern began to repeat itself. When Emily's daughter was born, Jane left her own three-month-old baby to fly to California to assist Emily, teaching her and Mickey how to diaper, when to pick up the baby or let her cry, showing them the ropes. Now, as their kids grow older, the ropes are more and more shared, tangling with a little less strain, as they compare notes and alternate counsel about children's tantrums and terrors, quirks and delights, nudging each other when each threatens to overidentify with her children, remembering the sweet stab of identification with each other. Through marriage, babies, children, they remain each other's intimate, each other's "only family." When Emily's second child, Simon, was born, she sent her sister a photo of him at birth, eyes still tightly shut, hands and feet still waving from the struggle to be born. With it she sent a note which now sits proudly in Jane's living room among photos of the two sisters and their families, displayed prominently, the way other families might hang a diploma or an autographed picture of the president. "Dearest Janie," scrawled her sister, weak and victorious from the birth, "Here he is at 2:45 AM. Normal shits. I feel a little better. I love you, E."

Stella and Megan are another pair of sisters where the boundaries of identity and sexuality, of intent and art are intimately enmeshed, and like the Lazarres', their story lies in the echoes and overlaps between them and in their interlocking choices as adults. Both are feminists and poets, though Stella keeps her art underground, gives readings of her poetry in the women's bar she runs, but shies away from publication. Megan has more outward ambitions and worldly success and has published several books of poetry and prose. Both are intense, brooding, Bohemian, and obsessed with their art. Stella is thin and angular with sharp features and short-cropped silvery hair and a profile that in some moods strangely suggest Julius Caesar. She is a chain-smoker with skittish moods, effusive and remote, hot and cold. Like Jane and Emily Lazarre, Stella and Megan take after different sides of their family, so Megan is shorter and rounder than Stella, angles softened, hands slightly pudgier, body more grounded. Stella calls herself an outlaw personality, "with a continual history from high school of being the outsider," a "wanderer into the labyrinth," a rebel and dabbler in movements, from beatnik to hippie, macrobiotics to feminism. She has been jostled by the subculture from city to city and relationship to relationship, and, at forty-one, the journey shows. For now, at least, she has settled down in a giant white elephant of an old warehouse, reconverted studio and living space for dozens of artists, loosely connected in a fringe and funky family.

Megan has had her share of rough times, too, bad health and a bad marriage, scrounging for money and little time to write. But now she has come out the other side into better days. She lives with her ten-year-old daughter in a cozy clapboard house, which the poet's eye has decorated with warm earth colors and hand-carvings and books of mysticism and poetry. Her study is a glassed-in porch looking out at the trees and the stars, and she seems to be settled there for a while.

Like Emily and Jane Lazarre, Stella and Megan's intimacy growing up was all the more intensified by the early breakup of their family. When Stella was twelve and Megan six, their parents split up and took off, and at times the girls were left entirely to their own devices. Stella's memory of this time is grim: "Although my total thing was taking care of Megan and playing with her, I was never taught anything about how you take care of a house or cook, so we'd be literally living off cornflakes. I spent a great deal of time protecting her from what was going on. It sort of kept my head cool to keep her head cool." Eventually, the girls were sent to live in the care of another pair of sisters, Megan with her grandmother, and Stella with her great-aunt.

Stella remembers the sisters raising the sisters this way: "I grew up with a woman who was unmarried, very shy, a Virgo, an extremely proper person, socially and professionally high in the community. A lot of my rebellion was directly caused by having lived in that atmosphere. I had to go wild when I finally got free. Megan lived in a situation with my grandmother where she learned to become a scrapper, fight and stand up for herself. So the differences in those two households contributed in many ways to our being different people.

"Even the times that we weren't quite able to meet each other in terms of the different lives we were living, there was always a substratum of love going on, which for a long time made us not able to recognize that we weren't quite meeting."

Along with the substratum of love went a deep substratum of influence, both intellectual and sexual. "I gave her Ezra Pound when she was thirteen, and that changed her life," Stella offers matter-of-factly. "I took it on myself to teach her the things that I knew she wasn't getting anywhere else." It was also at this time that Stella returned from college with the news that she was gay—and that, too, changed the sisters' lives more than they realized at the time. For even though they saw each other only intermittently, summers and holidays, their lives were two hands in a cat's cradle, and though their sexual choices appeared to make different patterns for years, they were formed from the same unbroken piece of string.

For years they followed the stars of their differing sexual preferences. Megan dated men and married the one who seemed the best catch, a language scholar, the perfect match. They had a daughter, and not long after that, the marriage fell apart. Stella, meanwhile, was having affairs with various women, living on a houseboat with one, moving to New York with another. Occasionally she would get involved with a man. Once she made a conscious and concerted effort to go "straight," thought about "getting married and having babies and stuff like that"—at the very moment when her sister's marriage was breaking up. So confused were her choices with her sister's (and so deeply out of her control) that she chose to follow her sister's path at the moment her sister's life had bottomed out.

This was a period of feeble communication and hurt and misunderstood feeliings. But soon after, their courses realigned, their choices, which had so radically diverged, came together at the crossroads. Megan had come out, too. "It took me a while to really believe it," Stella confesses, "because most of the women I had known who were gay were pretty much like me, they were gay from very young." But with the growth of the Women's Movement and the women-identified culture, more and more women who for years had loved, married, and had children with men were switching their allegiance and the spectrum of their loving to women.

For Stella and Megan this recent period has been one of closeness and newfound camaraderie. The shared language and experience of sexuality has become their common denominator—they have even, on occasion, slept with each other's lovers. "Megan slept with a woman that I broke up with," Stella mentions, "and found the same thing that I did—on the surface she was very attractive, but she had a lot of crazies going on.") The "older-younger thing" has given way to the common ground of equals, and now they feel they've become twice sisters: outside the family and within. Choosing to be lesbians, Stella explains, "has helped us understand each other a lot, because now Megan understands the problems that I've gone through and am going through, and definitely vice versa. Whereas before we were living in two different worlds with virtually two different sets of rules, and neither of us had quite grasped the reality of those worlds.

"During these past years our relationship has been growing

and changing, so that I feel that on both of our parts it's far more open than it has been since we were children."

Given their history, the early loss of mother love, its deep-wedged replacement with sister love, the strong female models who raised them to young womanhood, the intricate enmeshment of their sexual lives—it is no wonder that for these sisters coming out felt like coming home.

"As for the matter of what causes lesbianism, there is no agreement among psychotherapists," writes Dolores Klaich in her sympathetic study *Woman Plus Woman: Attitudes Towards Lesbianism*, but she sums up decades of speculation on the subject:

> Some of those who believe that lesbianism is a psychological illness generally lay the cause at the feet of the lesbian's mother or father (the mother is rejecting, thus the daughter seeks the mother in other women; the father unconsciously manifests a seductive attitude toward the daughter, thus the daughter, frightened of incest, fears all men). There are, of course, many variations on the parental-relationship theme. Other theories that are held, to name only a few; disappointment by a male; a refusal to accept women's traditional societal role; narcissistic regression—that is, in loving one's own sex one is in reality loving oneself; and so on.[9]

In *Of Woman Born*, Adrienne Rich digs further into the connection between mothers and lesbian daughters. She doesn't blame the mothers for their daughters' sexual preferences, as traditional psychotherapists have, but rather probes the delicate bond of woman-love and inadvertently sheds some light on sister love:

> . . . despite the realities of popular ignorance and bigotry about lesbians, and the fear that *she* has somehow "damaged" her daughter in the eye of society, the mother may at some level—mute, indirect, oblique—want to confirm that daughter in her love for women. . . . For those of us who had children, and later came to recognize and act upon the breadth and depth of our feelings for women, a complex new bond with our mothers is possible.[10]

Then, to pursue the thread between mothers and lesbian daughters, she quotes the poet Sue Silvermarie:

> I find now, instead of a contradiction between lesbian and mother, there is an overlapping. What is the same between my lover and me, my mother and me, and my son and me is the motherbond—primitive, all-encompassing, and paramount.

> In loving another woman I discovered the deep urge to both be a mother to and find a mother in my lover. . . . Now I treasure and trust the drama between two loving women, in which each can become mother and each become child.[11]

Not only is the mother bond intrinsic to the unfolding of lesbian love; so, too, can the sister bond be central. In families where the boundaries between sisters are particularly enmeshed and the shared language of sexuality particularly intense, in families where sisters have lost a mother and turn to each other for nurturance and support or in families where sisters are equal (or more powerful) sexual models than mother ever becomes—in these families, early intimacy between sisters may turn out to be a precursor of, model for, or a deep influence on lesbian relationships later on.

"Having a sister has provided a model for my relationship with other women: loving, natural, based on an expectation of equality and openness," says a thirty-six-year-old lesbian. Her happiest memories of growing up with her younger sister are the early physical intimacies (when she held her sister on her lap or when, at eight, little sister put a sleepy arm around her neck) and the times their sexual histories most closely overlapped (when they shared their stories about losing their virginity or being in love). Just as Sue Silvermarie, calling her mother-bond the model for her relationships with women, notes within these relationships the flexibility of playing "mother" or "daughter," this woman used her sister bond as the model yet draws a similar conclusion. "Sometimes I detect a tacit element of big sister/little sister (as with my present lover) but the roles are usually reversible. With women friends, I often refer to my sister and to my friendship with her as an example of how I like to relate to women. I'm sure I was in love with my sister as a child, and that this was a desirable model for my adult lesbian relationship." What, in part, made her childhood relationship with her sister so desirable a model was, by her own admission, the room for anger as well as warmth, conflict as well as cuddliness. "Our parents wanted us to get along without fighting," she explains, "but didn't grasp the fact that we got along even though we did fight."

"This is just one of those crazy ideas," broods Kate Millett, who has made her name hawking "crazy" ideas, "but I suspect that a great deal of the violence of sibling relationships is a kind of repressed sexuality. It is a love that dare never express itself in any kind of physical way so instead they fight, verbally or physically." She slouches in a rocker by her Franklin stove, bearish, yet fragile in a beat-up gray sweater and blue sneakers, sipping a martini against the edge of winter creeping into her loft, six flights up on the Bowery, the depths of New York. She rocks and talks, surrounded by her art and artifacts, shelves of her own books and clusters of her own sculpture, sturdy wood floors warmed by Persian throw rugs and huge expanses of wall softened by plants and drawings (a lamb chop drawn by her once husband, Fumio, an inner landscape by Judy Chicago). She is alternately shy and assertive, retreats like a turtle and spars like a cub. From her family's Irish past, she has kept the musical rhythms of speech, the broodiness and earthiness, the near-sensual pleasure of phrasemaking. The basking in outrageousness is distinctly her own. "I've always found the incest taboo kind of a stupid idea. The obvious people to love are the ones you know the best. But you're not supposed to."

Kate Millett falls in the middle of three strong-willed women. Five years older is Sally, who has recently divorced her husband of twenty years and his life of "bourgeois respectability" and become a slow-boiling feminist and a lawyer. ("No wonder," says Kate. "She has the mind of a Jesuit. A steel trap. At times it seems a guillotine blade.") Five years younger than Kate is Mallory, an erstwhile actress, divorced mother and free spirit who likes to complain that she feels like Milton Eisenhower to Kate's Ike, but is, by all accounts (including her own), a tough and talented cookie, who, as Kate puts it, "would correct Christ." ("Mallory's great talent is talk," boasts her half-proud, half-cowed sister. "She can talk the lid off a garbage can if it's on there with a lock.")

Kate's history with both Sally and Mallory makes a checkered path of loyalty and vendetta, fondness and fierceness. She is alternately praising them to the skies or not speaking to them. She claims her older sister once committed her to the loony bin—for which Kate swears she'll never forgive her ("I was locked in without my address book," she moans, the worst indignity). And she has had raving, bitching, screaming fights with Mallory—verbal and physical; one was unforgettably recorded on film by a mutual friend. "She acts out a tremendous defensiveness, a younger-sister defensiveness," observes Kate, "but she's got cannons and I've got a water pistol. That's the difference. I don't think she understands how powerful she is." Yet Kate and Mallory are also inseparably intimate, seeing each other or talking on the phone every day.

Her love affairs with women mirror her relationships with her sisters in form and content. As she says, "One recapitulates with lovers the relationship with one's sisters if one loves women. Almost every relationship I have is either my older sister or my younger sister." Cases in point: her first woman lover in college, who was exactly five years older and had Sally's surprising "kind of fragility," and her most recent lover, Cynthia, a photographer whom Mallory introduced her to. Cynthia, like Mallory, is exactly five years younger than Kate and has Mallory's kind of feistiness—with one critical difference. "I can argue with Cynthia for hours and enjoy it thoroughly, and I'm sure she does, too. I know she isn't devastated or saddened by it, no internal bleeding, whereas if you are blood sisters, then it becomes mystical and terrible."

Mallory, who is as passionately, theatrically into her affairs with men as Kate is involved with women, also sees sibling patterns leaving traces on her romances. "The way I relate to a man is modeled after how I relate to Kate. Since she was my big sister, I tended to look up to her, seeking approval. I saw myself as a child whereas she was the big girl. So now I tend to see myself as helpless with men, letting them be in control. The problem is my powerlessness versus their powerfulness."

Meanwhile, Mallory sees her sexuality versus Kate's as "a big dichotomy." "I find Kate rather resents my being involved with men. I may be projecting, but it's as if I'm consorting with the enemy. I find her being with women upsetting, too."

It is no mere coincidence that Kate's most recent lover, Cynthia, in Mallory's phrase, "served to lessen the gap between Kate and me." Exactly Mallory's age and chosen by her for Kate, Cynthia is a kind of go-between, closing in the already enmeshed boundaries between them. The symbolism is not lost on Kate, though she transforms it to make it more manageable. At the heart of the heart of the sister knot, Kate

Millett jokes, "We call Mallory our mother-in-law, laughingly, which is a title she loves."

For most sisters, sharing the language of sexuality is a natural part of growing up, comforting and comfortable to varying degrees, depending on age and circumstance, history and inclination. Over the course of the years, boundaries may shift and realign, alternately closer and more distant, and sexual identities may mirror or part, choices alternating in patterns of similarity and difference. Only occasionally do the boundaries merge so thoroughly that neither sister is sure where one identity ends and the other begins. Only occasionally do the interlocking patterns of sexual choices also lock in the sisters so that all choice is circumscribed and all growth stymied. Only then has the shared language of sexuality become more static than communication.

Eva sits on her bed, hugging her knees. At thirty, she looks both younger and older, with girlishly innocent eyes and subterranean fears, boyish short curls and coltish energy, and the presence of a woman still discovering and defining her womanliness, which is still unextricably tied in with her three-year-older sister, May. "May and I had an *extremely* tight relationship," she begins, and then grimaces as if a cord has suddenly been pulled too tight around her neck. "She would interpret what I was saying when I babbled as a baby. Even today, when I can't get my words out, I flash on that.

"My identity was so wrapped up in her," she goes on, "it was confusing. I thought she was great, smart, pretty. I thought I was nothing." For years Eva measured herself so exhaustively against her sister that neither the similarities nor the differences gave her any comfort. "Physically, there are and have always been some similarities, but she's relaxed whereas I'm tense. She's willing to say, 'Look at me, I'm pretty,' while I'm just beginning to say that. She's someone who loves to flirt, both with women and men. It has always been easy for her to ask a favor ('As long as you're up, will you get me a Kleenex?'), where I'd never do that."

For all the years of growing up, their closeness spread over them like a blanket, warm and cozy, muffling and stifling. "When we were younger, we always had the same opinions. We almost always had the same friends. We could just look at each other and know what the other thought. I have a nice memory of that closeness." But the cuddly blanket of closeness finally revealed the bed of thorns. "I also have a memory of being made fun of for wanting to be just like May. 'Be your own person,' my mother would say. 'Get your own friends.'" The merger of identity was so complete and so devastating that to this day, when Eva forgets a detail of her past, she will telephone her sister to ask, "What did I do when I was four?" Opinions, friends, even the footprints of her own past were entrusted to the care of her old sister.

Nor did her sister ever prove herself entirely trustworthy. About their shared language of sexuality, the whispered secrets, the awkward demonstrations, Eva now realizes, "She gave me a lot of bad information. When she was about thirteen, I asked her what orgasm felt like and she said, 'It's incredible! All this stuff will come gushing out of you.'

"Also, she taught me to masturbate. First, I heard her masturbate on the other side of the partition between the two halves of our room. I stayed quiet. I could have killed her for intruding on my privacy." *I could have killed her,* she says, and as if hit between the eyes with the shock of her sister's trespass, her blue eyes lose all trace of girlishness.

For years the sisters walked the taut tightrope between like and not-like, hers and mine, rage and merger, and then finally, without warning, the tightrope snapped. One summer May went to Berkeley and came back exultant and in love. "'I'm so excited,' she told me, 'I met this woman and fell in love with her. And she looks just like you.'" Eva pauses in her narrative, clutching her knees for dear life. "In the next breath, she asked, 'Would you be willing to sleep with me?'" The last line had been crossed, the last taboo shattered.

"I was livid," Eva remembers, and more than five years later, the shock has not worn off. "I screamed at her, 'Get out of here.' I had doubts about my own sexuality and she touched my sorest point. She pursued it, kept pushing. A couple of times afterward she tried to get me to spend the night at her apartment, even though mine was only a few blocks away. I started not wanting to spend time with her. *I wanted to kill her.*"

Five years later, the betrayal of their intimacy still hurts, the merger of their boundaries still strangles, and the fallout of that rage has not entirely dissipated. Though she insists that "being close to May helped me feel able to be close to women," when I ask her whether she feels the threat of that closeness as well, she blushes to her curls and says, "Yes, that was a good question." When I last hear from her, she has left

the man she was living with for years, the man she was
thinking of marrying, and is hurtling through the throes,
through the highs and lows of a new relationship—this one
with a woman who happens to look a lot like her sister.

8

SISTERS AS ARTISTS

When [Emily] is ill there seems to be no sunshine in the world for me. The tie of sister is near and dear indeed, and I think a certain harshness in her powerful and peculiar character only makes me cling to her more. . . . Day by day, when I saw with what a front she met suffering, I looked on her with an anguish of wonder and love. I have seen nothing like it; but indeed, I have never seen her parallel in anything. Stronger than a man, simpler than a child, her nature stood alone.[1]

—CHARLOTTE BRONTË

She rides in the front seat, she's my older sister
She knows her power over me
She goes to bed an hour later than I do
When she turns the lights out
What does she think about?
And what does she do in the daylight
That makes her so great?[2]

—CARLEY SIMON, *"Older Sister"*

FROM ONE ERA TO THE NEXT COME THE HARMONIES AND CA-cophonies of sister artists: from the remote and rarefied Gothic enmeshment of the Brontës to the proud and public pop songs of the Simons, from the contrapuntal and complementary visions of Virginia Woolf and Vanessa Bell to the contemporary and connected pieces of feminist performers Holly, Timothy and Laurel Near. Just as sisters share a special language of sexuality with its intimate patterns of mirroring, overlapping and diverging, they may also share a language of art. Not in every family, certainly, not as primitive and wordless as the powerful messages of the body, more often a matter of inclination than birth, of opportunity more than blood. But when it is rooted in a family (as it has from the Brontës to the Pointers, from Virginia Stephen Woolf and Vanessa Stephen Bell to Lillian and Dorothy Gish, from the Andrews to the McGarrigle Sisters), it lodges with a life of its own. This chapter will listen in on how a language of art is spoken and shared in several creative families: when it begins, how it is practiced, how it is nurtured or envied within the family and how it influences and sustains continued creative work.

Countless critics have, of course, tried to analyze how the artistic temperament is born, the mystery that one Brontë biographer calls "that strange mingling of influence, that incalculable blend of experience and heredity."[3] What particularly interests me here is how the sister bond influences artistic development, how sisters working in the same artistic genre or different genres make a mark on each other's work. And finally, how even in the most creatively enmeshed families there remains this paradox: that a language of art may be intimately shared—plays performed, songs sung, poems read together, but ultimately the muse comes in private and the artist works alone. Sisters may grow up for years together exchanging a language of art, but ultimately each must find her own voice and speak it on her own.

The language of art may be fueled by the creative sparks a parent, already flaming bright (the mother, like Judy Garland, hands on the torch of her torch singing to her daughters, or the father, like publisher Richard Simon, is a brilliant after-hours pianist, so the children learn to sing before they talk). Or it may be fired by a parental light hidden under a bushel, only later to emerge in the voices, gestures or words of the children (the father, like Reverend Patrick Brontë, scribbles poems between ministerial duties, and though the poems are amateurish, the passion for words finds immortality in Charlotte, Emily and Anne). And naturally, parental encouragement and creative reinforcement do not necessarily occur justly and equally for each and every child.

In her nightclub act, with the spotlight making her brave and giddy, Lorna Luft, Judy Garland's second daughter, remembers the past this way: "Mama would get up and sing. Liza would get up and sing and sing and sing. I would ask to sing. Mama would insist I go out of the room and make a proper entrance. When I came back, everybody would be gone."

Though the language of art may first be learned from parents, it is often in the nursery, in the private sphere of childhood, where its most important practice takes place. Pull back the curtain on the playrooms of families that produce artists and find the children engaged in fantasies as rich and as richer than those in their everyday world. The games and plays of childhood, the byzantine secret languages and elaborate fantasy worlds are often a premonition of later creative work. In her study *Literary Women* Ellen Moers points out that

Several Victorian women writers—the Brontë sisters and Christina Rossetti among them—derived a valuable professional leavening from starting out as infant poets, dramatists, or tellers of tales with an audience of enthusiastic and collaborating siblings. That not only much of the technical expertise but also some of the material of their adult work derived from the nursery circle should not surprise us.[4]

In Charlotte, Emily and Anne Brontë's romantic and excessive Angria and Gondal fantasies lies a hint of their unsurpassed Gothic classics, *Jane Eyre, Wuthering Heights* and *Agnes Grey.* In the girlish, but mordant wit and shrewd observances of Virginia Stephen's *Hyde Park Gate News,* the chronicle of family doings, begun when she was nine, lies an inkling of the mature literary presence which blooms in the novels of Virginia Woolf. "Like other children she enjoyed playing at being grown-up," observes her biographer (and nephew) Quintin Bell, "but whereas they usually do so with the aid of hats, skirts, trousers and umbrellas, she played the game with words and phrases; half giggling at her own audacity, half seriously, she apes the grandest journalistic style."[5]

For Holly, Timothy and Laurel Near—three sister artists of modest reputation, magnetic presence and talents which fit together like the features of one face—the creative play of childhood is a resource which they still return to as adults. They grew up on a farm in northern California without electricity but with a generator which ran the record player for the Broadway show tunes their grandmother sent to "give them culture." They all have misty-eyed memories of the music, dance and drama performances that were their childhood stock-in-trade. Holly Near, who is thirty, is a folksinger who got her start in the anti-War movement and now has become a balladeer of feminist culture with a devoted underground following. Timothy Near, who's a few years older, is an actress who was with the National Theater of the Deaf for many years, and Laurel Near, the youngest, is a dancer with the Wallflower Order modern dance troupe.

One of Holly Near's most exuberant songs is an ode to her older sister, "You've Got Me Flying," which immortalizes the hours of creative childhood play and imitation:

> I believed the world would lay before you
> All the passions—all the gypsy secrets that you knew

> I would wear the rose and cape
> When you were not at home
> Did I know that I'd grow to say
> You've got me flying, I'm flying[6]

No longer furtive, Holly Near now takes this song to center stage. She sits down at the piano, eyes and spirits dancing, and belts out the song, while her sister Timothy, with fingers as delicate as the rainbows thrown by prisms and as strong as their sisterhood has become, mimes the song in sign language. And somewhere, on another stage, Laurel Near and her dance troupe dance its patterns out, their bodies completing the story. Separated from each other and the confines of childhood, each has gone her own way, nourished her talent and found her own voice. Now they can return and share what they've discovered—this way the language of art is spoken from sister to sister to sister and offered to the world.

In every family of sisters there is a pull between the comfort and closeness of the sister bond and the urge to separate and be autonomous. In families of sister artists, this emotional pull is also translated into a kind of creative tension: between the enjoyment of an artistic sisterhood, creating together, nourishing each other, working side by side, and the need to break away and find an authentic and independent voice. How this process is negotiated in three different families of sister artists from three different eras is the concern of the rest of this chapter.

Branwell Brontë, wayward brother of three of the most notorious artist sisters in literary history, painted a portrait of Charlotte, Emily and Anne around 1838, which now hangs in the National Portrait Gallery. Though its facade is muted with age, its saga is unmistakable. The three sisters are clustered together in the family circle, but a pillar divides them: Anne and Emily stand on the shadow side of the pillar, shoulders touching and overlapping, Charlotte on the sunlit side, slightly removed yet inseparable from the whole. "Emily's countenance struck me as full of power," wrote Mrs. Gaskell, Charlotte's earliest biographer, "Charlotte's of solicitude; Anne's of tenderness."[7] The sculpted profiles and the somber dresses echo and repeat each other's, but it is in the eyes that the family's story is told. Sad and liquid as doe's eyes, deep-set and resigned as the grave, the eyes of the Brontë sisters manage to look outward and inward at the same time. And though their brother has painted them so that they seeem to be chiseled from the same piece of marble, nowhere do their eyes connect. Not one of them is looking at another. Even in their insularity and intimacy, in the interweaving of their genius lurks a distance which only their art can cross.

Virginia Woolf once wrote that Charlotte Brontë's classic, *Jane Eyre*, reflects "an acidity which is the result of oppression, a buried suffering smouldering beneath her passion, a rancour which contracts this book, splendid as [it is], with a spasm of pain."[8] Woolf's words are also powerfully descriptive of the Brontë family's life. For the three daughters and only son spoke in spasms of pain which were the outcry of oppression; by a driven and domineering father, by unending poverty which curtailed their mobility and narrowed their hopes, and by the disease which seized their mother as a young woman, their two oldest sisters, Maria and Elizabeth, as children, and eventually, in grim succession (just as the sisters had their first glimpse of fame), took each of them.

Their response to this unending oppression was an insularity so thick it hung over them like the clouds over their native Yorkshire. But the protective cloak of enmeshment, which took the chill off of fate, also stifled any exploration beyond the family sanctum. The tentative sallies into the world in their twenties as governesses and tutor ended in disasters: Charlotte fell silently and hopelessly in love with her married employer, and Branwell more brazenly with his. Both returned home broken and brokenhearted, Branwell numbing his pain with the opium and drink that led to his pitiful demise, his talent squandered, his spirit shattered. Almost thirty, Charlotte wrote to a friend about their return home to the parsonage, "I have done nothing yet ... I feel as if we were all buried here."[9] The years that followed proved her first statement hollow, but her second sadly prophetic.

Almost a century after the Brontës' death a clue was discovered to the feverish inner workings of the siblings' creativity, a clue to how the language of art was spoken and transmitted among them (as well as a clue to the psychic turbulence of their enmeshment). Fannie Ratchford, a Texas University librarian, spent years transcribing hundreds of tiny manuscripts, written as mock magazines in the Brontë children's microscopic hand. These turned out to be a complex series of stories, poems, novels, histories and dramas about two legendary kingdoms, Gondal and Angria, and their larger-than-life heroes and heroines. This secret fantasy life, begun before Charlotte was ten, was sustained and embellished by all the Brontës for sixteen years, from the nursery to the grave. One of their biographers ventured that the hills and plains of Gondal and Angria "provided a fantasy world which for all of them at various times, became a substitute for life," and beyond that, "even in maturity [they] remained addicted to it like a drug."[10]

"This habit of 'making out' interests for themselves that most children get who have none in actual life," wrote a friend of Charlotte Brontë's to Mrs. Gaskell, "was very strong in [Charlotte]. The whole family used to 'make out' histories, and invent characters and events. I told her sometimes they were like growing potatoes in a cellar. She said, sadly, 'Yes! I know we are!' . . . This is the epitome of her life."[11]

The epitomes of all the Brontës' lives: this artistic inwardness and insularity, dark and dense as cellar climate, terrifying and airless as a live burial—and yet paradoxically invigorating. Even at twenty-seven, numb with unrequited love, Charlotte sought solace in Angria and reconnected with her family through its paths. "It is a curious metaphysical fact," she wrote her brother, "that always in the evening when I am in the great dormitory alone, having no other company than a number of beds with white curtains, I always recur as fanatically as ever to the old ideas, the old faces, and the old scenes in the world below."[12]

But most important, the fantasies proved the fertile ground in which the Brontës' mature work was planted and bloomed to passionate life. The way monks in a cabalistic sect learn and refine their code, the Brontës practiced the rituals of their art in private and then grew bold enough to offer their work to the world. Ellen Moers puts her finger on the centrality of their fantasies to their art and life:

We know at least that all the Brontë virgins, Charlotte, Anne and Emily, loved with brute passion, committed adultery and incest, bore illegitimate children, moldered in dungeons, murdered, revenged, conquered, and died unrepentant in the imaginary kingdoms they called Gondal and Angria. . . . We know the source of [*Jane Eyre's*] Rochester and [*Wuthering Heights's*] Heathcliff. . . . To the power of their imagination, and the woman's passion that drove their fantasies, we owe not only the fiction but the love poetry of Emily Brontë.[13]

The pulse of the world below beat at the heart of the three Brontë sisters' inspiration. Charlotte tried to stifle its murmurs in her first novel, *The Professor*—and the novel was so restrained and lackluster it turned out a failure. But she heeded the Angrian voices in her next book, and even in her own lifetime, *Jane Eyre* was a success. Emily Brontë transformed her elaborate fantasies into the wild florescence of *Wuthering Heights,* which so shocked and embarrassed her Victorian contemporaries that Charlotte had to mitigate the sting in a preface to the second edition, published after Emily's death. Like the older sister who decodes her infant sister's baby talk for the rest of the family, Charlotte Brontë had to translate her sister's language and intent for the world:

> My sister's disposition was not naturally gregarious; circumstances favoured and fostered her tendency to seclusion: except to go to church or take a walk on the hills, she rarely crossed the threshold of home. Though her feeling for the people round her was benevolent, intercourse with them she never sought. . . . Her imagination, which was a spirit more sombre than sunny, more powerful than sportive, found . . . material whence it wrought creations like Heathcliff, like Earnshaw, like Catherine. Having formed these beings she did not know what she had done.[14]

Of the three, Anne Brontë plunged least deeply into the reservoir of family fantasy for sources for her novels, and her work is more circumscribed, less cosmic than her sisters', although, as Ellen Moers sums up about her, she only "has the reputation among people who don't read her for being the most timid of the sisters."[15]

As the central source of the Brontë sisters' work was private and arcane, so, too, was the publication of their novels clandestine. A volume of the three sisters' poetry came first, closely followed by a novel from each: Charlotte's *Jane Eyre,* Emily's *Wuthering Heights* and Anne's *Agnes Grey.* All were published under pseudonyms: the sisters kept their initials but masked their sisterhood as a brotherhood which they felt the times would be willing to accept. They bowed into the world as Currer, Ellis and Acton Bell.

The novels written at the same time, under the same roof, drew from the family's shared vision. But gradually each of the sisters was beginning to discover her own voice, tone and tempo. And Charlotte, especially, was listening to her own

voice with an unflappable conviction, so that, Mrs. Gaskell
reports, even her sisters' remarks seldom had "any effect in
inducing her to alter her work, so possessed was she with the
feeling that she had described reality."[16] In her aesthetic
judgments, at least, Charlotte was beginning the delicate
process of differentiating from her sisters. Still, while they
were writing, they read, encouraged and criticized each other's work, making of their sisterhood a rare and rarefied
writers' guild. After the Reverend Brontë went to bed (for he
was not to know they were writing until long after publication), the sisters gathered in the dining room and, as Mrs.
Gaskell reported, they

> retained the old habit . . . of putting away their work at nine
> o'clock, and beginning their study, pacing up and down the
> sitting room. At this time, they talked over the stories they
> were engaged upon, and described their plots. Once or twice a
> week, each read to the others what she had written, and heard
> what the others had to say about it. . . . The readings were
> of great and stirring interest to all, taking them out of the
> gnawing pressure of daily-recurring cares, and setting them in
> a free place.[17]

But the "free place"—the place where the pressure of daily
cares was soothed, the place where the weight of private
fantasies was finally transformed into fiction, and the place
where keeping the bonds of sisterhood, each might still have
found some autonomy—that place was snatched away from
them no sooner than it was found. Anne wrote one more
novel, the surprisingly feminist *Tenant of Wildfell Hall;*
Emily fell gravely ill before she finished another novel. So
entwined was Charlotte's imagination with Emily's that when
Emily was sick, Charlotte mourned to her publisher, "Both
head and hand seem to have lost their cunning; imagination is
pale, stagnant, mute."[18] First Emily, dead at thirty, then a
year later Anne, at twenty-nine, and six years later, Charlotte,
at thirty-nine: at the moment they were finally finding their
own voices, the most remarkable sisterhood of the century
was silenced.

Between Virginia and Vanessa Stephen the language of art
was intimately shared from the nursery forward but its
messages were from the beginning expressed in different
forms—much to the pleasure, envy and admiration of them

both. The two were daughters of Leslie Stephen, the formidable editor of the *Dictionary of National Biography* and the equally formidable Julia Duckworth. But Julia Duckworth devoted much of her care to her husband and his dictionary and died when Virginia was thirteen, so the Stephen sisters turned early to each other for mothering. When their only brother, Thoby, died of typhoid ten years later, their bond only intensified. "From the first," Quentin Bell assures us, "it was settled between them that Vanessa was to be a painter and Virginia a writer."[19] He gives no specific evidence of the terms of that early settlement. But the lives that grew out of it provide the evidence: Virginia Stephen Woolf, to be one of England's great novelists, Vanessa Stephen Bell, to be a fine and respected painter, particularly of portraits, her talent not an awesome as her sister's, but her life much longer and less troubled.

What Quentin Bell underlines is the extraordinary closeness between the sisters, "the way in which they were drawn together as though by some capillary attraction"[20]—for better or worse, which for Virginia, at least, meant in health and in madness. Adds Nigel Nicolson, son of Virginia's great friend, Vita Sackville-West, "Sometimes [Virginia] loved [Vanessa] almost to the point of thought-incest. They were like a pair of fox-cubs with their verbal licks, little growls, a tumbling of limbs, the nipping of ears."[21] Writing to Vanessa's husband, the writer and art critic Clive Bell (whom Virginia alternately envied, flirted with and sought for literary criticism), Virginia paints her devotion to her sister in a letter of playful excesses:

> First [let us turn] to Vanessa; and I am almost inclined to let her name stand alone upon the page. It contains all the beauty of the sky and the melancholy of the sea, and the laughter of the Dolphins in its circumference, first in the mystic Van, spread like a mirror of grey glass to Heaven, next in the swishing tail of its successive esses, and finally in the grave pause and suspension of the ultimate A breathing peace like the respiration of Earth itself.

> If I write you of books you will understand that I continue the theme though in another key; for are not all Arts her tributaries, all sciences her continents and the globe itself but a painted ball in the enclosure of her arms? But you dwell in the Temple, and I am a worshipper without. . . .[22]

But the underside of this admiration was the bitter bite of envy, the nightside of this sun-swept swoon was despair. The partition which was drawn from the first between writing and art seemed also, to Virginia, to be drawn between their lives. And what was contrapuntal and complementary in art was agonizing to Virginia in life. As artists, their separate voices and talents gave each other room to breathe; but the separation of their life-choices was, at least for Virginia, unsettling and disturbing. Vanessa was the wife and mother of three, the lover of several, an adventuresome and life-embracing spirit; Virginia was the wife who feared sex, the mother of none, at times ebullient and madcap, but at times a nerve-wracked and life-fearing spirit. The same pen that burned with love for Vanessa in the letter to Clive Bell froze with fear, fending off madness, in a journal entry twenty years later:

> Woke up perhaps at 3. Oh it's beginning, it's coming—the hor-ror—physically like a painful wave swelling about the heart —tossing me up. I'm unhappy, unhappy! Down— God, I wish I were dead. Pause. But why am I feeling this? Let me watch the wave rise. I watch. Vanessa. Children. Failure. Yes; I detect that. Failure, failure. (The wave rises).[23]

Quentin Bell, Vanessa's son, does not shrink from interpreta-tion: "Vanessa has three children," he translates for Virginia. "I have none."[24]

But the need for closeness, the deep-seated need for con-nection invariably overcame the grimness and resentment. Despite Virginia's deadly bouts of envy and passing snipes of condescension ("Old Vanessa is no genius,"[25] she once wrote snootily to a friend) and Vanessa's matching flurries of impatience and perplexity at Virginia's erratic behavior, the sisters remained loyal and steadfast, crossing the gap between each other's lives and sharing the language of each other's art. Once, Vanessa dashed off a letter to Virginia about the moths circling her lamp, the moths she tried and failed to catch and chloroform. No sooner had Virginia received the anecdote than she was burning it for literary fuel:

> By the way, your story of the moth so fascinates me that I am going to write a story about it. I could think of nothing else but you and the moths for hours after reading your letter. Isn't it odd?—perhaps you stimulate the literary sense in me as you say I do your painting sense.[26]

Then, embarrassed and defensive about the novel she'd just published: "God! how you'll laugh at the painting bits in the Lighthouse!"

But Vanessa's reaction was anything but laughter. Virginia's *To the Lighthouse* (which would be acknowledged her masterpiece), with its central characters Mr. and Mrs. Ramsay closely and profoundly drawn after Mr. and Mrs. Stephen, shook Vanessa so that she wrote her sister: "It is so shattering to find oneself face to face with those two again that I can hardly consider anything else. In fact, for the last two days, I have hardly been able to attend to daily life."[27] Then she added the supreme compliment: "So you see as far as portrait painting goes you seem to me to be a supreme artist."[28] The boundary which had been drawn from the first between their talents ironically allowed Vanessa the freedom to praise her sister in the genre that was her own. And the gift her sister gave her in return was to illuminate the shapes and shadows of the family in a voice that was clearly distinct but that drew from their common history and drew them all the more deeply together.

Jump another half-century to another family of sister artists, as much the voices, the stories and temperaments of their time as the Brontës and the Stephens were of theirs. Joanna, Lucy and Carly Simon: three sister artists with a younger brother, Peter, a photographer and renegade, eclipsed, like Branwell Brontë, by his sisters' fame. Three sisters who learned the patter of art from musical, ambitious parents, spoke it together before they could talk, then grew up to make it their lives—both private and public—in opera, song writing, and the strong and cocky rhythms of pop music.

A magazine cover portrait catches them, and in the flash an image separates their saga from the fading portrait of the Brontë sisters in the National Portrait Gallery. The Simons are lush, dramatic and unabashedly public, eyes trained on the camera, like an orchestra on its conductor, and the piece they are playing is a concerto of sexual energy. They are all polished till they shine: lips, eyes and cheeks decorated like icing on a cake, earrings glittering, hair coiffed and cascading: the symbols and spirit of wealth and privilege. But like the portrait of the Brontës, whose faces are distinct but of a piece, the photograph of the Simons makes each unique, yet all entwined by masses of hair, binding them together like threads.

Three sisters, three years apart; each encouraged from the first to find her own voice, according to the temperament and talent and place in the family constellation. Joanna Simon, thirty-eight, is the oldest, the opera singer, all frosted blond curls and extravagant makeup, Papa's darling who had dreams of grandeur from an early age. The story the family likes to tell about Joey as a girl: When she was asked which she'd rather grow up to be—a pianist or an actress—she countered with "Which has more maids?"

"I think I picked the wrong one," she laughs, curling her legs beneath her on her flowery couch. Her New York City apartment is delicately decorated as a doll's house; she is the *dernier cri* of decoration. Across the room hang four large watercolors of Joanna Simon dressed like a fantasy figure in the opera costumes, and the image of the fairy-tale fantasy she was raised on hovers between the lines as she talks. "I tend to be grand and want a very grand life," she says, then demurs, "but I'm also very realistic. I certainly like luxury enormously. That was an aspect of my father. He wanted to go to the best restaurants and drive the most expensive car and go to the most gala party—and there's a lot of that in me."

Comparing herself to her sisters, the *grande dame* of the family says, "I think Lucy plays a particular role which is sort of well-adjusted family lady, and Carly plays the role of— how could I word it?—searching. Carly presents her problems to the world whereas Lucy doesn't so much. Lucy's much more reticent about expressing things."

Lucy Simon, thirty-five, the second sister, now a singer and songwriter, once trained to be a nurse, but certainly a "family lady," first of the family to get married, first to have children. The warmest, most accessible, most classically pretty of the three, with soft features and cocker-spaniel eyes and the wide smile all the sisters share, which opens suddenly like a fun-house door and changes the whole picture of their faces. Reticent about some subjects but candid about others —for instance, about the paleness of her success compared to Carly's and the sting of that. And candid about the strongest and most puzzling influence on the sisters' life: their mother.

In the photographic portrait of the Simon sisters, Andrea Simon is the fourth face in the family circle, the missing link in the story. "She's a very strong, dominating and controlling woman," says Lucy, sitting in Central Park across the street from her apartment and petting her tiny poodle as she talks. "She's a very appealing woman if you're not her daughter, and all three of us have tremendous problems being her daughters. We are all still very much affected by what she says or implies or her judgments, even as grown women, knowing better."

Joanna remembers a time during her eight-year psychoanalysis when she confronted her mother with "atrocious, horrible" accusations, and Carly admits with a guilty wince, "Before, Mother would find fault with me very easily and want to verbalize it, but now she thinks of me as being the reigning queen of the moment and therefore doesn't want to tamper with me. Now she picks on the other children more than she picks on me."

"She's never been an accepting mother, in the way 'Whatever my child does is marvelous,'" adds Lucy. "She's very critical. She's very unable to say that she likes what we do. When I play her my albums, which are very close to me, for my ego is very tied up with them, she will first point out the shortcomings, which is very painful. On the other hand—" She pauses, as they all do, for there is "another hand" for all of them. "On the other hand, she is the mother of four extremely creative children, and I certainly credit her with a lot of the creativity that we all have, because she always encouraged the expression of it."

The household the Simon sisters grew up in was vibrant with the language of music. Joanna began piano lessons at age four; Lucy and Carly started to follow suit, but switched to guitar when they couldn't keep up with her. But the lessons, the recitals, the crooning around the piano were marred with the false notes of parental double messages. Andrea Simon, in her daughter Lucy's words, was "the singer who never got a chance to sing," so her early encouragement of her daughters' talents was laced with some understandable resentment. And Richard Simon was a gifted pianist whose music was his hobby, but whose life was his role at the helm of Simon and Schuster. So he, too, alternately spurred on his children's musical talents and then sank into his work and became inaccessible to them. He died when Lucy and Carly were still quite young, so it was Joanna who felt the greatest boost and burden of his hopes. (When Joanna made her debut in the opera, her father had been dead two years, and Lucy remembers "sitting in the audience crying because he couldn't be there to see her.")

"I think one of the things that sums up our family," says Joanna, waxing sentimental, smoothing out the wrinkles, as if cold-creaming her skin, "are the times when we were young and would gather around the piano, and our father would play, and we would all sing harmony. We fit very well together, and we all have our own voice category. (Lucy's is a bright, pure sound, mine is a rich, deep, clear sound, more like Carly's, but I have a trained voice and their voices aren't trained. I can't compare them—it's like comparing steak and bananas.) We also all have our own life-style, and a lot of it has to do with music."

But the dulcet family harmonies which the oldest sister heard did not always sound so sweet to the youngest sister. At the end of the line of strong Simon women, the effort to keep in tune with her two older sisters was a wearying one and finding her own voice was a painful process of separation. Carly Simon, thirty-two, the third sister: now the brashest, boldest, most magnetic of the three. And with all the flashiness of her fame, the most outspoken. An hour before we are to meet, she calls groggily on the phone to postpone our conversation till later. Later she tells me she had an "overwhelming difference of opinion" with husband James Taylor, spent the night in a hotel—and got no sleep. He wanders in and out of the room strewn with their musical instruments while we talk, barefoot, blue-jeaned and in an obvious fog from the argument, bringing in tea and being solicitous—all of which Carly drinks up.

Her relationships with her sisters she calls "the most complicated I have" (among other reasons, "because you can't make up physically and totally clear the air"—as presumably she can after fights with her husband). Now she is less awed, less devastated and less involved with her sisters than she used to be. But as a girl, she cowed in both of their shadows and particularly worshiped Lucy (as, she adds, for a while younger brother Peter worshiped her). "I was very preoccupied with Lucy for ten years, from the time I was about ten to twenty," Carly realizes, her grandly gangly body slouching into her black leather couch. "I really lived vicariously through her for a long time, until I had some kind of a life that I liked of my own. I was just fascinated by Lucy and her friends and wanted to be like them and wear everything

they wore and look like them and feel like them and act like
them. I identified so much with her that I almost lost myself
in the bargain." Years later, having worked her way out of
this labyrinth of overidentification, Carly Simon transformed
that period into a lilting song of praise, merging Joanna's and
Lucy's stories into one "Older Sister":

> In her black gymnastic tights
> She was into some elastic nights
> Sophisticated sisters for the
> Soldiers of the soccer team
> Their silver I.D.'s and sororities
> They tinker with love in their model T's
> Oh Lord, won't you let me be her for just one day. . . .²⁹

The years when their lives overlapped and their identities
threatened to merge continued into their twenties. Joanna and
Carly shared an apartment, Lucy lived right next door; every
morning they would gather around the breakfast table, comparing notes about men and music and revelations from the
psychoanalyses they were each going through. This was the
period when Carly unfurled the full force of her emulation on
Joanna. "When I began to live with Joey," Carly remembers,
"I took on a little of her style. I started wearing a lot of
makeup and false eyelashes, dyed my hair blond, and would
borrow her jewelry sometimes. It always looked very classy
on her, but on me it was the wrong shoe. It just happened to
correspond with a time when I put on a lot of weight—and it
was like, when you saw me, you saw this hulk of outstanding,
unattractive mass coming down the street." She stretches out
her lanky frame, draped in the sheerest silk blouse and the
softest black-wool skirt, laughs the laugh that opens the
fun-house door and finishes, "It was like I was trying on a
glove that was just for the wrong hand. I was awkward doing
Joey."

This was also the period when Lucy and Carly picked up
their guitars, donned their black tights and started playing
clubs as the Simon Sisters. One night they auditioned at New
York's Bitter End—and immediately were offered a record
contract. "We were very tuned in to each other then," Lucy
remembers about this "sweet and innocent" time of their
lives. "We just sort of fell into playing together and then it
became a profession. We didn't realize how good we were
until good things were happening without any effort."

Lucy and Carly lasted as the Simon Sisters for about two

and a half years and then, for the first time in her life, Carly felt the itch to try her own wings. "I sort of wanted to hear my own voice" is how she puts it. "I know that that was the first time my ego seemed to emerge on its own rather powerfully. I wanted to break away from Lucy and sing on my own, even though I was scared to."

Taking that first step away from the bosom of the family was indeed scary, and the path was at first cluttered with false starts, broken love affairs and self-doubts. But the energy liberated from breaking away from her sister propelled her to find a persona of her own. And the person she found—that frank and gutsy, intelligent and sexy lady—is the person she remains today. Her voice is as powerful, as driving, as riveting as the voice which belted "That's the Way I've Always Heard It Should Be," and "You're So Vain" and put her name on the charts (her career, as one critic put it, taking off "like a champagne cork"). Her style is at least as sensual now as it was then, the cowboy shirts of her footloose, fancy-free dating days (with Kris Kristofferson, Warren Beatty and Mick Jagger) traded in for the silks and elegance of success and married life. Her wings may be a little clipped by marriage and mothering (Sarah, who is four, and Benjamin, who is eighteen months and intermittently tugs at his mother's blouse for a nip of milk). But her charisma is untarnished, her talent uninhibited (her latest album, "Boys In The Trees," on its way to being her first platinum record) —and her career has long since overshadowed her sisters'. Lucy Simon has made two albums on her own, "Lucy Simon" and "Stolen Time," both appealing and personable, as Lucy is, but neither of them big sellers. Joanna Simon sings mezzo-soprano with the New York City Opera but is not (her publicist's hype to the contrary) Carly's equivalent in the world of opera. Each of the Simon sisters has had to make her peace with the overwhelming discrepancy between one sister's success and the others'. For what Lucy calls "the myth of the equal dole" that the sisters were raised on has not entirely panned out. The language of music that was learned, more or less, in harmony is no longer sung in even thirds. Each of the sisters has had to come to terms with her own voice, her own talent and her own weight and presence in the world—rather than defining herself as one part of a picture, one third of a sisterhood.

And in the process they make explanations, like Carly's: "If my career had started at the phase my life is in now—

having young children—it wouldn't have moved along any faster than Lucy's. And there's also timing. I was lucky at the time that my first record came out, because the sound was very fresh then." Then, too, she admits, "Lucy and I have different energies: She tends to be more of a depressive personality, and I tend to be more anxious. But I exude much more onstage than she does. I knew this when we were singing together. She's got a meeker, quieter energy, like a madonna, like an angel. People were always attracted to that particular quality in her. Her energy would work very well on film. But my energy is very much out there and projects farther than hers does."

They also have their rationalizations, like Joanna's: "Occasionally the financial aspect of [Carly's success] is a little staggering to me, because I work terribly, terribly hard and make not even one-tenth of the fees she makes. Sometimes it's sort of ironic to me that I could have spent as many years as I have learning four languages and taking music courses and stagecraft, and yet, financially, the rewards are not nearly as great.

"On the other hand, if you say, what balances it out, I think that the emotional rewards are much greater. The emotional satisfaction from singing Bach or Beethoven or Brahms is much greater than the emotional reward of singing your own music—much as I think Carly is terrific. But the sense of history and universality I get from what I sing is really a great power for me."

Occasionally, the carefully hewn explanations and rationalizations disintegrate into downright irritation, like Lucy's: "There was no question about the fact that I had to do music, but it didn't have to be on a major scale. But Carly's success undeniably changed the perspective of that. Because I was being compared to her all the time. When my first album came out, whenever it was reviewed, it was reviewed as a comparison. That was destructive, I felt, more destructive for Carly than for me at the time because I was encroaching.

"Now I've had two albums that have not been successful, and I'm very disappointed about it. But I'm trying to figure out whether I need to be successful as a competitive thing or whether I'm just happy writing songs. I don't know. I need music in one way or another, but whether I need a major success might be more determined by the fact that I'm a Simon than that I need it for myself and my family." Then, she adds so quickly that it could almost be rehearsed, yet so firmly that it must not be, "But I never perceived star, and I never wanted star, and I don't want star. What I do want is to be successful enough so that I can call my own shots."

It is Carly, of course, who is easily successful enough to call her own shots but using her voice to exercise her options has not been entirely trauma-free. "I think that I am extremely ambitious," she muses, "but it didn't show itself for a long time. It was very hidden. I guess I felt if I was ambitious I was going to be punished for it, so I directed all of my thinking into wanting to be a wife and mother, making some man happy and staying in the background more.

"I didn't want to assert myself," she continues, digging deep into the past, into the sway of the tight-knit circle of sisters, "because I had never gotten any acclaim or recognition or applause for being assertive—especially from my sisters, who saw that as a threat to their reign. So it seemed that I succeeded by being an underdog and thought, If I'm going to be loved by my family I should hold myself back. I succeeded by not succeeding, by having a lot of phobias, by not getting it together, basically."

The sister who grew up to be one of pop music's leading voices, whose albums sold millions, who was offered twenty-five thousand dollars to sing a James Bond theme song, whose name is recognized around the world, was still terrified for years of performing in public, terrified to phobic proportions, which she has been notoriously candid about. Only recently has she ventured to perform in public at all—and still with strict limits and stipulations (small clubs, no more than ninety miles from home—and James Taylor in tow for moral support and the occasional bailout when the jitters overwhelm her). What she'll say about adapting her success to her sisters is "Sometimes, I try to minimize how good the success is and draw on the negative aspect of it like 'I have no time for myself.'" But what she's done—at least until now—is to keep succeeding by not succeeding, to keep up the pretense of the equal dole, and not to admit, as Adrienne Rich hints in "Transcendental Etude" in *Dream of a Common Language,* that even the language learned together, learned as sisters, must eventually be practiced alone, with

> a deeper listening, cleansed
> of oratory, formulas, choruses, laments, static
> crowding the wires.

For sisters as artists within the family and without, practicing their common music, exploring their common art, digging for their common language, "there come times" when

> We cut the wires,
> find ourselves in free-fall, as if
> our true home were the undimensional
> solitudes, the rift
> in the Great Nebula.[30]

9

SISTERS IN OLD AGE

Sisters is probably *the* most competitive relationship within the family, but once the sisters are grown, it becomes the strongest relationship. On the whole, sisters would rather live with each other than anyone else in their old age. Whereas brothers during their maturity may be totally noncompetitive; they may be in other parts of the country doing quite different things and there may be very little focus on each other. You very seldom find brothers who want to live with each other in old age.

—MARGARET MEAD

If you tell your sister to go to hell in twelve different languages and you need a quarter, you can say, "I need a quarter." And she'll give it to you. A friend may say, I don't want to see you again. And a friend you can give up. You don't give up a sister. You were born with them and you die with them. Or they die and leave you, and you feel absolutely discomfited.

—ELIZABETH MEAD STEIG

THERE ARE MESSAGES SISTERS LEARN IN THEIR MOTHER'S lap, at their father's knee and carry with them to the grave. "Beware small men," and "Never eat ice cream more than one a day," warned our mother, and our father advised, *The New York Times* is the single greatest invention of modern man," and "Never be a snitch-cat." So Annie and I will forever hear these words of wisdom echoing between the lines of our lives. Whether or not we follow them, whether or not we tangle with small men or have that death-defying second dish of ice cream, the messages always haunt us and link us. There are words and images sisters learn at a tender age that forever carry that special charge, the connotation and context of family. "I can say 'Vernor's ginger ale' to my sister," says Gloria Steinem, "and she will understand." Or it could be Missoula, Montana, in 1943 or Mohonk or mohair sweaters or being the only two people in the world who know that Aunt Billie's name is really Beulah.

There are the manners and mores, often sanctified to the level of myth, which sisters observe at parents' kitchen, table, office, car and forever carry on their own journey: slicing apples into the turkey salad, swearing feverishly at the wheel, answering the phone with a millisecond pause before "Hello." Or the rituals sisters initiate among themselves and never entirely forget: checking the piece of roast beef for gristle and then turning it over and checking the other side, or like the Simon sisters, saying "kettles" for "breasts" and "logs" for "penises," or like my grandmother, bending to bless the Sabbath candles, and knowing that every one of her sisters was bending at her own house to bless her candles, too. These rituals, these manners and mores remembered as myths, these words and images, these messages learned in Mother's lap, at Father's knee, make up the common language of sisters, binding them together under the skin, in the blood—whether or not, on the face of things, they remain close and connected, drift continents apart or wade forever through the murky waters of ambivalence.

Seventy-five years ago, in New York, the third of three sisters is born and grows up side by side by side her sisters, sleeping together in a bed as big as a meadow and dreaming dreams of marrying princes, kings and doctors. They all do marry (a tailor, a pharmacist and a furrier), have children, keep house according to their mother's rules, serve the community according to their father's code, and live near enough each other so that they can visit every Sunday afternoon for thirty years. For thirty years they cluster and talk every Sunday, through sickness and health, joy and *tsouris*, friendship and vendetta, births and deaths. At sixty, one moves to California to grow old in the blaze of the sun, at seventy another follows. One Sunday afternoon, as always, the two in California sit chatting and gossiping in the living room filled with the identical furniture—the cut-velvet covered couch, the overstuffed armchair—they sat in for thirty-odd years of Sundays in New York. They are having a grand old time, as always, telling stories, trading secrets, trading recipes, weaving together the myths of past and future. In the midst of it all, they stop and almost with one voice they say to each other, "Let's call Ruby and ask her to come over," for she is the third sister, the missing voice. Then they stop and look at each other again, this time without exchanging words. In the gossip and the secrets, in the words of advice offered and exchanged, in the web of language woven between past and future, they have for a moment forgotten that Ruby lives three thousand miles away and cannot join the circle in the instant of a call.

For three-quarters of a century, Margaret Mead and Elizabeth Mead Steig shared the common language of sisters, the manners and mores, the rituals and messages, the memories of the same home, and as Margaret Mead wrote in her

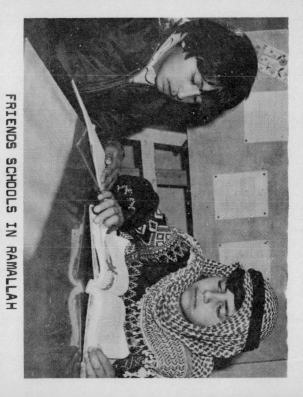

FRIENDS SCHOOLS IN RAMALLAH

FRIENDS SCHOOLS IN RAMALLAH — On the West Bank in Occupied Jordan, close to Jerusalem, are located the Friends Girls and the Friends Boys Schools. Lew and Joy Curless are at the Girls School, Lew being the principal, and Joy assisting with the instruction and bookkeeping.

Principal of the Boys School is Fuad Zaru, whose wife is Jean. There are some American "volunteers" who teach at the schools for two-year terms.

The administration and teachers find it most difficult these days because of the political unrest in the Middle East.

PRAY and **GIVE** to help meet the INDIANA YEARLY MEETING missions 1980-1 goal of $1500 for Friends Schools in Ramallah.

autobiography, *Blackberry Winter*, "the same small prejudices about housekeeping that carry the echoes of their
mother's voice as she admonished them, 'Never fill the teaket-
tle from the hot-water faucet,' and 'Wash the egg off the
silver spoons at once,' and 'Dry the glasses first.' "[1] I spoke
with the Mead sisters shortly before Margaret Mead died.
Margaret was seventy-five, Elizabeth, sixty-eight: They were
the last remaining of five siblings (the others were Richard,
who followed Margaret; Priscilla, who followed Elizabeth;
and Katherine, born between the older and younger sets, who
died as an infant). They spoke the common language of
sisters for years: from childhood outside Philadelphia when,
Margaret remembered, "Elizabeth became my delight"[2] and
the faithful follower in the family pageants that Margaret
directed, and they continued through education and maturity
that carried them in opposite directions: Margaret, with a
thorough academic background, to follow a single-minded
and ground-breaking course in anthropology, Elizabeth to
follow her training at the progressive School for Organic
Education at Fairhope, where, as her sister put it, "She
learned practically nothing at all—except how to teach, how
to waken children, and how to treat each individual as a
person."[3] They continued to thread the shared language
through marriage and motherhood (Margaret's only child,
Katherine, born six months before Elizabeth's oldest daughter, Lucy) and even through vastly different mothering styles,
and also through the unfolding of their careers (Margaret to
worldwide prominence and influence as an anthropologist,
Elizabeth through a checkered path of artistic jobs to her
recent retirement as a teacher of art teachers at Lesley
College in Cambridge, Massachusetts). From the dictates of
birth order (Margaret, the "loved and wanted" oldest, Elizabeth born into more ambivalence as the "next-to-youngest")
and the strong parental wills within the family crucible, the
Mead sisters were profoundly influenced by family. They also
continuously influenced each other during the cycles and
transitions of their lives, the exploration and achievement,
marriage, children and divorce, breakthroughs and respites.
They played out patterns of rivalry, which Margaret Mead
the anthropologist believed are intensified for sisters by having and comparing children, while Margaret Mead the sister
swore characteristically, "I've never been threatened by anything." (Elizabeth, however, admitted to a period as a young
mother when she got so peeved at Margaret that she didn't

speak to her for six months.) They also played out patterns
of polarities over the years and certainly rambled down the
roads of their proscribed family roles: Margaret, the family's
foreman and intellectual and academic star, Elizabeth, the
"changeling," the artist and uncategorizable spirit. And
through the changing cycles of closeness and distance, involvement and separation, they continued to share the common
language of sisters: the messages of sexuality (the passwords
of marriage, the lessons of childbirth and raising children),
the influences of art and work. Their lives span and sum up
the important themes of this book.

In old age, having spent decades apart, having often lived
on opposite ends of the earth, the sisters drew together again.
Elizabeth kept a room in her tiny Cambridge apartment
always ready for Margaret's visits. It is a room with bare
wood floors and a daybed, full of shadows, shared history and
Elizabeth's paints and easels. (Once, years ago, when Margaret's daughter lived in Cambridge and had just had her first
baby, the sisters sat together in Elizabeth's apartment "and
waited until Kathy wanted to see Margaret, which seems
awfully long to grandmothers and very, very short to parents.") But Kathy long since moved away, and in recent
years when Margaret visited, she filled her room with her own
energy and productivity, still burning with white heat at age
seventy-five and secretly ill with cancer: up at three A.M.,
typing till eight, churning out the thousand words which she'd
show to her sister when the sun came up. "She's the best guest
you ever had," chuckled her sister. "As my son said, she takes
up less than the optimum room." And Margaret's perspective
was to make the connections she was famous for between her
personal history and the history of the culture: "I think the
important thing about sisters is that they share the same
minute, familiar life-style, the same little sets of rules. Therefore they can keep house with each other late in life, because
they share the same bunch of housewifely prejudices. The
important thing about women today is, as they get older, they
still keep house. It's one reason they don't die, but men die
when they retire. Women just polish the teacups."

For all the years of sharing a common language, they also
spoke it with the same voice—something each sister remarked
on within the first five minutes I met her. "When I was in
college," Margaret Mead remembered, "Elizabeth used to
come visit me, and people would say, 'It's the same voice, but
what different words.'" When I met the sisters, the voice was

still the same, firm and only a little gravelly with the years, and the words were as different as ever: Margaret Mead was as definitive as a drill sergeant, as focused and precise as a surveyor; Elizabeth Steig was as vivid and impressionistic as the "artist to her fingertips" she has always been. Margaret followed tangents the way she might follow unruly children: the better to make them heel to the sway of her argument. Elizabeth followed tangents the way she would follow a shooting star. For the older, digression was mere interruption to resolute purpose; for the younger, digression was all. "The family could never tell if what I was saying was truth or fantasy," smiled Elizabeth with the relish of a child. "There used to be a phrase in the family, 'If it wasn't six million larks that Elizabeth saw, it was at least six.'"

There is a story each often told on the other by way of illustration that became a shared private joke they both told on the world. Once Margaret invited Elizabeth to an anthropology class in which she was teaching the delicate art of interviewing informants in the field. Margaret introduced Elizabeth as Mrs. Steig, a New York City school teacher—which at the time she was—but never once indicated they were sisters. Twenty years before, but and Elizabeth remembered the occasion vividly. "They started out by saying, 'Where do you teach?' and I said, 'Manhattan.' 'Now could you narrow it down?' and I said, 'No, I'm sorry, I can't.' So that one went down the drain. So the next one said, 'What about discipline?' and I decided to list seventy-nine things which we weren't supposed to do.

"Then they asked me what my grandmother did, and I said I thought she smoked a pipe, and they asked me what my great-grandfather did, and I said I thought he was a part-time preacher and carpenter."

Meanwhile, remembered Margaret, "As she was giving the facts, I put on the blackboard behind her what the facts really were"—that it was Great-Grandmother who smoked the pipe and that Great-Grandfather was a district judge and a covenant minister. When Mrs. Steig had finished her spiel, her sister asked—using the same voice, the same gestures—if she called to mind anyone in the room. In the silence that followed, Margaret Mead announced (the triumph still in her voice twenty years later), "Well, she's my sister." Then she drew the strands of the personal and the cultural together. "Now what you've got to remember when you go into the field is that the informant may be telling you all sorts of things about her own sister who belongs to another clan and whom she's not supposed to be talking about. Now, factually, you must not believe every word she says."

Visit one of them and ask about the other, and in the same voice and gesturing fingers, hear the colorations of two different portraits, as revealing of each speaker as of each subject. One hot summer day, in the Cambridge apartment where she lived for years, modestly furnished but bright with her own paintings and knickknacks, Elizabeth Mead Steig sat chain-smoking and weaving together the past and present. She is a thin woman, at once fragile and enduring, her bones slightly brittle, her hair auburn and jauntily tousled. She was wearing a long green bathrobe and a heavy necklace of Samoan shells, a cherished gift from her sister worn for my benefit. The occasion made the incongruity of her outfit oddly appropriate and appealing.

On the subject of her sister, she was enthusiastic, occasionally to the point of reverence. "I've never known Margaret to be depressed for more than an hour, maybe two," she told me, then gestured wildly. "Whereas I go from up there to down here, and recently the periods have become larger. I'll sometimes go for two years thinking that the world's falling apart. But then all of a sudden it's not." She smiled a cat-that-swallowed-the-canary smile, the smile that must have been getting her through the up periods and the down since childhood. On the subject of her sister, she was also expansive and elaborative, following memories as if they were butterflies, flying into her vision, from out of the blue, from years and years ago. Her train of thought went this way:

"I'm awfully cautious about making generalizations. Do you want a cigarette? Margaret does strange things in some ways. One year she said to me that I had to stop smoking, because I was getting addicted. But the last time she was up here, she said, 'I'm not sure you should stop smoking because you enjoy it so much.' And this is fairly typical. She provides for me enormously in material ways and giving me ideas and contacts. She got me a job at Vassar, so I could afford to pay the rent, because I was earning twenty-five dollars a week then. And then she came up and talked at Vassar. Oh, we had such a nice time up there. And for the first time in my life, I realized how lonely she's been on many occasions. Everyone took off after her speech, because they were afraid to ask her to go out with them."

The details, the skittish memories, the openness, the absorption in her subject: From the evidence of speech and attitude Elizabeth seemed more involved with her sister's life than Margaret was with Elizabeth's. On the subject of her sister, Margaret was no less affectionate, but considerably more hurried, more circumscribed, as if reminiscing about her personal life and sketching in the colors of the family circle interrupted the real business of living, which was conjecturing about the culture. Margaret Mead's domain was the same office she had had since 1926, in a tower in New York's Museum of Natural History, several stories above the dinosaurs, past cases upon cases of bones and specimens, and impenetrable without strict security clearance. Here she created the Museum's well-traveled Hall of the Peoples of the Pacific and was Curator Emeritus of Ethnology; here she wrote, met with former students (every one of the twenty-five hundred filed on an index card with a photograph for instantaneous reference), organized her research (with a staff of feverish and protective research assistants) and got ready for the frequent traveling that described her life as much as the quiet Cambridge apartment described her sister's. "For all my years of traveling," she wrote about this office, "I have always had somewhere to return to, somewhere where everything is just where I put it away twenty, thirty, or forty years ago."[4] Here she reigned, surrounded by the trophies and symbols of her uniquely productive and innovative career: tables and shelves bulging with books (she wrote two dozen herself, from her first anthropological study, *Coming of Age in Samoa,* to her most recent book, *Letters from the Field: 1925-1975*), treasures from the field trips on which she studied and restudied seven disparate cultures, and everywhere, taped-up photographs of family and friends: her daughter, her granddaughter, her beloved mentor and professor Franz Boas. And leaning against a cabinet was the crowning symbol of them all, the extension of her words and will: the gnarled and well-worn walking stick which supported her in her travels and was brandished for emphasis from the streets of New York to the floor of the Democratic National Convention, from the inner sanctums of Presidents who sought her wisdom to the conferences she presided over around the world.

Margaret Mead leaned intently across her desk with her head cupped in her hands, her face stern, but compassionate, softened by a fringe of gray bangs and short hair framing her face like a skirt. She was wearing a bright-green pants suit with a polka-dotted jacket. Where Elizabeth seemed more will-o'-the-wisp, Margaret was sturdy and firm; where her sister was speculative and relished circularity, Margaret was more insistent and direct. "I've always adored Elizabeth," she began emphatically, as if she might be challenged, "always found her very delightful and interesting. As I pointed out in *Blackberry Winter,* she seemed a replacement for the little sister I lost and gave me faith that the things you lost you got back. She was very unusual in the family setting. She was the musical one, the one who could dance and the one who could paint. She was an artist in a family of primarily academic-type intellectuals. And as such she was a delight."

Every articulate family—no less one where Margaret Mead is the eldest daughter—generates its own stories, explanations and myths to illuminate the differences in temperament and talent among its children, the lines of allegiance and influence between parent and child. The explanation that Margaret and Elizabeth Mead offered about their utterly different pasts and presents was simply that, metaphorically speaking, they were born to different parents, in different families. Margaret was the wanted, cherished child, born to parents in their intellectual and emotional prime. Margaret's mother was active and absorbed in her graduate work, her father was a young and energetic professor at the University of Pennsylvania. Later, Margaret would write with remembered devotion and characteristic lack of ambivalence, "The content of my conscience came from my mother's concern for other people and the state of the world and from my father's insistence that the only thing worth doing is to add to the store of exactly known facts."[5] Two years after Margaret came Richard, a sickly child, but also a "gorgeous" and coveted one, and then two years later, a sister, Katherine, who lived for only nine months. Her death forever clouded the emotional climate of the family, "drove a wedge" between father and mother and made a gap between the two oldest children and the two youngest who were born soon after, Elizabeth and Priscilla.

"My father decided after Katherine died that he was never going to care about a child as much again. So his commitment to the younger children was quite different," Margaret explained. Mother was also a different woman, saddened by her infant's death and so depressed after Priscilla's birth only eighteen months after Elizabeth's that she withdrew to the country for a rest, leaving the babies in the care of their grandmother and of Margaret.

"Next to Margaret, I was the most privileged child," remembered Elizabeth about those early years. "It was a combination of Katherine having gone and the fact that I was often ill and that I was able to upset my stomach at a moment's notice. And the fact that Margaret and my grandmother had adopted me. My first memory of tender hands was Margaret's."

During the years of surrogate raising of her sisters, Margaret was discovering that she had the tender hands of a mother—and the shrewd eye of the anthropologist she was already practicing to become. In *Blackberry Winter* she remembered formulating her observations:

> . . . while we were growing up I was fascinated by the contrasts between my sisters. Elizabeth was enthusiastic, loving, and devoted. Priscilla was more self-centered and was devastatingly honest about her motives. She would pay someone a compliment and then remark, "But I only told you that so you would take me along." Except for a brief period in her adolescence . . . she had an extraordinary beauty. But she thought of it as a burden—a talent she had to cultivate but never could really enjoy. . . . [She once described herself as] "the usual child of an unusual family." It was Elizabeth who was the real changeling in our midst, the child whose imagination illuminated—and often transformed in some very special and personal way—the ordinary facts of the workaday world.[6]

In later life, Margaret felt, it was Elizabeth whose talents flowered and enriched the lives around her, while neither Priscilla nor Richard "cared very much for their personal gifts. Priscilla was not made happy by her beauty, and Dick, in the end, made little of his beautiful tenor voice."[7] Dick went on to become a professor like his father, married twice (the second time to his first wife's sister), and died of cancer several years before Margaret. Priscilla, whom Elizabeth, hedging, called "a little competitive," moved to California, married the writer Leo Rosten and lived the grand life in Beverly Hills. "I do remember Priscilla feeling poor when she had thirty thousand dollars in the bank," said Elizabeth who, twenty years after Priscilla's death, calls her her "kid sister." "She was a brilliant kid, but she was interested in competency rather than innovation," observed Elizabeth. "According to Margaret, she made all kinds of innovative things around her house. Like having a silver dish for ashes—a silent butler—

which she would open to show the sparks were dead before she threw them out. Or using the kitchen sink to wash the kids' hair, because they could lean back and be comfortable." Priscilla had just returned to graduate school for a degree in social work when she died.

Of all the siblings it was Margaret and Elizabeth—the intellectual and the changeling, the academic and the artist— who formed the most close-knit friendship, who sustained, supported and influenced each other over the years, with varying degrees of intensity and intimacy, but never a loss of interest or faith. "I loved Priscilla as a sister, not as a friend" was how Elizabeth explained it. "Margaret I can love as a sister and a friend and a super colleague." They saw each other through marriage: Margaret's three to three anthropologists in succession, Luther Cressman, Reo Fortune and Gregory Bateson ("They were all beautiful, and they were always nice to me," recalled Elizabeth. "I remember Gregory explaining the whole structure of flowers to Kathy one morning. It took about twenty minutes and was the most brilliant thing I have heard in my life"), and Elizabeth's marriage to *New Yorker* artist and cartoonist William Steig, whom Elizabeth married after knowing him three weeks, because he said she "made him feel like bedroom slippers." The sisters saw each other through divorce from all these marriages—and also, and not entirely with equanimity, through years of motherhood. For the early years, they lived in the same neighborhood, belonged to the same support network, but followed styles of mothering as different as their eccentricities. "I was a very obsessional mother," Elizabeth described. "I didn't leave my kids for ten minutes. I walked the floor with them till they stopped crying—which they didn't. Whereas Margaret got a nurse, which was partly because of economic necessity and partly because she always believed that children should be brought up by a lot of people, so they're not dependent on just one parent. She got a nanny and taught at the Museum and when she went on lectures took Kathy along. I didn't leave my kids unless I had to go shopping. I drove them crazy. I sang to them all the time. When they were three, they told me I didn't sing in tune."

But where as mothers their domains sometimes collided and they found themselves occasionally treading on each other's toes, as professionals their domains were totally distinct. Over the years, they continually influenced each other's work, directly and indirectly, the artist's vision nourishing the anthropologist, the anthropologist's scope and knowledge deepening and enlarging what the artist saw. Elizabeth began her career baby-sitting for Margaret's daughter, Kathy, teaching her how to do medieval lettering and illumination. From there she took her teaching and artistic talents to "seventeen different jobs between the first and the last": from drawing sketches of spear ornaments at the Museum of Natural History to illustrating for *V*ogue, from teaching art to mothers at Vassar summer institutes and children in Harlem public schools to fifteen years of teaching teachers-to-be at Lesley College. Through it all, she felt Margaret's presence behind her, ready on request with advice and support; from suggesting topics for art classes (" 'How about islands?' she'd say, 'or outer space or drawing good and bad scientists?' ") to sending along cartons of books ("Most of the literature that really influenced me was what Margaret used to read us in the afternoon when we were children," Elizabeth remembered. "I didn't really learn to read till I was fifty") to buying Elizabeth's paintings to give to her friends "to make me feel professional." "Margaret has a way of endowing other people's projects with a lot more meaning than they originally had," Elizabeth observed, characteristically modest about herself and flattering about her sister. She also remembered a pivotal exchange when she told her sister that she wanted a Ph.D. and her sister countered with the voice of the family stage-manager from years ago, "You're a good M.A. Stay that way." But if there were any hard feelings, the years long since softened them, and Elizabeth Steig would only say, "When you speak of jealousy, I've always wanted to do a good enough job so that Margaret would be proud of me. I always felt that what I was doing had a double purpose: to gather interesting ideas for her and to do a good job myself." She smiled and fingered the necklace of Samoan shells. "I don't know whether I'm lying or not. One never does know."

And Margaret Mead, writing of Elizabeth's influence on her life and work, summed it up this way:

> . . . whichever of [Elizabeth's] talents she used, she used it differently from the rest of us. Her perceptions, so different from ours, have nourished me through the years. Her understanding of what has gone on in schools has provided depth and life to my own observations on American education. And her paintings have made every place I have lived in my home. I

have the first watercolor she ever painted and a painting of the New York Stock Exchange Building . . . and another of the view from our windows in Philadelphia. . . .

All my life I have felt that a painting or a poem composed by someone I know is far more meaningful to me than work by a greater artist or poet whom I do not know. I like to have my experiences buried deep in a personal context. . . .[8]

That sharing of experinces deep within the personal context is what Elizabeth gave Margaret over the years: a reference point during marriage, motherhood and divorce, a starting point for journeys deep into other cultures and into our own, a point to return home to after the vigorous demands of travel, actual and theoretical. Elizabeth was also specific about what Margaret gave her in return. "She has, in a sense, kept me within the range of reality, in a way I probably wouldn't have otherwise." She smiled and for a moment was again the little girl who, when she saw her first film, *Jack in the Beanstalk*, thought that it was real. "Margaret can identify the fantasy and also the reality," she said. "You can't have one without the other in this world." Then she gathered the waist of her long green bathrobe with a slim gold belt, threw a shawl around her shoulders, picked up her own gnarled walking stick and followed her vision into the blazing summer sun.

Occasionally, or perhaps more than occasionally, the shared language of sisters is so strong that it is spoken up to, even beyond, death. "Sister, dear sister, come home and help me die": so began a letter from her younger sister to Jessamyn West, giving the grim news she was dying of cancer, making a final request, Jessamyn West recorded this story in her memoirs, *The Woman Said Yes: Encounters with Life and Death,* and I found no more stunning record of the endurance of the sister bond.

They were a Quaker California family: "brought up in the stubble of barley fields . . . near foothills . . . beyond the blue mountains":[9] an older brother and two sisters: Jessamyn and, four years after her, Carmen. "She had been put into my arms as I sat in a child's rocking chair on the morning of her birth," remembers Jessamyn West. "Had that act given me a feeling more maternal than most children have for their younger sister?"[10] It is a memory West comes back to again and again in her vigil with her sister: that primitive moment of their first and irrevocable connection.

Easy to recognize the differences between them, says West, harder to pinpoint the likenesses which were nonetheless there. Jessamyn was "big-boned, five feet seven, square-jawed, square-shouldered, freckled, bookish, athletic"; Carmen was "five feet five, small-boned ... small-waisted, with a full bosom, taut bottom, and rounded calves" that made strange men devise reasons to stop and photograph her.[11] And though the two sisters did not have many years at home together—Jessamyn graduated from high school and left home at sixteen—Carmen's life and doings retained a kind of glamour for her sister, a kind of "star quality." "I looked forward to being with her," West writes, "as I would to being with an actress. But with an actress who was my sister."[12]

So it was against the background of this almost charmed attachment that West received Carmen's news: first a letter to say she had cancer of the lower bowel, next to say it was inoperable. She needed her sister to be with her, Carmen wrote, no, to help her die. "From one's parents one is prepared to receive grim news," West observes, stunned. "Not from one's younger sister. The bell that tolls for them will toll for you, but the bell that tolls for a younger sister is much closer; its knell doesn't stop reverberating and it says, 'You next. You next.' "[13]

Jessamyn went immediately to Carmen in Palm Springs, and she made her one promise: that she would not cry. She broke the promise only once. Together, like "planners, plotters, technicians,"[14] they began their last mission together. For Carmen had decided that when her pain became too unbearable, she would end her life with an overdose of sleeping pills, and Jessamyn would be her accomplice. "I want someone to hold my hand at the last," she told her sister. "Bill [her husband] can't do it. There's no one but you."[15]

Jessamyn slept in the room next door to Carmen; they installed an electric bell to ring between rooms. When Jessamyn slept through it one night, she panicked and moved her bed into Carmen's room. They drew closer and closer together. Under the cover of literary curiosity, Jessamyn researched the appropriate number of sleeping pills necessary; she questioned and probed the doctor for advice which went against his code to give. She assisted in her sister's last rituals: giving away her clothes (friends' daughters came to Carmen's bedside to try them on), planning the funeral. Once "the planning was taken care of, tickets bought, destination accepted,"[16] the sisters talked more and more of the past: sharing memories, images, family stories, as if to hold on the more tightly to life by treading over it again. "There had always been the two qualities, one in me, one in her that bound us. Or bound me," Jessamyn West admitted. "Her beauty; and the fact that of my family, she alone understood that fever and excitement of words: reading them, writing them. There was one other quality: the motherliness in me, augmented by my being the oldest in a family with an ailing mother, and of being childless after marriage."[17]

Finally, after several months of daily increasing pain, the time arrived. "Do I have to wait any longer?" Carmen asked her sister. "No," replied Jessamyn. She brought her sister, already dressed in her prettiest silk nightgown, her silk panties and a bottle of Givenchy's L'Interdit, which Carmen anointed herself with. Then Jessamyn brought her the pills, and, with Carmen's husband, sat in her room until the end.

The next day Jessamyn went to the funeral home and stood over her sister's casket, opened for her as for no one else. She read "the words James Baldwin had written for the death of Rufus," which Carmen had hoped would be spoken at her funeral. "They weren't said there," Jessamyn West writes at the memoir's end. "They were the last words I ever spoke aloud to Carmen; though in my mind, silently, I speak to her almost every day."[18] Even after death, the language of sisters endures.

CONCLUSION:
SISTERS OUTSIDE THE FAMILY

graciela and smoke waz like outta the same womb
cept it waznt so
graciela waz born some where in a different time from
  smoke
but even when they spoke different languages
the voice waz the same
           —NTOZAKE SHANGE, *"For Thulani"*[1]

ONCE UPON A TIME THERE WERE TWO LITTLE GIRLS WHO were not sisters but wished passionately that they were. One was blond and freckled and rather spindly with a body that was all legs and arms and a face that was perpetually framing the question, Why? And the other had dark curls, a solid frame and a manner that suggested the answer, Why not? The two were, of course, inseparable: played together, schemed together, whispered in a private language about their families, told secrets, told jokes, fought with each other, then, in the next breath, made up. And despite their obvious differences in face and frame, they were convinced, at some deep and wordless level, that they looked alike, that they were alike. In fact, at the deepest and most wordless level, they were convinced that they were related. And they were determined to show this to the world.

So one day, after elaborate preparations and in deepest, darkest secrecy, each pricked the other's index finger till it bled. Then each dipped a finger into the other's blood and mixed it with her own. And from then on, they called each other "blood sisters." For now what they knew in their hearts, they had made symbolically real: They shared the same blood.

The desire to be and have a sister is a primitive and profound one that may have everything or nothing to do with the family a woman is born to. It is a desire to know and be known by someone who shares blood and body, history and dreams, common ground and the unknown adventures of the future, darkest secrets and the glassiest beads of truth. It is not exactly like the yearning for a mother (just someone as compassionate or wise as a mother), or for a father (just someone as savvy or protective as a father), or for a lover (just someone as intimate and involved as a lover), or even for a friend (just someone as dependable and present as a friend). It is a wish for someone to be as involved in our own process of figuring out who we are as we are involved in theirs: that person who is that mysterious combination of exactly like and exactly unlike ourselves, that mystery which we spend a lifetime trying to decipher and define.

The equation between sisterhood inside the family and sisterhood outside is not always predictable, and even after writing this book to gauge it, I find the variables continuing to shift. For the woman who does not have a sister in her own family, the search for one outside the family may be all the more intense (I cannot count the number of times during my research that women without sisters shared their wish for a sister, even volunteered to describe the "fantasy sister" whom they had carefully etched out). But some women who have never known the intricacies of the sister connection might not know what they're missing, might not even know whom to look for as a sister surrogate beyond the family.

The woman who has a sister by birth might also feel no need to look beyond the family for another. One thirty-six-year-old identical twin, for instance, felt such a second-skin closeness to her twin that she found it difficult to "confide in anyone but her." And another woman felt "no need to have close relationships with women other than my sister. I do have good friends, but not that many and not that close." For other women, the experience of having a sister, of knowing the special intimacy of that connection is an impetus to seeking it outside the family again and again. Then, too, there are women whose relationships with their sisters inside the family are so tense and disappointing that they look outside the family for their supportive sisterly bonds. "Although we love each other, we do not like each other, and were we not related, we would probably not want to know each other" is one woman's typical response. She adds, "I feel more sisterly to other women than I do to my own sister." Or this from a woman who begins to make some political connections between sisterhood inside the family and outside:

> I feel that as children my sister and I were pitted against each other, as women are in the world in general. Neither of us was taken seriously as human beings—she the charming little doll who could do no wrong, and I as the thing too sensible to be a child and too unimportant for an education and serious pursuits. Had we had a collective strength perhaps we might have had a supportive relationship and withstood the destructive sexist atmosphere in which we tried to grow up; perhaps we'd even be mentally healthy, whole human beings. I was not a good sister to her, nor she to me.

Her recent awareness of feminism and the political ideal of sisterhood has led her to reexamine her relationship with her own sister and "spurred me to sympathize with my sister and to begin a new, strong relationship based on sisterhood and honesty." And though "the past has taken its toll," and the process is painstaking, the possibility for change is alive. For many women who call themselves feminists, discovering their sisters outside the family has led them to rediscover their sisters at home.

Inside or outside the family, the urge for a sister can be both wordless and spilling over with words. Two very different women, among many, offered testimonials in two recent interviews.

In a television interview, Anne Morrow Lindbergh recalled the grim aftermath to the kidnapping of her child, and especially the pervasive lack of privacy, even after the Lindberghs retreated to England. Her husband warned her not to write any letters that she wouldn't mind seeing blasted across the front page of *The New York Times*. Nevertheless, she remembered, she insisted, "I had to write letters to my sisters. It was like breathing."

And then, in a magazine interview, poet Maxine Kumin remembered her extraordinary friendship with fellow poet Anne Sexton, who had committed suicide four years earlier:

> Anne and I were inordinately close. We were more like sisters, I suppose.

I never had a sister. Somehow I think for both of us we filled so many of each other's needs that I didn't feel any particular push to have another, close, woman friend. And also, Annie was all-consuming. It was a rare day we didn't see each other, and if we didn't see each other, we talked on the phone. We each had a separate line in our houses so that we didn't tie up the family line. We frequently would dial one another in the morning and stay connected all day. I don't know what Ma Bell would have thought if they had known. It was not unusual for us to have the phone down on the deck and each be going about our day doing other things, and whistle into the phone when we wanted the other one. Very peculiar relationship. That's for seventeen and a half years.[8]

From comments offered casually in conversations, I mark the poles of intensity both inside and outside the family. There is the woman who, like Anne Morrow Lindbergh, names the tie with her sisters as basic as breathing. It is that need, in the midst of chaos and confusion, to stay in touch with them through letters—and it is also that need to stay in touch with herself. And there is the woman who, like Maxine Kumin, calls another woman a sister and names that tie "stay[ing] connected all day," the phone a kind of lifeline, a kind of bloodline for two who are not, strictly speaking, connected by blood. And though these are women in rather extraordinary situations—the one recovering from the trau-matic kidnapping of her son, the other the support and solace of a friend who would ultimately take her own life—their extraordinariness speaks only more intensely an ordinary need, which is felt as keenly inside the family as out: the urgency to have a sister and be one.

With the recent resurgence of the Women's Movement, there has of course been a rediscovery and a reaffirmation of sisterhood outside the family, of its power and primordial-ness. But though the Women's Movement may have given a new contemporary relevance to the term, the notion of sisterhood outside the family was discovered neither by the Women's Movement nor by the other groups of sympathetic and like-minded women who have called themselves sisters over the past several centuries: religious orders of sisters and Jewish sisterhoods, union sisters, black sisters, sorority sisters, or Big Sisters, who noticed what girls in the ghettos missed who had no sistering and created an organization to provide it. But the idea of sisterhood outside the family, the idea that women unrelated by blood are nevertheless related, goes back to the earliest roots of the culture. In fact, as Evelyn Reed ably demonstrates in *Woman's Evolution: From Matriarchal Clan to Patriarchal Family,* the use of the term "sister" to describe all the women in a given group or clan predates by innumerable eras its more limited contemporary use to describe the daughters of one specific mother and father. Tracing the terms "sister" and "brother" back to their usage in the earliest primitive clans, Reed explains:

> Family kinship terms came into existence late in history with the advent of the family institution itself. To be sure, the terms "mother," "brother," and "sister" as family terms grew up out of the equivalents in clan terminology. But this occurred only after the clan system broke apart and was succeeded by the family. . . . In primitive society, where the facts about biological relationship were unknown and irrelevant to the communal mode of life, kinship was exclusively social. . . . In our contemporary family system of kinship the term "brother" [or "sister"] signifies that a man [or woman] is a member of a specific family and that he [or she] is blood-related, i.e. biologically related, to the other members of the family. Under the primitive classificatory system of kinship the term did not mean either of these relationships. It signified only that the child was a "born" member of a group of mothers, his matrilineal kin, and a group of mothers' brothers, his fratrilineal kin.[3]

In other words, as anthropologist W. H. R. Rivers puts it, "a term like that of brother [or sister], which, except in the metaphorical sense, is limited among ourselves to the male [or female] children of our own parents, is in the classificatory system extended to all the male [or female] members of the clan of the same generation."[4]

Furthermore—and also relevant to contemporary usage—by a ritual called the "blood covenant," as Reed describes it, "men who were formerly strangers became bound together as "blood brothers."[5] Originally, the blood covenant "converted separate hordes into parallel clans"; later, it became a pact between individual men. To become such blood brothers, two men might open their veins and suck a little of each other's blood, or they might smear some of their own blood on each other or on a piece of food which they would then eat together. In certain of the blood covenants between men, it would be required at the same time that the women become sisters, with a ceremonial phrase such as "Our women shall be sisters and our men brothers."[6] Anthropologist Robertson Smith describes the force of the blood ritual this way: "The reason why it is so binding is that he who has drunk a clansman's blood is no longer a stranger but a brother, and included in the mystic circle of those who have a share in the life-blood that is common to all the clan."[7]

So the secret and carefully orchestrated ritual by which two little girls of today become blood sisters and complete their own mystic circle has its origins in the earliest primitive societies. And the primitive need among all men and women—related by blood or not—to be joined and defined as brothers and sisters is still fiercely alive today. Even in an era when the links among members inside the family are radically reorganizing—given optional or single parenthood, abortion and vasectomy, and the spiraling rate of divorce—the quest for connections outside the family, named by the same familiar names, carries on. It is no small coincidence that members of this century's most important political movements—labor, civil rights and black nationalism, and feminism—call each other sisters and brothers, making a mystic circle out of a political ideal. In the struggles inside labor unions, in the search for common strength and sympathy of civil rights groups and later of black nationalists, and in the emerging shared bonds of the Women's Movement, the need for sisters and brothers beyond one's own family is discovered and expressed with all its ambiguities and ideals.

And the patterns that describe sisters' relationships inside the family are also relevant to relationship among sisters outside. If we look at those movements whose members call each other sister—and particularly at the Women's Movement, which I am most familiar with—we see reflected the same themes that color life between sisters throughout the sweep of the life-cycle: the fluctuations of closeness and distance over time, and always the constancy of ambivalence; the gradual recognition of similarity with the simultaneous awareness of difference; and the urge for connectedness mingled with the need for independence and the haunting knowledge of aloneness. These are the themes first discoverd in the family crucible which circumscribe the quest outside the family and become woven into the history of political movements: the changes in attitude and intensity of political activists over time; the exhilarating gauging of similarity and commonality, with the subtle but intense delineating of differences, which often creates factionalism; and the passionate need for solidarity even with the constant and stubborn insistence of the individual. And if we look specifically at several self-defined sisters outside the family, we will see patterns familiar to us from looking inside: patterns of multiple roles, of rivalry, of opposites and of the shared and inspiring language of sexuality and art.

One afternoon, four women sit together at a table at Sardi's, musing and conjecturing about sisterhood. Two of them—my sister and I—are sisters by birth, as intimate with the details of the other's life as with our own. The others are sisters by choice, but their intimacy is as easy and complex as our own. One is playwright Ntozake Shange, whose choreopoem *For Colored Girls Who Have Considered Suicide, When the Rainbow Is Enuf* rocked Broadway audiences with its nitty-gritty rhythms of sisterhood born of the joys and struggles of black women. The other is Shange's best friend, Thulani, soul sister and sidekick extraordinaire. "Once," Thulani will tell us, "Zaki [Ntozake's nickname] and I were jumping up and down singing with the TV, and her mother shook her head and said, 'I know because I was there that you all came out of different wombs, but I swear that you came out at the same time.'" This turns out to be a key piece of mythology in a friendship that does not lack for mythology or mythmakers. And it is the story which Zaki transposed in the poem dedicated to Thulani about the rainbow sweep of their friendship, which begins, "graciela and smoke waz like outta the same womb/cept it waznt so."

At Sardi's, all the waiters know Shange, for she has adopted this place, of all places, as her second home. She asks for a bib and then grins with pleasure. "I'm such a big baby. This is how I get my baby stuff out. A lot of times in the winter when I was being very lonely, because getting famous made things weird for me, I would come here to get something that really made me feel secure. I would really feel like nothing was wrong. I would get steak and mashed potatoes with gravy, and the whole world would just cool right out."

"Mashed potatoes and gravy," agrees Thulani, "are definitely home." She says it in a way that makes the incongruous acceptable, that way that sisters have of confirming each other's world and making each other's life more real to them. And though the high-pitched theater crowd and bustling waiters do not spell home to me, Ntozake Shange and

Thulani are clearly in their element here: the twenty-eight-year-old Broadway *wunderkind* and hip explicator of black sisterhood and her attentive and worldly-wise friend, who boast proudly of themselves, "Both of us wanted to be what we thought Simone de Beauvoir would have been if she'd been a colored lady."

Both Ntozake and Thulani each have two sisters of their own, who, in their fashion, they are also close to. Thulani's sisters are much older, a different generation, really, and though they struggle to make sense of Thulani's freewheeling, they do not quite speak the same language. Ntozake's sisters are Ifa and Bisa (they all took African names around the same time; Ntozake Shange means "She who walks like a lion" and "She who comes with her own things"). The three sisters are close in age and perhaps too close in inclination. They are all artists, all writers besides, and occasionally tread too close to each other's heels. The criticism Ntozake gets from her own sisters may be their way of making their jealousy manageable.

The relationship between Ntozake and Thulani, however, does not carry with it all the emotional baggage of the past, the scores unsettled, the comparisons unresolved. They never knew each other with the rough edges and bloody knees of childhood. They met as college freshmen, coincided as their adult selves were bursting from the cocoons of their pasts. And now, exotic butterflies, they fan and intensify each other's poses, without losing touch with the heart beneath. In Sardi's, where the crowd is sleek and sinewy, they are the exotic gypsies at the cocktail party, the earth mothers at the black-tie soiree. They are both heavy, sensuous women, who dress the way they eat, as if luxuriating in the process. Their clothes, draped in layers, both hide and accentuate their bodies. Shange wears an ink-blue sleeveless shift, and over it a shawl of pink and red roses, so vivid it appears to hum. A black scarf is tightly wrapped around her head, so that her features are starkly distinct, wide and smooth, petulant and delighted. Thulani is as intense, though not as striking, swathed in a billowing slate-blue blouse, dangling rows of necklaces and earrings shaped like the goddess Isis.

They have been friends since they were Barnard freshmen, and from the day they met, they have been completing each other's sentences, humming each other's tunes, echoing and repeating each other in style and story, heart and intellect. When they chat to each other, they lapse into a kind of

Black English, a patois of privacy, history and affection. When they talk to others, when they say hello over the phone, like sisters their voices are interchangeable. "I was walking down the street singing the theme from Lester Young, one of my favorite pieces," Ntozake reminds Thulani about the time they met, "and you finished up the last chorus." She sings it gently to herself—da, da, dum, da—and then goes on, "Then we started walking together to Chock Full O' Nuts. We did that for four years."

"I always tell people," adds Thulani, spinning out the myths, "that intellectually we're twins. We've read all the same things and felt similarly about them. When we came to college, we were both into Sartre and we signed up to take a course in modern German literature and were both interested in Brecht. We were into existentialism and—"

"Russian poets," Zaki cuts in, unable to contain herself. "I was a big Mayakovski fan. And both of us were into studying the new wave of French theater. And both of us were raised on black music, on jazz, and so that was endemic to our relationship." Thulani was also the first person Ntozake showed her writing to, a poem called "Heart Failure," which Thulani remembered was "so good it upset me." Thulani, at that point the writer with the wider reputation, recommended it be published by someone she knew on campus. Says Zaki, "She's really responsible for me ever being a writer, because I didn't tell anybody but her and wasn't getting support from anyone else."

"I didn't see why you couldn't write," Thulani answers, relishing her role as patron, for by now her protégée has long since passed her by. "But at that time we were more different than we are now. My mother was a dancer who died when I was about five, and my father raised me to do something. I was a much more unrepressed person, much more impulsive than Zaki, and I had been to a school that stressed art quite a bit. So I didn't see why she didn't do anything she wanted to do."

So their friendship grew from a common intellectual ground, from a faith in each other's future as artist and a fine tuning to the details of each other's past. Both had grown up in black, middle-class, professional families. Ntozake (born Paulette Williams) was the daughter of a surgeon and a psychiatric social worker; Thulani's parents were a chemistry teacher and a dancer. Both came from close-knit families, lively with intellectual and artistic spark. But even with the advantages of their particular households, as black women struggling to make their way in a world run by whites, they were subtly cautioned not to ask for or expect too much. Shange wanted to be an art historian, but remembers bitterly that "my mother said she wouldn't pay for college if I did, because they don't hire niggers to be no art historians and my parents couldn't afford that." And while she was muddling out of this thicket of double messages, along came another woman who, like a sister, "had experienced the contradictions of my life that I hadn't resolved." Out of just this common awareness of the contradictions that shape us (and out of a common commitment to bring them to light, even change them) are sisters outside the family born.

By now, after almost ten years of friendship, Ntozake and Thulani are almost as familiar with each other's family as with their own. When they talk about Ntozake's mother, they sound the way any two sisters do, sorting through their roots, looking for (and revealing) themselves in the process. But there is an extra edge of self-consciousness, that literary mythmaking that marks their friendship. For they are not only sisters, but also each other's first and best audience. "My mother," muses Ntozake, "is like a good mixture of Myrna Loy and Claudette Colbert in a movie without Clark Gable." She pauses as if knowing she will get a laugh—which she does—and then Thulani picks up her cue. "She's also like *Dinner at Eight*, where the world is going on and she says, 'But no one seems to understand. I'm having dinner at eight.'"

"She's also," adds Ntozake, rising to the occasion, "like Alice Adams when the ice cream melts because they don't have no air conditioning. Or like in *Stella Dallas* when the children come to the birthday party. There's that nagging fear of not being accepted, which makes my mother function on a socially acceptable level at all times.

"And for years," she adds, "I was running around being a forty-year-old woman, because I had no personality that wasn't my mother's. I was having the fears that a forty-year-old repressed person has and not even knowing what my own fears were."

"She kept her mother's rules when she wasn't even around her mother," is how Thulani explains it, "and that didn't make sense to me, because they were things you don't have to keep. The important thing was to keep safe mind and body, and beyond that it was up to you." So, from the first, the only ground rule of their friendship was to keep safe mind and body, and beyond that it was up to the two of them. And before long, the twenty-year-old Ntozake locked inside the forty-year-old frame was floating free. When they describe the high jinks and high times of their friendship, they turn as giggly as little girls. "One of the fun things about our friendship," says Thulani, while Zaki hangs on her every word, "is that there's room for a lot of possibilities that start within us. I could say, let's do such and such, and she would not question the validity of my idea. One year I said I really wanted to go to Atlantic City to hear this rock-and-roll show. She didn't tell me I was crazy. She said, 'That's a great idea. Let's go!' " Or there was the time they traded in a check earmarked for a doctor's bill for an "incredible French meal" which they paid for "to the penny." Or the time they went to hear jazz at the Apollo and walked home from Harlem for hours in the pouring rain. Or their most recent caper, a trip to Paris, which was kind of a last bachelor fling for Zaki, who married—for the second time—soon after. As she tells it, savoring the story like her dinner of spaghetti and wine, they went to "the Moulin Rouge and picked up these two Brazilian dancers and went out dancing with them and then went home with them, and they fixed this marvelous Brazilian breakfast."

"It was so funny," Thulani tacks on, "because we both liked both of them."

"We both liked the ones we were with," insists Zaki.

There have, of course, been times when romance did not shake out quite so neatly, when, as they phrase it, "We both had the same man talk to us about the same time." That happened only twice, and it was, they admit, troubling and "incestuous in a certain sense." "Most of the crises Thulani and I have," Zaki explains, "either have to do with violating each other's territory or with men." Once they even stopped speaking for a year. "I was in what the French call 'good form,' which means you do everything correctly," remembers Zaki. "And Thulani and another friend disappeared with my fiancé on my wedding night for half an hour, and I didn't speak to them anymore." But today, when she retells the story (on the eve of her second marriage, which Thulani will preside over), the air has been long since cleared. The two of them have a good laugh over the old vendetta, even take the opportunity to pin down a few details that had never been explained.

Like sisters, their friendship is strong and elastic enough so that it can occasionally be pulled to the breaking point without snapping. But where for blood sisters the shared history of growing up in the same family becomes the bottom line, for sisters outside the family there must be something else to fall back on. Even Ntozake Shange, who does not ordinarily lack for words of any kind, finds it elusive to name. "There's some kind of indelible something," she offers. "It has to do with a style of life, how we think, what we expect from one another, what we're willing to listen to."

Like sisters born to the same family, these two have been rivalrous and complementary, fallen out of favor with each other, not even spoken for periods and then rushed willy-nilly back together and picked up where they left off. And from the first certainty of friendship and throughout, they have profoundly influenced each other's intellectual and sexual lives, providing a reference point at their turning points, a port in each other's storms. And what it is about their friendship that Shange can't quite put into words, what it is that makes them sisters, she speaks instead inside a poem:

> . . . found out my friend who went out wid my
> ol boyfried went cuz she was lonely & he was nice.
> & I was outta my mind
> no one cd listen to music like her & walk to the apollo in the rain/
> eat chock fulla nuts franks in sauerkraut while analyzing brecht & baraka/
> she waz the only friend i had cd read me like a miles davis solo/
> > she waz like a sister/ i remembered what mama said/
> > > so
> i went & got her
> she was also alone/ we made a pact/ brought ice-cream/cried/ cuz we
> > was not betrayers but sisters/ widout the same mama/ but sisters
> > > cuz we loved each other/ & wanted no more pain.[8]

In the unlikeliest section of a dense American city, in the unlikeliest house on the block (so turreted, byzantine, and spacious that it is called The Castle), live five young women in their twenties and thirties, who were not born sisters but who nevertheless consider themselves sisters now. As a group they are one of a kind; but as a phenomenon, they are one of many scattered around the country, in the fringes of cities or the rural heartlands; collectives of women creating and defining a notion of sisterhood, and outside the families they were born to, living together as sisters.

For the past several years, the women of The Castle have worked, played, cooked, eaten, gardened, partied, sang, bickered and joked together, shared secrets and alliances, talked behind each other's back and eyed each other's boyfriends, coveted each other's clothes and freely lent their own, hankered to be different, to be special and yet sought the comfort of similarity, of commonality and solidarity. During this charged and delicate period of separating from home—yet before the separation is complete—they have gone looking for themselves while looking after each other. For several years they have pursued jobs and romances, involvement in the counterculture and allegiance to the Women's Movement, a commitment to sisterhood that is both personal and political, both close to home and far-ranging as the world. And the totems of their individuality as well as of their shared commitment are displayed all over the house.

The Castle is so big and rambling that each of the five women can have two rooms of her own—a study and a bedroom—and each has unleashed the full sway of her personality on decorating her space. One sleeps on sleazy black sheets; another has two different beds—one on the floor, one on stilts—for two different moods; still a third has converted a cranny into a sewing room where years of handmade Halloween costumes are on display: among others, giant Minnie Mouse hands and pincushions sewn in the shape of a clitoris. In the common rooms—kitchen, living and dining rooms—the energy is more tempered and the images more harmonious than eccentric, symbols of their shared vision. Gauguin prints circle the living room, earth mothers bearing baskets of food, sturdy female archetypes. And everywhere, the walls blaze with posters of the feminist culture, the creative sisterhood they nourish and are part of: the health collective and radical theater group, the quilt exhibit and self-defense classes, the day-care center and all-women's rock band. And in the kitchen is the communications network of The Castle: a message board where each of the five has her own space. And only once was a message tacked up in the wrong space, and the wrong woman went to meet someone else's friend at a café.

Five women who call themselves sisters live in The Castle, and as in any family of five, they have chosen roles for themselves and each other, needing to etch themselves out as individuals, needing the cozy solidarity of the group. Greta is the oldest and the tallest, almost six feet, a strapping figure of a woman with pre-Raphaelite curls streaming down her back and a strange array of costumes plucked from attics, second-hand stores and the occasional trash can. She is a midwife and the surrogate mom, the unacknowledged but carefully followed leader in a group that stubbornly insists it is leaderless. She has been with the same man—off and on—for eight years; she doesn't want to marry, but is trying to have a child with him. "I want to have a baby," she says, "and if it's a girl, I want to raise it here, because I think a little girl should have this experience growing up. I was never really close to women until I moved here two years ago. Now I'm making up for what I missed." A relative latecomer to the promises of sisterhood, she is now the utopian visionary of the group, with dreams of one day transforming the sorority into a matriarchy.

Marie is the cutup, the madcap of the family, tells stories on herself and on the others that are both piercing and endearing. Before bedtime, with cocoa at the kitchen table, she entertains them with their own legends, and their laughter at themselves makes their mythology more real to them. But beneath Marie's laughter, emotions burn and questions lie in wait like jungle animals. All day long, Marie works at a home for battered wives, women who have chosen each other by default. And at times the contrast with her own chosen sisters makes her uneasy, so she holds the unease at bay by making her sisters laugh and take themselves lightly.

Fran works in a woman's bookstore and is the intellectual, the ideologue, the bookworm of the family, the one who has recently worked her way through every volume of Anaïs Nin's diaries and is now tackling Rosa Luxemburg. She is the sage of the group, the philosopher, quoting Rosa Luxemburg at dinner, leaving cryptic messages from Anaïs Nin on the community bulletin board.

Samantha, called Sam, is a marathon runner who makes her living in an all-women's plumbing collective. She is the family's surrogate son, the one who has sweated away her shape so that her clothes hang limp on her body, swallow her like an old man's overcoat. As the only gay woman of the group, she alternately takes the offensive and defensive, challenging the others' commitments to their sisters as less authentic than her own, fending off what she imagines to be their slurs. She lives as if she has one foot out the door, one foot in another, more sympathetic camp. But though she keeps running, she has not yet left the fold.

And the fifth is Pearl, who calls herself Tango, to give an air of sophistication to looks that are not, for she is round and dimpled and full of curls. The artiest, the sexiest, she is the family baby, who is trying to grow progressively less demure, using her years in The Castle to get ready to shed her skin. She will be the one to break away when a more seductive opportunity comes along. "I'm getting ready to leave this house," she whispers, "because it's too female an atmosphere. I want to live with some men, too. I grew up in a house full of women, too, have two sisters of my own, and now I want a different experience." But until she finds a new partner and slithers off in the opposite direction, Tango will settle in right here.

Five women who call themselves sisters, and they have learned to live with each other for years in spite or because of the patterns of roles, of rivalries, of polarities, familiar inside the family, played over again outside. They have variously fallen in love with the same man, courted the friendship of the same woman, competed for the same job, had a jillion trivial arguments over who does the dishes, who cleans the bathroom, had some bitter political disputes where the undercurrent was always, I am more radical than thou. And in spite or because of their rivalries (those fierce, these delicate struggles between your territory, mine–or ours). Their solidarity has carried on. Then, too, they have played out their polarities, muddled through oppositions: the gay sister versus the straight, the middle-class versus the working-class, the radical versus the liberal, the separatist versus the ones willing to work alongside men, the leader versus the ones who believe there is no leader. But they have also stayed up all night with each other when times were grim, brought chicken soup when they were sick, cheered each other's successes, boosted each other's spirits after disappointments, lent each other money, listened to each other's poems, found each other jobs. They have heard each other's dreams unraveled the morning after at the breakfast table, and watched each other's dreams woven into their life experiences. They have seen the mystic circle of their sisterhood grow wide and wider.

Throughout it all, they have kept hammering at the difficulties between like and not-like, between the urge to be independent and the need to be linked, looking for the right balance, the resolution. And the sisters in The Castle (like their sisters in the Women's Movement, for whom they are, of course, a symbol) have not found that balance, that resolution yet, for as difficult as it is inside the family, it is even more puzzling beyond. But still, their solidarity carries on. So now when they talk (as they invariably do) about how sisterhood is powerful, they are beginning, just beginning, to know what they mean.

NOTES

INTRODUCTION

1. Robert White, *The Enterprise of Living*, p. 106.

2. THE FAMILY CONSTELLATION

1. Alfred Adler, *What Life Should Mean to You*, p. 154.
2. Ibid. p, 144.
3. Ibid. pp. 144–152.
4. Lucille Forer, *The Birth Order Factor* (with Henry Still), p. 21.
5. M. Sewall, "Two Studies of Sibling Rivalry, I. Some Cases of Jealousy in Young Children," *Smith College Studies in Social Work*, 1 (1930), pp. 6–32, as discussed by Robert White, *The Enterprise of Living*, p. 86.
6. Adler, *What Life Should Mean to You*, p. 153.
7. Yvon Gauthier, M.D., "Observations on Ego Development: The Birth of a Sibling," in *Bulletin of the Philadelphia Association for Psychoanalysis*, Vol. 10, no. 1 (March, 1960), p. 84.
8. C. Schooler, "Birth Order Effects: Not Here, Not Now!" in *Psychological Bulletin*, 78 (3), 1972, pp. 161–175, as quoted by Guy Manaster, "Birth Order: An Overview" in *Journal of Individual Psychology*: Vol. 33, No. 1 (May, 1977), p. 5.
9. E. Douvan and J. Adelson, *The Adolescent Experience* (John Wiley & Sons, Inc., New York, 1966), p. 227, as quoted by Margaret Hennig in "Family Dynamics and the Successful Woman Executive" in *Women and Success: The Anatomy of Achievement*, ed. Ruth B. Kundsin, Sc. D., p. 90.

10. Forer, op. cit. p. 50.
11. Ibid. p. 89.
12. Alfred Adler, *Understanding Human Nature*, p. 222.
13. Sigmund Freud, *The Standard Edition of the Complete Works of Sigmund Freud*, Vol. X, p. 132.
14. Simone de Beauvoir, *Memoirs of a Dutiful Daughter*, pp. 44–45.
15. Ibid.
16. Margaret Mead, *Blackberry Winter*, p. 64.
17. Forer, op. cit. p. 101.
18. Ibid. p. 57.
19. Harry McGurk and Michael Lewis, "Birth Order: A Phenomenon in Search of an Explanation," in *Developmental Psychology*, Vol. 7 (3) (November, 1972), p. 336, as quoted by Forer, op. cit. p. 58.
20. Forer, op. cit. p. 58.
21. James H. S. Bossard and Eleanor Stoker Boll, *The Large Family System*, p. 209.
22. As reported in *Ms.* magazine (May, 1978), p. 20.
23. Forer, op. cit. p. 27.
24. Ibid. p. 63.
25. Walter Toman, *Family Constellation*, p. 75.

3. INSIDE THE FAMILY CRUCIBLE AND BEYOND

1. Margaret Mead, *Blackberry Winter*, p. 70.
2. Nancy Friday, *My Mother/My Self*, p. 11.
3. Ibid. p. 63.
4. Ibid. p. 379.
5. Holly Near, "You've Got Me Flying," copyright Hereford Music, 1975 (Redwood Records).
6. Friday, op. cit. pp. 229–230.
7. Mel Gussow, "Elizabeth Swados–A Runaway Talent," *The New York Times Magazine* (March 5, 1978), p. 20.
8. I'm thinking in particular of Eric Berne, *Games People Play*; Claude Steiner, *Scripts People Live*; Hogie Wyckoff, *Solving Women's Problems Through Awareness, Action & Contact*.
9. Everett R. Howes, "Twin Speech: A Language of Their Own," *The New York Times* (Sept. 11, 1977), p. 54.
10. Holly Near, "You've Got Me Flying."

4. SISTER ROLES: SISTERS AS LITTLE WOMEN

1. Nina Auerbach, *Communities of Women*, pp. 68 and 60.
2. Carolyn Heilbrun, as quoted in "Jo's Girls: The Literary Women of the '20's" (no author) in *San Francisco Chronicle* (April 13, 1978), p. 26.
3. Louisa May Alcott, *Little Women*, pp. 6–7.
4. Alfred Adler, *What Life Should Mean to You*, pp. 153–154.
5. Carly Simon, as quoted by Jane Shapiro in "The Extraor-

dinary Simon Women," *Ms. magazine* (February, 1977), p. 53.

6. James H. S. Bossard and Eleanor Stoker Boll, *The Large Family System*, pp. 203–204.
7. Ibid. pp. 212–219.
8. Ibid. pp. 219–220.
9. Robert White, *The Enterprise of Living*, p. 98.

5. SISTER RIVALRY

1. Robert White, *The Enterprise of Living*, p. 106.
2. Margaret Mead, *Blackberry Winter*, p. 70.
3. Adapted from *Perrault's Classic French Fairy Tales*, pp. 77–99.
4. Bruno Bettelheim, *The Uses of Enchantment*, p. 236.
5. Iona and Peter Opie give a concise history of the Cinderella tale in *The Classic Fairy Tales*, pp. 117–121.
6. Bettelheim, op. cit. p. 243.
7. Ibid. p. 248.
8. Karen Horney, "The Genesis of the Castration Complex in Women," *Feminine Psychology* pp. 45–46.
9. Bettelheim, op. cit.; also Donald M. Marcus, M.D., "The Cinderella Motif: Fairy Tale and Defense" in *American Imago*, Vol. 20 (1963), pp. 81–82; and Ben Rubenstein, "The Meaning of The Cinderella Story in the Development of a Little Girl," in *American Imago*, Vol. 12 (1955), pp. 197–205.
10. Marcus, op. cit. p. 84.
11. The material of the slipper varies according to the version of the story, sometimes silk, gold or fur (or in French, *vair*, which Perrault may have misunderstood to be *verre*, or glass, as the Opies suggest, op. cit. p. 121).
12. Bettelheim, op. cit. p. 248.
13. Ibid. p. 275.
14. Brothers Grimm, "Cinderella," *Grimm's Fairy Tales*, p. 165.
15. Helene Deutsch, *The Psychology of Women*, Vol. 1, p. 249.
16. Bettelheim, op. cit. p. 245.
17. Marian R. Cox, *Cinderella: Three Hundred and Forty-Five Variants*, as quoted by Bettelheim, op. cit. p. 245.
18. Arpad Pauncz, in "Psychopathology of Shakespeare's *King Lear*," *American Imago*, Vol. 9 (1952), p. 60.
19. Freud in "The Theme of the Three Caskets" in *Collected Papers*, Vol. IV, works analytically with themes of three sisters in "Cinderella," the Three Fates, and *King Lear*. About the three sisters in *King Lear*, he concludes, "One might say that the three inevitable relations man has with woman are here represented: that with the mother who bears him, with the companion of his bed and board and with the destroyer. Or it is the three forms taken on by the figure of the mother as life proceeds: the mother herself, the beloved who is

chosen after her pattern, and finally the Mother Earth who receives him again" (p. 256).

6. SISTERS AS OPPOSITES

1. Carl Gustav Jung, *Collected Papers on Analytical Psychology*, p. 149.
2. Brothers Grimm, "Snow-White and Rose-Red," *Grimm's Fairy Tales*, p. 298.
3. Ibid.
4. Bruno Bettelheim, *The Uses of Enchantment*, p. 91.
5. Ibid. p. 96.
6. Ellen Moers, *Literary Women*, p. 159.
7. George Eliot, *Middlemarch*, pp. 9–10.
8. Frank Kermode, "Afterword" to George Eliot's *Middlemarch*, p. 817.
9. Robert White, *The Enterprise of Living*, p. 96.
10. Ibid.
11. Queen Elizabeth, as quoted by Peter Evans, "16 Famous Sisters," *Cosmopolitan*, May, 1976.
12. Dena Kleiman, "True Story of City Gang Life: No Glittery 'West Side Story,'" *The New York Times* (March 6, 1978), p. B1.

7. SISTERS IN LOVE:
THE SHARED LANGUAGE OF SEXUALITY

1. Louisa May Alcott, *Little Women*, p. 5.
2. Margaret Mead, *Male and Female*, p. 61, as quoted by Adrienne Rich, *Of Woman Born*, p. 226.
3. Rich, *Of Woman Born*, pp. 225–226.
4. Adrienne Rich, "Sibling Mysteries," *The Dream of a Common Language*, pp. 51–52.
5. Maria Katzenbach, *The Grab*, p. 104.
6. Erica Jong, "For Claudia, Against Narrowness," *Loveroot*, p. 20.
7. Salvador Minuchin, *Families and Family Therapy*, pp. 53–56.
8. Cathérine Deneuve, as quoted by Peter Evans, "16 Famous Sisters," *Cosmopolitan*, May, 1976.
9. Dolores Klaich, *Woman Plus Woman*, p. 90.
10. Rich, *Of Woman Born*, p. 232.
11. Sue Silvermarie, "The Motherbond," *Women: A Journal of Liberation*, Vol. 4, No. 1, pp. 26–27, as quoted by Rich, Ibid.

8. SISTERS AS ARTISTS

1. Charlotte Brontë as quoted by Margaret Lane, *The Brontë Story*, pp. 238–239.
2. Carly Simon, "Older Sister," Copyright 1974 by C'est Music ASCAP for "Hotcakes," Elektra.

3. Lane, op. cit. p. 37.

4. Ellen Moers, op. cit. pp. 159–160.

5. Quentin Bell, *Virginia Woolf: A Biography*, Vol. I, p. 28.

6. Holly Near, "You've Got Me Flying," Copyright Hereford Music, 1975 (Redwood Records).

7. Mrs. Gaskell, as quoted by Lane, op. cit. p. 113.

8. Virginia Woolf, as quoted by Ellen Moers, op. cit. pp. 23–24.

9. Charlotte Brontë in a letter to Ellen Nussey, as quoted by Lane, op. cit. p. 187.

10. Lane, op. cit. p. 78.

11. Mary Taylor to Mrs. Gaskell, as quoted by Lane, op. cit. p. 93.

12. Charlotte Brontë, as quoted by Lane, op. cit. p. 173.

13. Moers, op. cit. pp. 261–262.

14. Charlotte Brontë, as quoted by Lane, op. cit. pp. 218–219.

15. Moers, op. cit. p. 236.

16. Elizabeth Gaskell, as quoted by Lane, op. cit. p. 205.

17. Ibid.

18. Charlotte Brontë, as quoted by Lane, op. cit. pp. 237–238.

19. Bell, *Virginia Woolf*, Vol. I, p. 23.

20. Bell, *Virginia Woolf*, Vol. II, p. 147.

21. Nigel Nicolson in *Introduction to The Letters of Virginia Woolf*, Vol. 1, ed. Nigel Nicolson and Joanne Trautmann, p. xvii.

22. Virginia Woolf in a letter to Clive Bell, in Nicolson and Trautmann, eds., op. cit. (February, 1907), p. 282.

23. Virginia Woolf, as quoted by Bell, *Virginia Woolf*, Vol. II, p. 110.

24. Ibid.

25. Virginia Woolf in a letter to Violet Dickinson in Nicolson and Trautmann, eds., op. cit., (January, 1907), p. 276.

26. Virginia Woolf, as quoted by Bell, *Virginia Woolf*, Vol. II, pp. 126–127.

27. Vanessa Bell as quoted by Bell, *Virginia Woolf*, Vol. II, p. 128.

28. Ibid.

29. Carly Simon, "Older Sister."

30. Adrienne Rich, "Transcendental Etude," *The Dream of a Common Language*, pp. 74–75.

9. SISTERS IN OLD AGE

1. Margaret Mead, *Blackberry Winter*, p. 70.

2. Ibid. p. 63.

3. Ibid. p. 66.

4. Ibid. p. 17.

5. Ibid. p. 54.

6. Ibid. pp. 65–66.

7. Ibid. p. 67.

8. Ibid. p. 69.

9. Jessamyn West, *The Woman Said Yes*, p. 107.
10. Ibid. p. 89.
11. Ibid. p. 91.
12. Ibid. p. 92.
13. Ibid. p. 95.
14. Ibid. p. 120.
15. Ibid. p. 121.
16. Ibid. p. 145.
17. Ibid. p. 146.
18. Ibid. p. 180.

CONCLUSION: SISTERS OUTSIDE THE FAMILY

1. Ntozake Shange, "For Thulani," in *For Colored Girls Who Have Considered Suicide, When the Rainbow Is Enuf* (San Lorenzo, California: Shameless Hussy Press, 1976).
2. Maxine Kumin, as quoted by Susan Allen Toth, *Ms.* magazine (June, 1978), p. 37.
3. Evelyn Reed, *Woman's Evolution: From Matriarchal Clan To Patriarchal Family*, pp. 170–178, passim.
4. W. H. R. Rivers, *History of Melanesian Society*, Vol. I, p. 7, as quoted by Reed, op. cit. p. 178.
5. Reed, op. cit. p. 178.
6. Ernest Crawley, *The Mystic Rose*, Vol. I, pp. 295–296, as quoted by Reed, op. cit. p. 181.
7. Robertson Smith, *The Religion of the Semites*, pp. 315–316, as quoted by Reed, op. cit. p. 179.
8. Ntozake Shange, "For International Women's Day," in *For Colored Girls*, op. cit.

BIBLIOGRAPHY

Adler, Alfred. *Understanding Human Nature*, trans. Walter Béran Wolfe, New York: Greenberg, Publisher, Inc. 1927.
——*What Life Should Mean to You*, ed. Alan Porter. Boston: Little, Brown and Company, 1931.
Alcott, Louisa May. *Little Women*. New York: Thomas Y. Crowell Company, 1955.
Auerbach, Nina. *Communities of Women*. Cambridge: Harvard University Press, 1978.
Austen, Jane. *Pride and Prejudice*. New York: Dell Books, 1959.
——*Sense and Sensibility*. New York: Oxford University Press, 1970.
Baez, Joan. *Daybreak*. New York: The Dial Press, Inc., 1968.
Bell, Quentin. *Virginia Woolf: A Biography*: Volume One: Virginia Stephen: 1882–1912. London: The Hogarth Press, 1972.
——*Virginia Woolf: A Biography*: Volume Two: Mrs. Woolf: 1912–1941. London: The Hogarth Press, 1972.
Bettelheim, Bruno. *The Uses of Enchantment*. New York: Vintage Books, 1977.
Bossard, James H. S., and Eleanor Stoker Boll. *The Large Family System: An Original Study in the Sociology of Family Behavior*. Philadelphia: University of Pennsylvania Press, 1956.
Chodorow, Nancy. *The Reproduction of Mothering: Psychoanalysis and the Sociology of Gender*. Berkeley: University of California Press, 1978.
Daly, Faye Kennedy. *Good-Bye, Diane*. New York: Berkley Publishing Corporation, 1976.
de Beauvoir, Simone. *Memoirs of a Dutiful Daughter*. New York: Harper and Row, 1974.

Deutsch, Helene. *Psychology of Women*: Vols. I–II. New York: Grune and Stratton, 1944.

Diner, Helen. *Mothers and Amazons: The First Feminine History of Culture*, ed. and trans. John Philip Lundin. New York: Anchor Press/Doubleday, 1973.

Drabble, Margaret. *A Summer Bird-Cage*. Great Britain: Penguin Books, 1967.

Eliot, George. *Middlemarch*. New York: The New American Library, 1964.

Erikson. Erik H. *Childhood and Society*. Second edition. New York: W. W. Norton & Company, 1963.

Forer, Lucille (with Henry Still). *The Birth Order Factor*. New York: David McKay Company, Inc., 1976.

Freud, Sigmund. *Collected Papers of Sigmund Freud*, trans. Joan Riviere. London: The Hogarth Press and the Institute of Psycho-Analysis, 1946.

————*The Standard Edition of the Complete Psychological Works of Sigmund Freud*, trans. ed. James Strachey. London: The Hogarth Press and the Institute of Psycho-Analysis, 1955.

Friday, Nancy. *My Mother/My Self: The Daughter's Search for Identity*. New York: Delacorte Press, 1977.

Gaskell, Elizabeth. *The Life of Charlotte Brontë*. Middlesex: Penguin Books, 1975.

Gissing, George. *The Odd Women*. New York: W. W. Norton & Company, Inc., 1971.

Godwin, Gail. *The Odd Woman*. New York: Alfred A. Knopf, Inc., 1974.

Goethals, George, and Dennis S. Klos. *Experiencing Youth*. Boston: Little, Brown and Company, 1970.

Gornick, Vivian, and Barbara K. Moran, eds. *Woman in Sexist Society: Studies in Power and Powerlessness*. New York: Basic Books, 1971.

Griffin, Susan. *Like the Iris of an Eye*. New York: Harper and Row, 1976.

———— *Voices*. New York: The Feminist Press, 1975.

Grimm Brothers. *Grimm's Fairy Tales*, trans. E. V. Lucas, Lucy Crane and Marian Edwardes. New York: Grosset & Dunlap, Inc., Publishers, 1945.

Hamilton, David. *Sisters*, text by Alain Robbe-Grillet. New York: William Morrow & Company, Inc., 1973.

Hammer, Signe. *Daughters and Mothers: Mothers and Daughters*. New York: Signet, 1976.

Hennig, Margaret, and Anne Jardim. *The Managerial Woman*. Garden City, New York: Anchor Press/Doubleday, 1977.

Horney, Karen. *Feminine Psychology*, ed. Harold Kelman. New York: W. W. Norton & Company, Inc., 1973.

Howard, Jane. *Families*. New York: Simon and Schuster, Inc., 1978.

Jong, Erica. *Fear of Flying*. New York: Holt, Rinehart and Winston, Inc., 1973.

———*How to Save Your Own Life*. New York: Holt, Rinehart and Winston, Inc., 1977.

——— *Loveroot*. New York: Holt, Rinehart and Winston, Inc., 1975.

Jung, C. G. *Collected Paper on Analytical Psychology*, trans. and ed. Constance E. Long. New York: Moffat Yard and Company, 1917.

Katzenbach, Maria. *The Grab*. New York: William Morrow & Company, Inc., 1978.

Kennedy, Flo. *Color Me Flo: My Hard Life and Good Times*. Englewood Cliffs, New Jersey: Prentice-Hall, Inc., 1976.

Kennedy, Joy. *The Neurotic Woman's Guide to Non-Fulfillment: How Not to Get A Man*. New York: The Viking Press, Inc., 1976.

Klaich, Dolores. *Woman Plus Woman: Attitudes Toward Lesbianism*. New York: Simon and Schuster, Inc., 1974.

Koch, Helen. *Twins and Twin Relations*. Chicago: University of Chicago Press, 1966.

Kundsin, Ruth B. *Women and Success: The Anatomy of Achievement*. New York: William Morrow & Company, Inc., 1974.

Laing, R. D. *The Politics of the Family*. New York: Pantheon, 1971.

———and A. Esterson. *Sanity, Madness and the Family*. Middlesex: Penguin Books, 1970.

Lane, Margaret. *The Brontë Story*. Glasgow: Fontana/Collins, 1969.

Lawrence, D. H. *Women in Love*. New York: The Viking Press, Inc., 1968.

Lazarre, Jane. *The Mother Knot*. New York: Dell Books, 1977.

Lehmann, Rosamond. *The Ballad and The Source*. New York: Reynal and Hitchcock, 1945.

Masters, R. E. L. *Patterns of Incest*. New York: The Julian Press, Inc., 1963.

Mead, Margaret. *Blackberry Winter: My Earlier Years*. New York: William Morrow & Company, Inc., 1972.

——— *Male and Female: A Study of the Sexes in a Changing World*. New York: William Morrow & Company, Inc., 1949.

——— *Sex and Temperament in Three Primitive Societies*. New York; William Morrow & Company, Inc., 1963.

——— and Martha Wolfenstein, eds. *Childhood in Contemporary Cultures*. Chicago: University of Chicago Press, 1966.

——— and Ken Heyman. *The Family*. New York: The Macmillan Company, 1965.

Miller, Jean Baker, M.D., ed. *Psychoanalysis and Women*. Baltimore: Penguin Books, Inc., 1974.

Millett, Kate. *Flying*. New York: Alfred A. Knopf, Inc., 1974.

—— *Sexual Politics.* Garden City, New York: Doubleday & Company, Inc., 1970.

—— *Sita.* New York: Farrar, Straus and Giroux, 1977.

Minuchin, Salvador. *Families and Family Therapy.* Cambridge: Harvard University Press, 1974.

Mitford, Jessica. *Daughters and Rebels.* Boston: Houghton Mifflin Company, 1960.

Moers, Ellen. *Literary Women: The Great Writers.* New York: Anchor Press/Doubleday, 1977.

Morgan, Robin, ed. *Sisterhood Is Powerful: An Anthology of Writings from the Women's Liberation Movement.* New York: Vintage Books, 1970.

Neisser, Edith G. *Brothers and Sisters.* New York: Harper and Brothers, 1951.

Nicolson, Nigel and Joanne Trautmann, eds. *The Letters of Virginia Woolf:* Vol. I: 1888–1912. New York: Harcourt Brace Jovanovich, 1975.

Opie, Iona and Peter. *The Classic Fairy-Tales.* New York: Oxford University Press, 1974.

Patch, Susanne Steinem. *Blue Mystery: The Story of the Hope Diamond. Washington,* D.C.: Smithsonian Institution Press, 1976.

Perrault, Charles. *Classic French Fairy Tales.* New York: Meredith Press, 1967.

Reed, Evelyn. *Woman's Evolution: From Matriarchal Clan to Patriarchal Family.* New York: Pathfinder Press, Inc., 1975.

Rich, Adrienne. *The Dream of a Common Language: Poems 1974–1977.* New York: W. W. Norton & Company, Inc., 1978.

—— *Of Woman Born: Motherhood as Experience and Institution.* New York: W. W. Norton & Company, Inc., 1976.

Rosaldo, Michelle Zimbalist, and Louise Lamphere, eds. *Woman Culture and Society.* Stanford: Stanford University Press, 1974.

Rossner, Judith. *Looking for Mr. Goodbar.* New York: Simon and Schuster, Inc., 1975.

Rubin, Lillian Breslow. *Worlds of Pain: Life in the Working-Class Family.* New York: Basic Books, Inc., 1976.

Sand, George. *Lélia.* Paris: Colmann-Levy, 1958.

Satir, Virginia. *Conjoint Family Therapy.* Palo Alto, California: Behavior Books, 1964.

—— *Peoplemaking.* Palo Alto, California: Science and Behavior Books, 1972.

Scheinfeld, Amram. *Twins and Supertwins.* Philadelphia: J. B. Lippincott Company, 1967.

Senn, Milton J. E., M.D., and Claire Hartford, eds. *The Firstborn: Experiences of Eight American Families.* Cambridge: Harvard University Press, 1968.

Shakespeare, William. *The Tragedy of King Lear,* ed. George Lyman Kittredge. Boston: Ginn and Company, 1940.

Shange, Ntozake. *For Colored Girls Who Have Considered Suicide/When the Rainbow Is Enuf* (play). New York: The Macmillan Company, 1975.

———— *For Colored Girls Who Have Considered Suicide/When the Rainbow Is Enuf* (poems). San Lorenzo, California: Shameless Hussy Press, 1976.

Sheehy, Gail. *Passages: Predictable Crises of Adult Life.* New York: E. P. Dutton & Company, Inc., 1974.

Shorter, Edward. *The Making of the Modern Family.* New York: Basic Books, 1975.

Spock, Benjamin. *Baby and Child Care.* New York: Pocket Books, 1976.

Sutton-Smith, Brian, and B. G. Rosenberg. *The Sibling.* New York: Holt, Rinehart and Winston, 1970.

Toman, Walter. *Family Constellation.* New York: Springer Publishing Company, Inc., 1961.

Walker, Alice. *In Love and Trouble: Stories of Black Women.* New York: Harcourt Brace Jovanovich, 1973.

West, Jessamyn. *The Woman Said Yes: Encounters with Life and Death.* New York: Harcourt Brace Jovanovich, 1976.

White, Robert W. *The Enterprise of Living.* Second edition. New York: Holt, Rinehart and Winston, 1976.

Winnifrith, Tom. *The Brontës.* New York: The Macmillan Company, 1977.

APPENDIX:
SISTERS
QUESTIONNAIRE

Name (optional):
Address (optional) *or state you live in*:
Age:
Occupation:
Occupation of parents:
Number of sisters and brothers and their ages:
Names and addresses of sisters and brothers (optional):
   (Indicate if sisters and brothers would be willing to fill out a
   questionnaire. If so, indicate on returned questionnaires that
   family members are related, using a family pseudonym, if you
   like)

Occupations of sisters and brothers:

1) Briefly describe your present relationship(s) with your sis-
   ter(s): i.e. how often do you see each other? how close are
   you emotionally? are you satisfied or unsatisfied with the
   relationship(s)?
2) Briefly describe your mother and your relationship with her.
3) Briefly describe your father and your relationship with him.
4) What is your earliest memory of your sister(s)? If you are
   older, can you remember how you felt when she was born
   and how your life changed?
5) At age 12 or 13, what is your most vivid memory of yourself
   with your sister(s)?
6) What is the closest or happiest with your sister(s) you've
   ever been?
7) What is the angriest at your sister(s) you've ever been?

8) If you have brothers, how were your relationships growing up with them different than your relationships with your sister(s)? If possible, tell a story to illustrate the difference.

9) How did (does) your birth position (eg, oldest, middle, youngest) affect your sense of yourself? (For instance, your self-image, your relationship with siblings, your relationships with friends, your work? Briefly describe any or all of these topics.)

10) How did/do your parents influence how you relate(d) with your sister(s)?

11) What is your worst jealousy of your sister(s)? Hers of you?

12) What different parental messages did you and your sister(s) and brothers get about what you could be or do when you "grew up"?

13) How are your sexual attitudes and experiences similar to or different from your sister(s)?; ie. early relationships, first lovers, sexual experimentation, relationships with women, monogamy or nonmonogamy?

14) If you or your sister(s) are married, divorced or widowed, how did those experiences affect your relationship as sisters?

15) If you or she have children, how does that experience affect your relationship? How are you different or similar as mothers? How do you feel about her children and she about yours?

16) What is the most shocking thing you ever learned about your sister(s)?

17) What is the most vivid dream you've had about your sister(s)?

18) What is the most precious gift—tangible or intangible—your sister(s) has given you?

19) How does having a sister affect your relationship with other women?

20) If you consider yourself a feminist, did/does that affect your relationship(s) with your sister(s)?

21) What stories or books about sisters influenced your thinking about sisters?

22) Is there anything else you'd like to add to fill out the description of your relationship(s) with your sister(s)?

ABOUT THE AUTHOR

ELIZABETH FISHEL was born in New York in 1950. She graduated with honors in 1972 from Radcliffe, where she was on the editorial board of the *Harvard Crimson*. In 1974, she received her Master's from Stanford. During the past ten years, her articles have appeared in numerous publications, including *Ms, The New Yorker, Human Behavior, Ramparts,* and *Newsday*. She also teaches writing, and now lives with her husband in Berkeley, California. This is her first book.

WE DELIVER!

And So Do These Bestsellers.